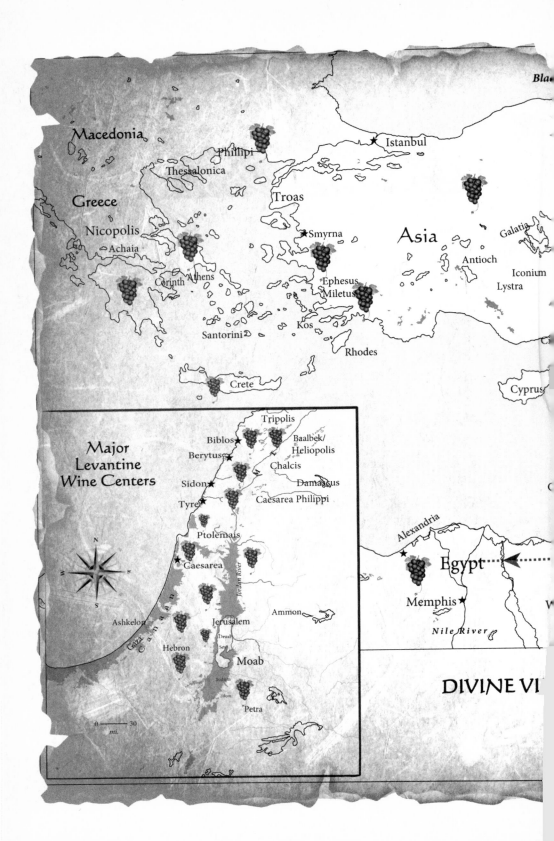

Black[Sea]

Macedonia

Philippi

Thessalonica

Istanbul

Troas

Greece

Asia

Galatia

Nicopolis

Smyrna

Antioch

Iconium

Achaia

Lystra

Corinth Athens

Ephesus
Miletus

Kos

Santorini

Rhodes

Cyprus

Crete

Major
Levantine
Wine Centers

Tripolis

Biblos★

Baalbek/
Heliopolis

Berytuss★

Chalcis

Sidon★

Damascus

Tyre★

Caesarea Philippi

Ptolemais

Alexandria

Egypt

Caesarea

Jordan River

Memphis★

Ashkelon

Ammon

Gaza

Jerusalem

Canaan

Dead
Sea

Nile River

Hebron

Moab

Sodom

Sidon

DIVINE VI[NE]

Petra

0 — 30
mi.

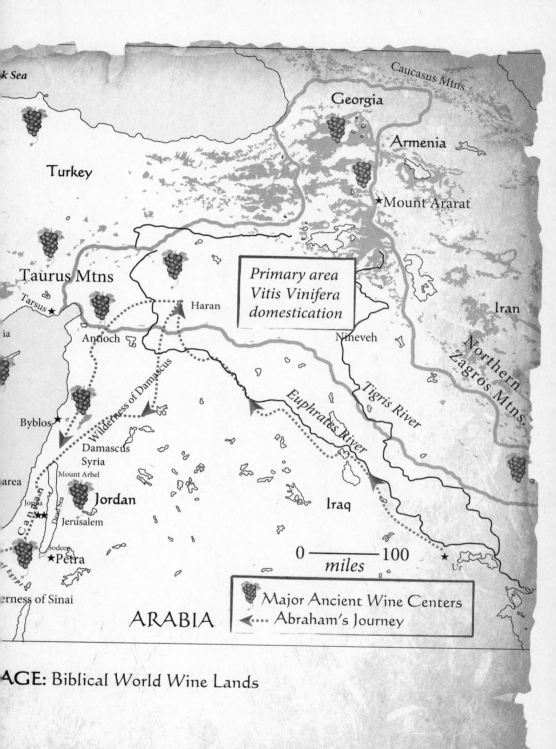

IMAGE: Biblical World Wine Lands

Divine Vintage

FOLLOWING THE WINE TRAIL FROM
GENESIS TO THE MODERN AGE

RANDALL HESKETT & JOEL BUTLER

palgrave
macmillan

For our daughters
Hannah, Karin, and Allison

DIVINE VINTAGE
Copyright © Randall Heskett and Joel Butler, 2012.
All rights reserved.

First published in 2012 by PALGRAVE MACMILLAN® in the United States—a division of St. Martin's Press LLC, 175 Fifth Avenue, New York, NY 10010.

Where this book is distributed in the UK, Europe and the rest of the world, this is by Palgrave Macmillan, a division of Macmillan Publishers Limited, registered in England, company number 785998, of Houndmills, Basingstoke, Hampshire RG21 6XS.

Palgrave Macmillan is the global academic imprint of the above companies and has companies and representatives throughout the world.

Palgrave® and Macmillan® are registered trademarks in the United States, the United Kingdom, Europe and other countries.

ISBN 978-0-230-11243-8

Photograph of Mt. Ararat © A_Sh / Shutterstock.com
Photograph of assyrtiko root © Boutari Foundation

Library of Congress Cataloging-in-Publication Data
Heskett, Randall.
   Divine vintage : following the wine trail from Genesis to the modern age / Randall Heskett and Joel Butler.
      p.   cm.
   Includes bibliographical references and index.
   1. Wine and wine making—History. I. Butler, Joel. II. Title.
TP549.H52   2012
641.2'209—dc23
                                                                2012019320

A catalogue record of the book is available from the British Library.

Design by Letra Libre, Inc.

First edition: November 2012

10   9   8   7   6   5   4   3   2   1

Printed in the United States of America.

Contents

Part 1

IN THE BEGINNING

HISTORICAL WINES, BIBLICAL BEVERAGES

Eight pages of color photographs appear between pages 50 and 51.

Part 2

THE MODERN DIVINE WINE TRAIL

Eight pages of color photographs appear between pages 146 and 147.

Preface

When we set out to write this book, *Divine Vintage*, we consciously understood that the word *divine* had a double meaning of "divine" and "of or pertaining to the vine." Wines from the Bible wine trail actually have a divine purpose and come from a long history of viticulture where the vine itself is sacred.

We not only aimed to describe the historical, social, and spiritual dimensions of wine in the Bible, as many have already attempted to do, but also to characterize what the people of the ancient world actually drank. This work tries to answer that question by making our observations using ancient texts and our sensory perceptions of wine made today, accounting for differences in grape growing, climate, and wine-making techniques over the millennia. We sampled wines produced today and crafted through "ancient" methods in order to answer the elusive question, *WWWJD: What wine would Jesus drink?*

We assert in this book that one role of wine in the biblical traditions serves metaphorically for the spread of human (certainly Western) civilization from the origin point(s) in the Near East and all of its positive aspects. On another level, wine represents the most profound and revealing connection between humans and their need for "connectedness" to something we call the "divine." By its use, new visions and understandings become "realized" from an entirely new perspective.

Chapters 1–6 pursue these questions through our study of the Bible, other ancient texts, and a variety of modern secondary works on climate, winemaking, history, and archaeology. Chapters 7–12 actually take the reader along the wine trail of the Bible today, describing what we have tasted and what these biblical "terroirs" have produced. The Bible describes itself as a human testimony to divine revelation (Deut 29:29; John 5). For those who believe, the Bible is the "word of God," transmitted by humans, which civilization then spread across the earth. It depicts wine as the symbolic gift of God to humans, and it played a key role in spreading the "word of God" throughout the ancient world. On the earthly plain, we maintain that wine contributed strongly to the spread of cultural values we associate today with both Judeo-Christian and classical humanism. Indeed, wine provides the connective skein between these often contentious viewpoints.

Before we embark on this journey along the Bible wine trail, we want to clarify what we are *not* attempting in this book: We are not treating the Bible as a "history book." We realize that the books of the Bible often provide more of a history of faith or metaphorical history than a literal one. That said, there is much written in the Bible that is supported by modern archaeological and scientific studies.

We treat the biblical records on wine according to biblical chronology, aware that the earliest books in the Bible were not necessarily written and assembled by the earliest writers. We will not treat all of the pointless claims that promote abstinence from alcohol or assertions that the wine in the Bible was not fermented. We will argue, instead, that wine consumption not only linked God's covenant with Israel, continuing within the rites of Judaism today, but is also linked to the very core of Christian theology.

The Modern Renaissance of viticulture and enology in biblical lands embodies a return to past glory and gives modern-day wine lovers three areas to focus on: New World (everywhere but Europe and the mid-east), Old World (Europe), and Ancient World (the original "home" territories of wine culture in the Fertile Crescent, Levant, Egypt, and even Greece)—the original birthplace of wine. We agree with Patrick McGovern, who beautifully describes the role of wine in the development of the human being:

I contend instead that the driving forces in human development from the Palaeolithic period to the present have been the uniquely human traits of self-consciousness, innovation, the arts and religion, all of which can be heightened and encouraged by the consumption of an alcoholic beverage, with its profound effects on the human brain.

We employ various theological and wine terms throughout the book. Particularly, we leave the unspeakable divine name, often pronounced "Yahweh" (YHWH), in its non-vowel-pointed form in reverence for Jewish heritage.

We use the nondenominational abbreviations for dates: BCE and CE.

We have tried to be as accurate as possible in our evaluations of wines, our judgments about the biblical literature, and reconciling historical data with interpretative narrative. In the end, any errors or omissions are solely the authors' responsibility.

Joel Butler MW
Randall Heskett PhD
June 2012

Acknowledgments

Our thanks go to:

Our editors at Palgrave Macmillan, especially Laura Lancaster, for her patience and encouragement.

Marion Brewer. We owe our old college friend great gratitude for helping us to initially plot the course of our work and navigating through much of the contractual and legal attending issues that neither of us honestly wanted to deal with, nor understood at first. *Grazie tante,* Marion!

Prof. Patrick McGovern, of the University of Pennsylvania's Museum of Anthropology and Archaeology, forced us to write this book. By that we mean his many books on ancient wine and the origins of alcoholic beverage use inspired us immensely. His enthusiasm for the subject and deep knowledge illuminates this wonderful history and provides countless readers like us great pleasure and inspiration.

Prof. Stephen Cook, Prof. Brian Irwin, and **Dr. Randy Verarde,** for directing us to resources, assisting us in finding them, and being a sounding board for difficult issues.

Father Ed Buelt and **Rev. Ron Roschke,** for helping us to think theologically about some passages.

In Georgia: Jim Kriegbaum and **Levan Davitashvili,** for introducing us to the culture, producers and history of Georgian wine, and the remarkable character of its *qvevri* wines, which are today's closest links to ancient wine.

In Greece: Konstantinos Lazarakis MW; Sophia Perpera and **George Athanas** of New Wines of Greece; and **Nico Manessis** for their incredible generosity, time, and knowledge in the daunting task of furthering our understanding of modern Greek wine. A bevy of Greek wine producers gave bountifully of their time and their wines. To all of them, *Efkaristo!*

In Israel: **Asaf Paz, Sasson ben Aharon, Adam Montefiore, Prof. Amos Hadas** and **Dr. Michal Dayagi-Mendels,** who provided us with a "road map" to modern Israel's fine wines, and graciously furthered our understanding of the intimate link between ancient Israel's wines and today's. Prof. Hadas also guided us in revising our thinking about ancient wine-making methods and consequences. We also generously thank all of the producers we visited for sharing their wines and experience. To all, *L'chaim!*

In Jordan: **Omar Zumot,** who organized our visit to the key sites in Jordan and, most importantly, showed how good Jordanian wine can be from his own vineyards. Without his tireless help and true love of wine, our book would be much diminished.

In Lebanon: **Joe "Assaad" Touma** of Clos St. Thomas; we cannot thank you sufficiently for your hospitality and assistance in organizing our stay in Lebanon. Your connections to the who's who of Lebanese wine-growing made our visits much easier and informative. To all of the fine producers we visited, we praise your diligence in keeping alive the vinous heritage of your country, often under very trying conditions.

In Turkey: **Taner Ögütoglü**, director of the Wines of Turkey group. We thankfully acknowledge your support and counsel. Without your enthusiastic help and coordination, our Turkish wine journey would have been strongly diminished. To the members of Wines of Turkey and the other producers who hosted us, you are attempting a renaissance of fine wine in your country not witnessed for nearly 2,000 years!

Not least, we lovingly and gratefully thank our wives/partners Kimberly Beckman-Heskett and Betsy Ashburn. Their patience during the many weeks we were away traveling, and the hours spent hunched over a computer when we got back, probably did not seem expressly acknowledged at the time. We owe them a great debt for their sacrifices on many levels, knowing how much this book meant to us.

Part 1

IN THE BEGINNING

Historical Wines, Biblical Beverages

A NOTE ON METRICS

Production volume is noted in standard nine-liter cases, and land under vine is provided in both acres and hectares—1 hectare (ha) = approximately 2.5 acres. Altitude is noted in feet as well as meters (m) above sea level (one meter = 3.25 feet): eg. 1,000 m / 3,250 feet), and distances are in miles and kilometers [km] (100 km = 62 miles). Yields are in both tons per acre (tpa) and hectoliters per hectare (hl/ha): 1 ton per acre = 16 hl/ha. We have also included the alcohol percentage (for example, 14%) whenever possible, for wines that are described. When describing percentages of new oak barrels used for aging (eg. 50%), this means that half of the barrels used for aging are new barrels, being used for the first time.

One

THE ORIGINS OF WINE

How Wine Infiltrated the Biblical World

God said to Noah, "This is the sign of the covenant that I have established between me and all flesh that is on the earth." The sons of Noah who went out of the ark were Shem, Ham, and Japheth. Ham was the father of Canaan. These three were the sons of Noah; and from these the whole earth was peopled. Noah, a man of the soil, was the first to plant a vineyard."

—Genesis 9:17–20

THE BOOK OF GENESIS: WRITING THE BIBLE AND BEGINNING THE BIBLE WINE TRAIL

Both wine and the Bible evolved over time. We find our first stories about wine in the book of Genesis—in Hebrew Berə'šît, which means "in the beginning"—where we also learn about the origins of wine and the power of its intoxicating effects.

Early in the 1800s scholars began to realize that Moses could not have written the whole Pentateuch (the first five books of the Hebrew Bible/Old Testament, or Torah); rather, the Torah was written throughout a several-hundred year period. For example, Moses could not have written the account of his death, not to mention various striking anachronisms—such as references to the Canaanites and Perizzites "no longer in the land" (Gen. 12:6; 13:7; see other anachronisms in Gen. 36:31; Gen. 13:18, 14:14; Judg. 1:10, 18:29). Additionally, some parts of Genesis used YHWH for God's name before God had revealed this name to Moses in Exodus, while other parts of Genesis used Elohîm as God's name. These discrepancies reflect various time periods in which the book of Genesis was written and the various stages of development in viticulture.

Biblical texts are literary works of high order. As Sean Freyn, a noted Bible scholar, writes, "The Bible as a whole gives us theologically interpreted history." The Old Testament in particular represents on one level a story line, or "plausible myth," that explained to credulous humans the changes in their lives that resulted from evolution and civilization. Wine cultivation is one of several new adaptations humanity was developing, understanding, and appreciating on many levels.

IN THE BEGINNING

Early human beings discovered by accident that crushing fermented grapes and drinking the juice not only provided something naturally sweet, but also altered their conception of reality in a mystical way. Curious, humans began to experiment. After thousands of years they domesticated this wild fruit and planted vineyards.

The Bible does not discuss how the inebriating aspect of the grape was first discovered but does tell a postdiluvial story about one of Noah's first experiences with it.

NOAH, THE FIRST WINEMAKER AND FATHER OF THE TWELVE-STEP PROGRAM

In the Flood narrative, God responds to the wickedness of humankind by sending a flood on all the land but spares Noah and his family, who build an ark in which they float for 40 days and 40 nights. This account originated from two historical sources. Biblical scholars call the one we are concerned with the Yahwist (J); he wrote from the perspective of the monarchy in the ninth century BCE. Only the J source tells how Noah planted a vineyard after he left the ark (Gen. 9:18–28) and after he built an altar to YHWH: "Noah, a man of the soil, was the first to plant a vineyard" (Gen. 9:20). In J's telling, YHWH planted a garden and Noah planted a vineyard. The other source says only that Noah left the ark (8:4).

Of all ancient Near Eastern flood stories (for example, Gilgamesh and Atrahasis), J's is the only one that mentions vineyards and wine. Ironically the narrative says merely that Noah was the first person to plant a vineyard. J, who wrote with a distinctive style, never mentions that Noah then made wine, drank it, and became inebriated. Here the word for *plant* (*nāta'*) includes sowing the seeds and the harvest. Hence wine making was considered the end process of planting the vineyards after the harvest.

Perhaps Noah drowned his sorrows with wine because the world he knew had drowned. The passage tells us that "he drank some of the wine, became drunk, and he exposed himself inside his tent" (9:21). The next verse informs us that "Ham, the father of Canaan, saw the genital area of his father"—Noah (9:22). Some scholars think that the word *saw* is a euphemism for either rape or castration, as the medieval Jewish commentator Rashi suggests: "Some say Cham [Ham] saw his father naked and either sodomized or castrated him. His thought was 'Perhaps my father's drunkenness will lead to intercourse with our mother. . . . I will prevent this by taking his manhood from him!' When Noah awoke he said, 'Because you prevented me from having a fourth son, your fourth son, Canaan, shall forever be a slave to his brothers, who showed respect to me!'"

Leviticus 18:6 establishes the general law for such behavior: "None of you shall approach a blood relative to uncover nakedness." The consensus of Bible scholars is that the phrase "uncover nakedness" refers to sexual intercourse. In Genesis 9 Ham is cursed because he "saw the nakedness of his father," implying some sort of sexual violation (Gen. 9:22). However, the narrator makes no moral judgment about Noah's drinking. The narrator casts judgment only on Ham's act of either voyeurism or sexual violation, yet Noah's drunkenness clearly played a role.

Although the historic flood gave rise to stories about other heroes—including Utnapishtim in the Gilgamesh epic—Noah is unique because of his planting of a vineyard and wine making. Whether it was Noah or someone else, the first human to plant grapes began intentional viticulture, one of the earliest human activities that denoted our evolution from members of a hunter-gatherer society to participants in a pastoral, settled civilization.

It is significant that this story about Noah, the first winemaker, directly follows God's covenant with Noah and all of creation (9:8–17): "Be fruitful and multiply." This theme of wine, blessing, and covenant appears repeatedly throughout the Hebrew Bible.

Isn't it curious that one of the very first things Noah does is plant a vineyard after he sacrifices to YHWH? The links between Noah, the Flood, the planting of the first vineyard, and the first human civilizations in the biblical Near East are strong and plausible. Also quite intriguing is that the J source locates the origins of wine near where modern archaeology has found the oldest wineries outside Israel.

Contemporaneously, an intriguing ancient Greek legend addresses the origin of the wine grape: "Typical of the Thracian epiphany is the story of Orestheus and his dog (or should it be bitch?) Sirius, whose name apparently stands for midsummer heat. She gave birth to a piece of living branch—in fact to what gardeners call a 'cutting.' Orestheus . . . the son of Deucalion, the Hellenic Noah, buried this piece of wood and from it there grew a grape vine. It may be to the point that Orestheus means 'man of the mountain'; his grandson was named Oineus, the Vine."

In effect, this is the beginning of the Bible wine trail. Noah is presented mythologically or theologically as the primordial winemaker. The next step on our journey is to locate the first vineyards and to determine what the first wines were.

THE ORIGINS OF THE WINE GRAPE

Vitis vinifera L. ssp. *sylvestris,* the Eurasian wild grape vine, is the first character in our story. This hardy climbing plant evolved over millions of years in temperate upland areas of the Near East, as well as around the northern shores of the Mediterranean Sea and into southern Europe. The oldest evidence for it comes from the upland areas of eastern Turkey, Armenia, northwestern Iran, and Georgia. In this highland area near the Caucasus and Zagros Mountains, the neolithic peoples who lived there (8500–4000 BCE) would have noted the colorful berries in the fall, gathered them to eat, and enjoyed one of the only sources of natural sweetness available besides honey. As they carried the grapes back to their camps in containers, the berries would rupture. We don't know exactly where or when the first human took a drink of grape juice that had sat around for a few days.

THE ACCIDENTAL PERSIAN LUSH

An ancient Persian story credits a woman of the court with the discovery of wine. This princess or member of the king's harem had lost the favor of the king and attempted to poison herself by eating some table grapes that she believed had spoiled in a jar. She became intoxicated and giddy and fell asleep. When she awoke, she no longer was afflicted by the stresses that had made her life intolerable. When she drank some more days-old juice, her conduct changed so remarkably that she regained the king's favor. He shared the woman's discovery with his court and decreed an increase in the production of days-old grapes.

This Persian story shows how fermentation happened inadvertently, with no human knowledge of the process, and alludes to how people first became aware that ingestion of this marvelous fruit could change human behavior and thinking. To early humans this new grape juice was magic, but magic they could create again and again by allowing the grapes to ripen, crushing the fruit, and letting the juice steep. Humans were unfamiliar with the process of fermentation and the grape was magic to them because they did not need to add yeast for fermentation. They did not know that yeast on the grape skins causes the fermentation. Thus grape juice was not only a fine source of energy, but it gave their harsh, difficult, and simple lives a connection to the mystical. Recent archaeological digs in eastern Turkey (Körtik) and northwestern Iran (Hajji Firuz Tepe) have revealed that humans were drinking wine—or a mixture of wine, honey, and fruit juice—at least eight thousand years ago. These areas, particularly in Turkey, are not far from Mount Ararat, where the ark was said to have landed and where mythological-biblical Noah planted his first vineyard. Archaeologists have found pottery shards, grape pips, and other detritus that attest this region is where the *Vitis* species shows the most genetic variation and therefore where it was likely first domesticated. The first wine cultures emerged in these upland areas around 7000 BCE.

Our neolithic ancestors probably returned every season to gather the wild grapes and once again drink, entering a different reality that was both pleasurable and meaningful. People began to settle in larger groups, that is, settlements. Archaeological evidence suggests that it took a few thousand years to figure out how to cultivate grapes. Because *Sylvestris* could be propagated only from seeds, as there were male and female plants, it was difficult to grow a consistent and reliable plant. Moreover, the yield of the wild grape vine is smaller than that of a domesticated one, and the vines tend to climb trees, making them difficult to harvest. This didn't stop neolithic societies from trying to grow the fruit for more reliable harvests.

Domestication of wine grapes probably took place at the end of the Neolithic period, around 4000 BCE, as people, through trial and error, noticed that some vines were hermaphroditic—the male and female parts of their flowers were equally well developed—and yielded a more genetically stable plant that produced consistent progeny if propagated.

Seed remains that have been dated to the sixth through the fourth millennia BCE suggest that, as time progressed, humans figured out how to clone hermaphroditic mutations with greater success. They did this because the fruit from wild vines is not as sweet as fruit from domesticated ones. As humans experimented and gained experience, their domesticated grapes became sweeter, good to eat, and even better for wine making.

Over time these early vine growers figured out that by taking a cutting from vines that had sweeter flavors, or larger berries, they could grow a new plant that was more like its parent than one grown from seed. In short, humans were learning to domesticate the Eurasian wine-grape vine at an early stage.

THE NOAH HYPOTHESIS

The Noah hypothesis suggests that he (or persons like him) was the first winemaker, and that this part of the Near East was likely the "original" foundation for the domestication and propagation of Vitis Vinifera. Did he contribute to the dispersion of the domesticated wine grape, *Vitis Vinifera* L. ssp. *vinifera,* into more southerly, environmentally friendly areas for the vine? Was this a unique event a one time, one place proposition? That one of Noah's first acts after the ark came to rest on Mount Ararat was to plant vineyards, make wine, and drink it aligns the biblical story with the empirical evidence found throughout the region and thus leads to this conclusion.

After the ark landed on Mount Ararat, YHWH made a promise: "Now when the YHWH smelled the pleasing odor, the YHWH said in his heart, 'I will never again curse the ground because of humankind, for the inclination of the human heart is evil from youth; nor will I ever again destroy every living creature as I have done. As long as the earth endures, seedtime and harvest . . . shall not cease'" (Genesis 8:21–22).

The Eurasian grape, which we know existed at the end of the Ice Age (roughly twelve thousand years ago), now has nearly ten thousand varieties and produces virtually all of the world's wine. Further, wild grapes have grown in Israel for hundreds of thousands of years, and viticultural remains date back to the Chalcolithic period around 4500 BCE.

The Noah hypothesis offers a tantalizing and plausible explanation of why the wine grape's origins are associated with northeastern Turkey and nearby regions in Iraq, Armenia, and Iran. By planting the vineyard, Noah literally set down roots after the chaos of the Flood.

Growing wine required a fixed location—a settlement at minimum—with people creating a new organization for virtually everything they did, which was quite different from the nomadic society that existed before the Flood. Early societies used the sacred and profane consequences of wine growing to understand their relationships with gods as well as to make humans' living conditions more comfortable and pleasant. Through Noah's initial establishment of a vineyard, he subsequently made wine and fulfilled the mandate from YHWH (implicit in his covenant) to disperse that technology to all humans. The guiding insight is the metaphorical notion of humankind's becoming civilized, with the cultivation of grapes for wine as a principal component of humanity's development of a closer relationship to nature and to YHWH.

THE FIRST BIBLICAL INTOXICATION

In early human societies the vineyard was a status symbol. J was probably writing the Noah story in the ninth or tenth century BCE, during the time of the kings, when Israel was becoming a powerful regional entity and the aristocracy clearly enjoyed the finer things in life. Therefore it seems reasonable to assign wine a privileged place in Noah's story.

Yet the behavior that followed this act of planting was anything but civilized. Noah's drunkenness resulted in Ham's betrayal of his father. The Noah story illustrates that with the advancement of civilization comes great responsibility. That which has the power to advance peoples also has the power to destroy them when treated foolishly. Wine is a gift from God that must be treated prudently and delicately. It stands as a sign for how humanity must reverence the creation.

DRUNKEN MONKEY HYPOTHESIS

The drunken monkey hypothesis is based on the observation that when primates eat fermented fruit, they often continue to eat until they are drunk. The hypothesis states that many species, primates especially, are "hard-wired" to enjoy eating fermenting fruit until intoxicated. We posit that the desire to do so regularly was a principal reason for domesticating the grape vine.

Noah's drunkenness after drinking his wine is perhaps an early example of this behavior. His subsequent behavior (with his sons) shows humanity's recognition of the delicate nature of relations between God and humans. By succumbing to the intoxicating and negative side of wine, Noah had broken his covenant with God and had to make amends by encouraging humanity to propagate the vine and respect its power. Over time humans learned to control and domesticate this source of pleasure. Their relationship to the vine became symbiotic; human interaction with the vine helped to produce a more consistent organism that would in turn produce higher quality fruit in line with the new importance wine held in religious and cultural terms.

THE GILGAMESH EPIC

Noah's experiences with viticulture, enology, and wine drinking find a parallel in the Gilgamesh epic, which dates from the fourth millennium BCE. Gilgamesh, a king who is part god, enters a grove of trees that is described as bearing fruit that looks like the precious stones carnelian and lapis lazuli. Shortly after, on his way to the mouth of the rivers, Gilgamesh meets Siduri, the maker of wine. She owns a tavern and serves him either wine or beer she made from the "Tree of Life"—this is not clear because of a gap in the surviving tablet. Siduri functions as a wise female deity, associated with fermentation and selling this new and exciting grape wine.

In the same Gilgamesh story, Enkidu is a primitive man—he is unkempt, covered with hair, and lives in the wild like the biblical Adam. Enkidu becomes human when a harlot named Shamkatum seduces him, and he eats bread and drinks beer, or perhaps wine. "Enkidu knows not how to eat bread," she said, "nor how to drink beer." She then beseeched him: "Eat bread, Enkidu, as it is part of life! Drink beer as it is the custom of the land." The narrative continues: "The wild beast Enkidu ate bread . . . then drank beer, seven cups full. His spirit relaxed and became free. He started to talk in a loud voice. Well-being filled his body and his face turned bright. He washed his matted fleece with water and rubbed his body with oil, and Enkidu became human." Essentially the intoxicating beverage was what animated Enkidu. Drinking this brew civilized him—made him human. By making Enkidu's animal nature gentle, this intoxicant—whether beer or wine—helped to define who he was.

Something about intoxicating beverages like beer and wine tied humans to earth and to their humanity. Drinking these and experiencing the results, which combined physical with emotional effects that brought people potentially "closer" to the divine, helped the consumer have a unique mystical revelation and illuminated to people the great difference between other animals and themselves.

Who is to say that Adam's eating fruit from the tree of knowledge of good and evil was not fermented fruit? In 3 Baruch and 4 Ezra, both probably written in the first century CE, the tree of knowledge is clearly identified with the vine and wine, for divine wisdom comes from drinking the grape, as wine is the beverage of the gods, an ancient view. Like Adam's eating fruit from the tree, perhaps Enkidu's and Noah's first encounter with beer and wine introduced them to their mortality.

The oldest collection of laws, the Laws of Hammurabi (ca. 2250 BCE), established a daily ration of beer; how much you received depended on your social standing. A common worker received two quarts a day, civil servants three quarts, administrators and high priests five quarts. In the ancient Near East beer often served as a form of currency or was used for barter. Both Gilgamesh and Noah drank more than the daily ration prescribed in these most ancient laws. Both the Gilgamesh and biblical flood stories teach that the buzz of alcohol can either enlighten or damage.

EARLIEST WINE MAKING

The Bible helps us to understand the origin of wine and wine making, as do the stories of Gilgamesh and the Persian lush. The drunken monkey hypothesis gives us a plausible scientific basis for human desire and need for alcoholic beverages; wine is merely the easiest to understand and produce. The Noah hypothesis provides an explanation for where, when, how, and perhaps even why the wild grape became domesticated by humans.

Because the area around Mount Ararat was climatically hospitable to the grape, and thus open to the cultivation of other crops, human society began to settle in the valleys and along the lower hills that form the lowlands of the Taurus, Zagros, and Caucasus Mountains. This implies that *Homo sapiens* had become capable of "creating society." Domesticating the wine grape took several thousand years, and that time frame dovetails with when humans began to live more stable and meaningful lives. By Noah's time (late Neolithic/Chalcolithic period), human settlements were beginning to trade with other similarly evolving settlements farther south, in Syria, Israel, and Lebanon, as well as in northern Iraq and Iran, where the desire for wine would have been a newfound, even exotic, product. Jericho, located northeast of Jerusalem in the Jordan Valley and one of the oldest cities in the world, was likely one of these settlements. The more productive economies of these growing communities allowed for expanded farming and new vineyards where the climate and land were compatible with the domesticated grape.

Biblically speaking, the Bible wine trail led south and west as the mythical Noah repopulated the world after the Flood and, just as important, led to the revival of ordered life, including Man's pre-eminent position as Yahweh's instrument on earth to effect his Work. The grape vine and wine were among the most important instruments to lead to this new type of civilization from a world up-ended by the chaos resulting from the Flood. Whether historical or not, Noah serves as the prototype of the first wine grower and the first founder of a vineyard/winery, and his location coincides with archaeological findings today.

THE FIRST VINEYARDS: ARARAT, THE TAURUS, THE CAUCASUS AND ZAGROS MOUNTAINS

Plausible evidence from recent research reveals that the biblical flood was not just a myth, nor are other flood stories from Akkadian inscriptions or Babylonian sources mere fiction. Indeed, geological evidence supports the idea that around 5600 BCE, the last Ice Age warming period, which had been evolving for about one thousand years, greatly raised sea levels. The Mediterranean's saltwater breached the northern end of the Bosporus, rapidly creating a gigantic flood that inundated the fresh waters of the Black Sea, which sits below sea level, with massive force and rising water. Within a few years the Black Sea was level with the Mediterranean, its shoreline similar to today's.

What had been waterfront property, with fertile soils, forests, and isolated settlements with primitive farmland nearby, was deluged; only those who escaped to higher ground survived. This earlier culture had by then learned to cultivate the barley or wild wheat seeds it had, and these people took their culture with them beyond the rising waters. In 2000 Robert Ballard, the marine salvage expert, explored Black Sea waters 300 feet deep off the Turkish shoreline and found the remains of wooden houses, revealing that people had lived there before the Flood.

The wild grape vine would have thrived in this warming environment, and the knowledge of how to select the appropriate vine cuttings and plant them most likely traveled with them as they escaped the floods. Those surviving the initial flood shock-waves, who had lived on the southern and eastern shores of the Black Sea, went southeast toward the higher ground that culminated in the enormous, singular bulk of Mount Ararat, which rises more than 17,000 feet above sea level from the plain and low hills below.

Others likely traveled farther south toward the Taurus Mountains of southern Turkey or went east or northeast toward the lowlands of the Caucasus Mountains in Georgia and Armenia; the mountains would have been a forbidding barrier to further travel. Some headed southeast to the Zagros Mountains of northwestern Iran.

All these areas were then climatically hospitable to the grape vine and suitable for humans. According to Ryan and Pitman, other populations on the north shore of the deepening Black Sea likely traveled west and north, populating Europe and the colder, less hospitable, northern steppes of Ukraine, Russia, and central Europe.

THE CLIMATE AT THE DAWN OF HUMAN WINE GROWING

The wine grape grows best at latitudes of 30 to 50 degrees north or south; in Europe and western Asia this area extends from North Africa, including Egypt, to southern Germany and mid-Ukraine. The vine needs a period of true dormancy to grow best, and areas within these latitudes have both temperate climate zones and a true winter. Anyone who has been in the tropics, or near the equator, knows that these conditions don't exist at lower latitudes. In warm, humid climates grape vines will grow riotously, producing lots of vegetation but little fruit. Wine grapes planted in a semitropical climate, such as southern India or Thailand, often produce two crops a year of pallidly flavored fruit, even with sufficient pruning.

Less humidity in temperate climes allows the fruit to mature with less likelihood of disease, fungus, and other maladies. The grape vine evolved an ability to survive and grow in poorer soils, where water availability is less abundant, yet it doesn't tolerate severe cold weather, such as that found in higher latitudes like Russia or even southern Europe at the beginning of the last Ice Age incursion, approximately fourteen thousand to seventeen thousand years ago. The grape vine does require sufficient water (ca. 400 mm/16 inches a year) to survive and develop a root structure. That water must come in a relatively predictable and regular way, which is one reason that grape vines do not thrive naturally in desert areas. The cradle of grape cultivation falls well within that range, from a latitude of about 38 to 45 degrees north. From previous studies we know that by the end of the last Ice Age (ca. 6000 BCE), the habitat of the wild grape vine extended to the Fertile Crescent region and to Italy, Greece, and the coastal areas of Turkey.

Other factors also made these regions a natural fit for the grape vine. These zones were in upland areas, with forests, rivers, and hillsides with elevations as high as 6,500 feet; they were much more temperate than the arid, hellish climate of lowlands in southern Iraq. What seems evident from reading Genesis and the story of Noah is that, as a prototypical grape grower and winemaker, he planted cultivated wine grapes, not wild grapes. Eastern Turkey, northern Iraq, and Iran might not seem hospitable to vine growing today. What was different then, climatically or otherwise, that allowed humans (Noah) to plant vineyards and prosper?

Since the late twentieth century, excavations within the Fertile Crescent point to a rather different climate, one that provided the conditions for the domestication of the wild grape conducive to cultivation of *Vitis vinifera*. Beginning about twenty-two thousand years ago, the climate of the Middle East, encompassing the Fertile Crescent, the Levant (modern Syria, Jordan, Israel, and Lebanon), and probably Egypt, entered a glacial period that lasted for several thousand years in the late Pleistocene. About nineteen thousand years ago a fairly rapid warming began, with many fluctuations for several thousand years, culminating in an extended cooling period called the Younger Dryas, between thirteen and eleven thousand years ago. During the warming period the vast Ice Age glaciers and ice sheets retreated, leaving behind rocky deposits of all sizes that were high in mineral content. Also, the Near East was a volcanically active area; over the eons the volcanoes spewed lava, which then broke down into further mineral- and metal-rich soils, providing nutrients to vines.

The Levant saw a gradual but steady warming period, with more moisture, leading to the formation of underground aquifers and springs, especially in Israel. The period included two extremely wet cycles around 6400 BCE and 5600 BCE that were punctuated by a cool, dry period lasting a couple hundred years (ca. 6200 BCE). Melting ice caused sea levels to rise, and the consequently larger bodies of water reflected the sun's heat, moderating the climate in a positive way for humans and wine grapes. Paleoclimatologists note that the period from roughly 6200 to 2000 BCE was warmer and wetter than previously. Equally important was that the region also saw sequential, shorter periods of rapid climate change: dramatically warmer and drier conditions would prevail for thirty to one hundred years before another wet cycle began. Evidence at archaeological sites indicates that one such period of abrupt drought likely took place around Lake Van (Mount Ararat) around 4700 BCE, while farther west at Eski Acigöl, south of the Black Sea, the wetter conditions prevailed longer and dried out only gradually.

As the land dried out, survivors found higher ground that was arable, or they moved to less affected areas farther south and east. These alternating periods of wet and dry, cooler and warmer no doubt had a strong effect on human migrations, societal change, and the fortunes of later empires. Nomadic groups could settle down, raise animals, grow crops, and form a stable community, trading with other groups within a reasonable distance.

But drastic climate change also involved intermittent droughts (as after the Flood) that encouraged people to adapt and create new technologies and means of production, likely accelerating the domestication of the wild grape vine and its intensive cultivation on suitable sites.

The preponderance of classic terra rossa (soil of fine red clays over porous limestone rock) found throughout the region provided excellent land for vineyards, holding in groundwater as well as the vegetative cover that prevents the erosion typical of today's desert climate. In the southern Levant particularly, cultures created sophisticated irrigation systems to make use of the extra water. The situation had changed somewhat by 1900 BCE, but people like Abraham still settled in the Negev, for example, as it was more productive then than it is today.

The landscape of the Levant and the Fertile Crescent played a major, unquestionable role in the evolution of Bronze Age societies from subsistence cultures to more sedentary, village-based farming societies. These produced enough food (and wine) to enable them to expand their control of neighboring areas. Studies in the area have shown that the bare hills we see today were still covered by thick terra rossa soils, held in place by oak-pistachio (terebinth) forests and Mediterranean maquis in the north of Israel. Lighter loess (wind-blown deposits) soils covered by steppic vegetation predominated in the South. For the descendants of Noah, including Abraham, entering the Levantine areas on a journey from the arid east of Ur (southern Iraq) in the early second millennium BCE must indeed have seemed like entering a veritable garden, one most suitable to the vine.

At the neolithic settlement of Hajji Firuz Tepe in the Zagros Mountains of northwestern Iran, archaeologists have found some of the earliest samples of clay jars with wine residue; these date to about 5400 to 5000 BCE.

More recently, in early 2011, an excavation found an extensive winemaking operation, about six thousand years old, containing not only a fermenting vat but also the remains of a drinking cup made from animal horn, storage jars, dried grapes, and seeds. Botanical analyses showed the grapes were indeed cultivated, and the presence of malvidin, a compound that gives red wine its color, revealed that the wine being made was a red wine.

The discovery in southern Armenia was made less than 60 miles from Mount Ararat. The cave is located in an upland area about 1,100 feet above sea level and was carved out of the karst (porous limestone) rock typical of the region, an ideal geology for the wine grape. Dr. Patrick McGovern, a leading biomolecular archaeologist, called this the earliest wine-making facility yet found, further evidence that humans have been making wine for a very long time.

HOW WINE MIGRATED THROUGHOUT THE BIBLICAL WORLD

The Old and New Testaments use the words *wine* 280 times, *vine* 49 times, *vineyard* 72 times, *cup* 49 times, and *winepress* at least 15 times (New Revised Standard Version [NRS] 1989). The Old Testament commonly uses words like *tirosh* (new wine) and *yayin* (fermented wine) respectively to describe wine.

Deuteronomy 7:1 mentions the peoples of at least seven nations, from Hittites and Amorites to Canaanites, spread throughout what we call the Fertile Crescent and into the Levant. Hittite wines and Canaanite wines were highly regarded during the first and second millennia BCE. Even earlier, beginning in the mid- to late fourth millennium BCE, pharaohs hired Canaanite wine experts to create vineyards in Egypt.

Most of the very early evidence for grape cultivation appeared around 6000 BCE. As trade increased between societies in the region—down the Tigris and Euphrates valleys, west into Anatolia, and south into the Jordan Valley and Lebanon, among others—domesticated vines became disseminated farther afield. Grape pips unearthed at the site of Tell esh-Shuna tell us that cultivated vines had reached Israel in the Jordan Valley by the early fourth millennium BCE. McGovern notes that in lower Mesopotamia grapes could be grown only if they were irrigated and protected from the sun, and therefore they were available only to royalty. At the beginning of the third millennium BCE, vines were planted near Shiraz in the Zagros Mountains to the northeast to supply the lowland areas. The problem was that to get this wine, the king of Ur/Sumer would have to incur serious expenses to ship it by boat or mule train to his capital. It would necessarily have to be of finer quality to justify the expense. From economic documents that have been found, McGovern calculated that by the second millennium BCE, the equivalent of an inexpensive wine like Two Buck Chuck from California would have cost three to five times more in lower Mesopotamia to ship from Armenia or eastern Turkey south, than growing the same wine nearer to the royal residences. Indeed the highland area around

Shiraz became famous for the quality of its wines, which only royalty could afford to ship south to Ur.

New evidence shows that domesticated grape vines arrived in the northern Levant by the sixth millennium BCE. In fact viticultural knowledge may have arrived even earlier, probably because of trade between Anatolia and Byblos (in modern Lebanon).

By the middle of the fourth millennium BCE knowledge of wine making and domesticated viticulture had extended into Egypt and westward to Cyprus. In chapter 2 we turn toward Ur, Canaan, and Egypt. While the historic accuracy of much of Genesis remains conjectural, the story of wine now moves into recorded history. We shall focus our attention first upon wine's influence in the rising civilizations of the Fertile Crescent and Egypt and how the Hebrew patriarchs and their descendants regarded wine.

Two

FROM MESOPOTAMIA TO ISRAEL

Abraham, Wine, Salt, and Sex

Now may God give you of the dew of heaven,
And of the fatness of the earth,
And an abundance of grain and new wine.

—Genesis 27:28

UR: THE ROYAL USE AND SACRED NATURE OF WINE

A fine map in Patrick McGovern's *Uncorking the Past* shows the spread of technology for making fermented beverages that emanated from the upland areas around the Caucasus, the Taurus Mountains, and the northern Zagros Mountains beginning around 7500 BCE.

Wine became a significant facet of the cultures of the early Levantine societies, including those soon to arise in Turkey (like the Hittites'), as well as of the Uruk/Sumerian culture that was developing in the lower Tigris and Euphrates valleys of Mesopotamia.

Both Egypt and Mesopotamia developed a beer culture, a result of the cyclic nature of their river systems. Both regions have desert climates, and both have rivers that flood periodically, then carry silts and rich organic matter downstream to areas that local inhabitants soon found were well suited for growing cereal crops. The rivers' proximity also ensured a regular water supply. Beer making takes about ten times as much water as wine making. In contrast, having sufficient water to make beer was a challenge in the semiarid, nonriverine environments of much of the Levant, where rainfall was often scarce.

In Mesopotamia, as in Egypt, farmers relied on regular flooding to grow cereal crops like barley that provided both food and a main ingredient for beer. Besides, their alluvial soils, with poor drainage and a shallow water table, are not conducive to growing vines.

Wine was available only to royalty and the wealthy. According to a later Greek story, Dionysus, whose origins were associated with a more ancient eastern deity, fled from Mesopotamia because people there drank only beer. This was a Greek way of explaining the barbarian nature of Babylonian society: they drank beer and not wine.

Wine also was a luxury for Sumerian royalty, because of the great cost of transporting it down the Tigris River from the highlands. Excavations at Godin Tepe, a town in the highlands to the northeast of Ur and the city of Uruk in ancient Sumer reveal that wines were made there as early as 3500 BCE. The people of the lowlands, including Ur, sought out these places to grow crops like wine grapes that wouldn't grow well in their lowland environment, given the heat, the salinity of the soils, and other impediments.

Residue of tartaric acid scraped from a ceramic jar at Hajji Firuz Tepe in the northern Zagros Mountains of Iran revealed that the jar contained wine. This jar dated to an even older period, circa 5200 BCE. A second jar analyzed from the same site showed that the wine had been flavored with resin from a terebinth tree (*Pistacia terebinthus*), also common in Turkey and a known antioxidant, antimicrobial substance (so this would have been the original retsina). The royals of Sumer clearly had access to fine wine grapes grown in the northern highlands of their empire, such as at Hajji Firuz Tepe, albeit at a price. Further south, little evidence for viticulture in Mesopotamia around Ur exists before the middle of the third millennium BCE, though documents from the period of 2125–2110 BCE, during the reign of King Gudea of Lagash, note that the "lord of the city" built irrigated terraces protected by trees to be used for planting grape vines.

Mentions of wine in tablets from Ur that date from about 2400 BCE do not make clear whether they are talking about date or grape wine, though likely the latter. Grape wine (*kas-geštin* in Sumerian) existed in Babylonia but probably only for the elites. Intriguingly, in Mesopotamia the Fourth Dynasty of Kish, north of Ur near Babylon, was founded by a female wine merchant called Azag-Bau, who ruled about 3089 BCE and probably dealt in date wine. Vineyards in northwest Mesopotamia are described as plantations with thousands of trees; these supported the vines, at least as far back as Ur's Third Dynasty, around 2500 BCE. Free-standing vines did not yet exist, and tree-trained vines are consistent with pre-Sumerian imagery and the vine's basic biology as a climbing plant.

Wine was also a sacred drink in Uruk since it accompanied the sacred rites performed by priests, often with music. Drinking was a ritualized aspect of the Sumerian/Uruk culture. If wine became important in Mesopotamia early on, then its consumption and sacred use in ancient Turkey perhaps is even more so.

EARLY WINE GROWING IN TURKEY

Given the archaeological evidence from sites as diverse as Göbekli Tepe in the East, Troy in the West on the Hellespont, and certainly around the Hittite capital, Hattuşa, there's no question that wine was made and consumed in Turkey from earliest times. According to recent research by McGovern and colleagues, clay bowls and goblets found in southeastern Turkey at Hallan Çemi and dating from roughly 6000 BCE contain the residue of grape wine. Southeastern Turkey, as well as Georgia and Armenia, now are considered the origin points for the domestication of the *Vitis* species. Given recent linguistic findings that Hittite is an origin language, and evidence from biomolecular archaeology and grape genetic studies, researchers like José Vouillamoz consider that "South eastern Anatolia is the most likely primary domestication centre of the grapevine." The Hittites appear quite early in biblical texts (Gen. 23:10) and were known to the early Hebrews, as well as the later Israelites. The Hittites, who ruled from Hattuşa, their capital in north-central Anatolia, developed an appreciation for wine as early as the third millennium BCE. From the Hittite language comes what is perhaps the ancestral word for wine, *wiyana,* which meant grape and/or wine. Its other descendants today are *vinum* in Latin and *oinos* in ancient Greek. The Hittite texts also reveal that the same word/ideogram in Sumerian, *geštin,* was phonetically pronounced as *wiyana.* It too means grape, grape vine, and wine. Anatolia in Turkey is notable today for being the original home of two prized varieties, kalecik karasi and narince. Hittite royalty prized Anatolian wine; gold wine cups and grape pips dating from 1750 BCE have been found in tombs at Karahöyük. A superb Hittite beak wine jug with a grape motif that dates from 2000 BCE was found in the homeland of Narince near Tokat, providing further evidence of the high value placed on wine in Hittite culture.

As the Hittites conquered new lands, they spread their wine culture, introducing it to Babylon around 1600 BCE, the Mitanni kingdom in northern Syria three centuries later, and finally to Egypt, with which the Hittites signed a peace treaty around 1284 BCE. All these cultures showed an appreciation for wine, but it may have been less important to their culture than to the Hittites'. Cuneiform Hittite tablets tell us that the Hittites even had words to distinguish various types of wine, such as *geštin gibil*—new young wine; *geštin làl*—honeyed wine; and *geštin kaš*—a cocktail of wine and beer.

In time Assyria, the nascent power to the east, also adopted aspects of Hittite culture, including appreciation for banquets and distinctive wines. The Hittite reverence for wine eventually spread west to the Aegean coastal areas and to the far southern reaches of the Anatolian plateau, where it ran headlong into the evolving wine-loving cultures of Canaan and Babylonia to the east. We now return to these lands on our journey.

FROM UR TO ISRAEL: ABRAHAM
DISCOVERS WINE ON HIS JOURNEY

In Genesis, after the story of Noah and the Flood, wine does not show up again for several millennia and scores of generations, and then in a different place. After Abram ("father of many," who becomes familiarly known as Abraham, "father of multitude," after YHWH renames him while making a covenant with him, Gen. 17:5) defeats the soldiers of the kings of Sodom and Gomorrah's army near Hobah, north of Damascus, he turns south toward Jerusalem (Gen. 15) and passes by Shaveh, which is not far from Hobah. There the king of Sodom comes out to meet Abraham (Gen. 17), and Melchizedek, king of Salem (Jerusalem), then joins them, offering wine from local vineyards and bread.

What this vignette tells us is that Abraham had to deal with a range of kings, societies, and peoples who were living in the region, where *Vitis vinifera* had also taken up residence. It also hints at the closer ties in literature between the emerging culture of the lower Tigris and Euphrates valleys and the Levantine societies. The appearance of Abraham among Canaanites and other Levantine wine-drinking societies coming from Ur, where wine was primarily a noble drink and relatively uncommon otherwise, provides only the second mention of wine in the Old Testament after Noah. Yet this meeting between Melchizedek and Abraham has even greater implications. Is it possible that his meeting with Melchizedek provided Abraham's first exposure to grape wine? It ultimately symbolizes the coming together for the first time of two different cultures, Hebrew and Canaanite; one was in the infant stage of a novel religious evolution toward monotheism, and the other was entrenched in traditional polytheistic culture. Abraham, who has arrived in a new land, meets something both unfamiliar and novel, wine. He had come from a desert, beer-drinking region, and Canaan offers a vision of a new world, one promised by YHWH to Abraham, in which he would become a "great nation" (Gen. 12:2). Indeed Canaan—the countries of Israel, Lebanon, and Jordan today—by the seventh millennium BCE became a great new world for the grape as traders and new cultures took up its cultivation as they moved out of the Fertile Crescent.

The historical evidence for wine in Canaan, however, goes back only to the fourth millennium BCE, though likely even much earlier, with cultivated grape seeds found at Tell esh-Shuna in the Jordan Valley. This where we next pick up the Bible wine trail.

HARAN: TRAVELS AND TRAVAILS

The Abraham saga in Genesis (Gen. 11:10–25:18) moves the biblical narrative from the Garden of Eden to the migration and civilization of a people. Although the story of wine begins with Noah at Mount Ararat, it moves from there with Abraham as he journeys within the Fertile Crescent from Mesopotamia to the Promised Land. Noah may have been the first to plant vineyards and get intoxicated, but Abraham received bread and wine as a sign of a blessing.

On Abraham's travels from Ur to Canaan, his first major stop was in Haran. Haran lay on a trade route near the Tigris and Euphrates Rivers and was a strategic Assyrian city; it controlled the point where the road from

Damascus joined the highway between Nineveh and Carchemish. Because Haran had an abundance of goods that passed through its region, it became a target for raids.

Haran also was not far from Mari, where a royal wine archive was discovered. The archive contained letters written from Mari during Abraham's time; they describe the activities of a confederation of seminomadic tribes like Abraham's in the vicinity of Haran near the Balikh River. Abraham may have traveled through Mari, which was on the middle Euphrates, on his way to Haran. Both cities would have traded in wine.

While living in Ur and then settling in Haran, Abraham would have heard about the costly beverage that only kings, diplomats, and the wealthy could afford. He likely did not drink wine, because he had not yet become "very rich in livestock, in silver, and in gold" (Gen. 13:2). However, as he acquired some wealth in Haran (Gen. 12:5), the opportunity to purchase this prized beverage may have arisen.

When Abraham left Harran, he also left behind the local deities and his household gods, which his relatives kept there (Gen. 31:19). According to the Bible, YHWH told Abraham to leave the nation of Haran and go to Canaan, because the city of Haran was the chief home of the "heathen" Mesopotamian moon god Sin: "Now YHWH said to Abram, 'Go from your country and your kindred and your father's house to the land that I will show you. I will make of you a great nation, and I will bless you, and make your name great, so that you will be a blessing. I will bless those who bless you, and the one who curses you I will curse; and in you all the families of the earth shall be blessed'" (Gen. 12:1–4).

So Abraham left his country, his family, and his gods to follow YHWH to the land of Canaan. The narrative suggests that Abraham brought his wife, Sarai (Sarah), and his brother's son Lot, and all their possessions.

ABRAHAM'S JOURNEY

From Haran, Abraham journeyed to Shechem and probably would have traveled through Imar, Ebla, Qatna, and Damascus—all places where winepresses have been found—to get there. So he probably encountered wine during the trip. The city of Shechem lay between Mount Ebal and Mount Gerizim (central Israel). Shechem in later times was a place with vineyards, where the wine flowed freely (Judg. 9:27). An ancient winepress was discovered at Shechem, too.

Today Shechem (Nablus) lies on the West Bank in the middle of the Shomron (Samaria) wine region with several wineries nearby. A winery named Tura, where the wine is made by settlers, lies on the southern ridge of Mount Gerizim. A settlement called Har Bracha (Mount of Blessing) was established at the top of the mountain in 1982. This region, once rich in wines, is again considered to be fine land for vineyards; wineries such as Tishbi source grapes from its vineyards. From Shechem, Abraham's journey took him to the hill country east of Bethel, where excellent vineyards still produce fine wines today. There Abraham pitched a tent and built an altar to YHWH (Gen. 12:8).

Two ancient wine presses have turned up at a site where Bethel would have been located. A later biblical passage describes someone carrying a jug of wine in Bethel (1 Sam. 10:3). Today several wineries, including Psagot and Tanya, are located in the north Jerusalem Mountains near Bethel. Next, "Abram journeyed on by stages toward the Negeb" (Gen. 12:9). It's likely that the climate was cooler and slightly more humid before Abraham's time (early in the second millennium BCE). The edges of the Negev would have been more fertile and quasi-pastoral. The water tables were higher in the Negev then, and streams breached their banks and flowed into rich alluvial bottom-lands that were used for farming.

This weather slowly changed around Abraham's time and led to a horti-cultural breakdown that in turn depopulated the region. As the climate entered a prolonged dry period, people abandoned the land and the surplus cash-crop from the production of olives and wine. At the time Abraham settled there, overall rainfall was down, the forests were receding, and stream hydrology (the study of the movement, distribution, and quality of water), was changing, es-pecially in the south near the Negev. As a result Abraham and the other people in the area experienced famine. Because of the famine Abraham and his wife, Sarah, went to Egypt (Gen. 12:10).

Once the famine was alleviated by the fluctuating weather patterns, Abraham and Sarah left Egypt and returned to the Negev. Genesis (13:1–2) says, "So Abram went up from Egypt, he and his wife, and all that he had, and Lot with him, into the Negev. Now Abram was very rich in livestock, in silver, and in gold" (Gen. 13:2). Abraham would have been able to purchase wine in the Negev, where it was still possible to grow grapes. Although it is a desert today, the Negev produces wines (Kadesh Barnea Winery, Sde Boker Winery), thanks to irrigation; societies in Abraham's time probably developed new irrigation schemes to adapt to the weather changes. Some studies also conclude from analyses of ancient climate data that the Negev was more humid in ancient times than today. The Nabateans, who came later, probably adapted much of this technology from previous cultures.

Recently, the Negev has gained popularity for viticulture. Winemakers have built wineries near ancient winepresses such as those found at Shivta, a few miles from Sde Boker Winery, that date at least to 100 BCE. Viticulturists have planted vineyards in the higher elevations of the central Negev, as well as around Ramat Arad in the semiarid northeast Negev. The *terroir* (physical characteristics of a specific site/region) provides sandy to loamy soils (a mixture of sand, clay, silt, and organic matter). Temperatures range from extremely hot days to cold nights, which produce grapes with balanced sugars and acids. Early morning mists cover the vineyards. Just as the ancient prophets suggested—and Israel's first prime minister, David Ben-Gurion, dreamed when he established the National Water Carrier system to flow to the Negev—"the desert would again bloom."

SETTLEMENT

After wandering from the northernmost to the southernmost edges of the Fertile Crescent and sojourning in the Negev, Abraham remembered the lushness of the North. We speculate that if he had first tasted wines in Bethel and Shechem, then later in the Negev, his experience would no doubt be similar to tasting cabernet sauvignon and merlot in Lodi, California, after tasting the same varieties in Washington State: familiar flavors but riper and less refined because of the much warmer, drier climate of the desert. Hence, "he journeyed on by stages from the Negev as far as Bethel, to the place where his tent had originally been, between Bethel and Ai" (Gen. 13:3).

Abraham and Lot each had acquired so many herds, workers, and possessions that they could not settle together. They split up, with Lot choosing to move near Zoar, where the plain of the Jordan River was fertile and lush, ideal for vineyards such as noted at Jezreel, and Abraham settled in the land of Canaan, near the oaks of Mamre at Hebron, and built an altar to YHWH there (Gen. 13:14–18).

Hebron, one of the oldest cities in civilization, is located in the Jerusalem Mountains wine region, about 16 miles west of the Dead Sea and about 20 miles south of Jerusalem. The "oaks of Mamre" (*ēlōnê mamrēʿ*) most likely refers to a Canaanite cultic shrine just north of Hebron that in Abraham's time was dedicated to El, the supreme sky god of the Canaanite pantheon. Today, as in Abraham's time, Hebron is surrounded by rolling hills and vineyards. Abraham so prized the area that when his wife, Sarah, died, he purchased a burial site for her in Hebron. Numbers (13:23–24) describes an area called the Wadi Eshcol (Valley of Grape Cluster), where grapes grew in huge clusters.

THE GAME CHANGER: ABRAHAM'S MEETING WITH MELCHIZEDEK

Although Abraham was living in wine country, and Genesis (13:2) informs that he had become "very rich in livestock, in silver and in gold," the first mention of Abraham's drinking grape wine occurs during his encounter with Melchizedek.

The story of Melchizedek and Abraham has so affected the world of wine that the largest bottle made—30 liters, or just under 8 gallons—is the melchizedek bottle, which holds 40 bottles of wine. Abraham's encounter with Melchizedek represents his "first contact" with a local king who welcomes him to Canaan instead of waging war.

"Now King Melchizedek of Salem [Jerusalem] brought out bread and wine; he was priest of Ēl ʿelyôn. He blessed him [Abraham] and said, 'Blessed be Abram by Ēl ʿelyôn, maker of heaven and earth; and blessed be Ēl ʿelyôn, who has delivered your enemies into your hand!' And Abram gave him one tenth of everything" (Gen. 14:18).

Abraham acknowledges not only Melchizedek's kingship here but also his priesthood and temple by giving tithes and by grounding the story in the cultic setting. Abraham helped Melchizedek become the head of an alliance of Canaanite cities that would later be the tribes of Israel. In a sense Melchizedek serves as an agent of change who demonstrates for Abraham a link between wine and spiritual practices. Melchizedek, the first person known to share wine with the first Patriarch, sets a precedent for Isaac and Jacob whose wine heritage would create a blessing that would follow the history of Israel, as we will show in chapter 3.

Two sources of Bible stories (the J, discussed in chapter 1, and P, "Priestly Writer") contribute to this one story about Abraham and Melchizedek, but they describe different traditions and name different wine gods. The J source ends the story at Genesis 14:17, where the king of Sodom goes out to meet Abraham after the battle, but no exchange of goods takes place. However, at this first meeting, the P source says King Melchizedek of Salem brings bread and wine (*yayin*) to Abraham (Gen. 14:18–20). In the Semitic languages spoken in the northwestern part of the Fertile Crescent, *Salem* is an abbreviated form of *Jerusalem,* which meant "city of Salem/peace" in those languages.

No other account in Genesis even alludes to Jerusalem. Monarchies in the ancient Near East often built names around the city gods. In the P source these deities would have been Shalem and Zedek. Shalem is probably a wine god who is mentioned as early as 2000 BCE—he's mentioned in the Kultepe tablets. Zedek was the local deity of Jerusalem before David declared the city for the kingdom of Israel as opposed to the kingdom of Judah. So the writer avoided using *Jerusalem,* probably because it was so associated with the specific faith ideas of a later time. Thus, when Abraham acknowledged Melchizedek's kingship and tithed to his temple, Abraham was in effect accepting an older Canaanite system of worshiping three deities, Ēl ʿelyôn, Shalem, and Zedek, one of which was certainly a wine god (Ēl ʿelyôn).

This story takes another vinous twist. The J source refers to another wine god named Eshcol, who would have been subordinate to Ēl ʿelyôn. In Ugaritic literature Ēl ʿelyôn is the monarchic head of the Canaanite pantheon. The mention of Eshcol in Genesis 14:13 and 24 is similar to how the Yahwist portrays YHWH in Genesis 18. Throughout the J source's telling, even YHWH is less godlike—he works as a peasant farmer and walks with Adam as one human walks with another (Gen. 2). The J source had a tendency to anthropomorphize the gods. As a result J seems to refer to the three gods who came to see Abraham as "three men" but later reveals that one was YHWH (Gen. 18:2).

Similarly, J speaks of "three brothers"—Mamre, Eshcol, and Aner. The same J source elsewhere mentions three giants (Ahiman, Sheshai, and Talmai), who were in the Wadi Eshcol during the season of the first ripe grapes. In J, Mamre appears to be a god of oak groves (Gen. 14:13), and Eshcol, which literally means "grape cluster," seems to be the god of grapes or wine (Gen. 14:13). By the time the J source was written down, these three gods appear to have been anthropomorphized as brothers, men, or giants. Thus the wine god Eshcol may have already been absorbed into Ēl ʿelyôn by the time Abraham met with Melchizedek.

This foreshadows the fully formed monotheistic consolidation and sensibility of divine attributes, especially when pertaining to the giving and receiving of wine. As the Israelite identity becomes more associated with one god, this *one* deity takes on the attributes of all the local gods that influenced Israelite culture before Israel monotheism, and yet is still presented in Genesis in an anthropomorphic fashion. By naming the Wadi Eshcol after the wine god Eshcol, the attributes of this deity are brought into the fold of monotheism. Hence, the wine god is not severed completely from Israel's one God but is channeled into Ēl ʿelyôn and eventually YHWH, whereby the rituals that center around wine become part of the covenant and liturgy. From here on, one of the key attributes of YHWH is that of a wine god who would later anchor the patriarchal blessings within viticulture (Gen 27:28; 49:22–26).

Ironically, the traditions around the deity Ēl ʿelyôn later became part of Israelite religion. Even the psalmists seem to inherit these traditions (Ps. 46:5). Genesis 14 brings together cultures by designating the gods, wine gods, and chief god of the Canaanite shrine in a way that Abraham can acknowledge him. When Melchizedek blesses Abraham, he also uses the phrase "maker of heaven and earth" along with Ēl ʿelyôn, as another way of referring to YHWH. Since Ēl ʿelyôn is the creator and most high God, one of whose primary roles is as a wine god, his identification by Hebrews as YHWH aligns Abraham's people with the dominant wine-drinking culture of the region and attests to wine's importance within their future religious and cultural beliefs.

This event gave Abraham a new place on the stage of biblical history not only because he was victorious over these four kings (of Elam, Goiim, Shinar and Ellasar, Gen. 14:9) but also because he gained a new social status by receiving wine at a time when this beverage was costly and only privileged classes were able to drink it.

The breaking of bread and drinking of wine were woven into many religious rituals throughout the ancient Near East. Believers often offered drinks of wine to the gods. In Mesopotamia wine was linked to the concept of creation, for example, through the Babylonian creation story, the Enuma Elish. It describes Marduk's nomination as chief god at a banquet while the other gods lighten their hearts with wine. In a ritual and prayer to Ištar of Nineveh, one libation ritual suggested: "The diviner breaks one thin loaf for Ištar of Nineveh and crumbles it into the spring. Afterward he again breaks one thin loaf for Ištar of Nineveh and sets it down on the table. He sprinkles oatmeal before the table. Next he sprinkles meal into the spring. Further, before the table on the oatmeal he sprinkles sweet oil cake (and) meal. He libates wine three times into the spring and libates three times before the table."

This method of preparing wine appears in *The Iliad*, where Homer describes a Pramnian wine mixed similarly and drunk by Nestor before the walls of Troy, though more likely eaten, given the texture. Another ritual text, entitled "A Second Soldier's Oath," states: "[Aft]erwards he pours out wine, and simultaneously [he says as follows:] '[This] is not w[ine], it is your blood. [Just as] the earth swallowed (this) dow[n], may the earth swallow down your [blood] and . . . in the same way.' [After]wards he pours water into the wine and [simultaneously] says as [follo]ws: 'Just as this water [is mixed] with the wine, may these oath deities mix sick[ness] within your bodies in the same way.'"

LOT, SALT, SEX, AND WINE: A COMPLICATED STORY

Out of hope for progeny and eventually establishing two new nations, Lot's daughters used wine to intoxicate their father and then have intercourse with him. Such use of wine and sexual act provided ancestral roots for the two nations of Ammon and Moab and how the earth was populated (Gen. 19:30ff). Lot became so drunk that he did not even know that incest was occurring. Although the story explains that the daughters took turns on alternate nights, it includes no expression of shame, ignominy, or disapproval, unlike Sophocles's treatment, written some four centuries later, of Oedipus's marrying his mother, Jocasta. One could argue that Lot existed before there were laws about incest. But each daughter's need to inebriate her father with wine implies their awareness of breaking a taboo.

Of wine and women, literature is full of stories, some ribald, some romantic, some mean, and in this instance, strangely bizarre and offensive to modern ears, yet with symbolic importance. Does Lot's story carry a symbolic meaning relative to the spreading influence of the vine, and wine, as new varieties were created through breeding within the same family of vines, but in a new location, through cuttings? Certainly this is a stretch, but metaphorically the Canaanites would have had new vines (children), who would keep alive the older heritage in a new location. This was the only biblical account of its type. Otherwise, no other evidence was written in the Bible of marriage or intercourse between father and daughters.

Wine can serve in sacred rituals, as in the case of Abram and Melchizedek, or not so sacred. The inebriating effects of wine can also have less desirable, "earthly" consequences; witness Lot's daughters. Wine also turns up in the Bible as a relaxant. In Genesis 27:25 Jacob gives his father wine to further a plan to deceive the old man. In another story David tries to get Uriah drunk so he will have intercourse with his wife, Bathsheba, enabling her to hide the identity of her baby's father—David. One archetypal function of wine that pervades today's culture, its ability to intoxicate and therefore allow otherwise non-acceptable behavior, has not changed over thousands of years.

WINE IN EARLY CANAAN AND ITS NEIGHBORS

Wine grapes arrived in southern Canaan from the North (i.e., Anatolia) by the fourth millennium BCE, if not before; they reached Egypt around 3200 BCE from the port of Byblos, north of where Beirut is today. The story of Sinuhe (believed to be legend) comes down to us from papyrus fragments dating to Egypt's Middle Kingdom, about 2200 BCE. The story says that in the land of Palestine (Upper Retenu), "More plentiful than water was its wine" and that "wine was drunk every day." Bybline wine (from Byblos) was famous up through the Roman period and was drunk even earlier by the Egyptian royal family.

Egypt ruled Canaan until the thirteenth century BCE. Much Canaanite wine went to Egypt as tribute payments. The coastal cultures for the most part were heavily engaged in the wine trade, although Hebrews (*Hebiru* in Egyptian) were more often farmers and pastoralists. They lived primarily inland and despised trade; the word *Canaanite* became synonymous with *trader*. This attitude changed only later, and Jews became traders. Lebanese vintners today claim that their merwah grape is the Bybline vine and that it is related to the semillon today. In Lebanon today merwah is rarely used for table wine, but it is distilled for raki. Documents from Ugarit in northern Syria dating to the late third millennium BCE reveal huge wine exports from Tripoli and Ashkelon and that traders clearly distinguished wines by quality. Early Canaanite vintners usually mixed vines in plantings with other crops. The concept of a vineyard as we know it today, with neat rows of trellised vines marching up a hill, did not exist. Rather, vines generally were grown low to the ground and trained to grow up trees. Later, in Roman times, vines were formed up onto pergolas, with the canes trained along strings between the rows, not unlike pergola systems still found in older vineyards of Valpolicella, Italy.

By the fourth millennium BCE most vines were propagated from cuttings. More plants were added to the vineyard simply by running a cane from a mother plant underground to a nearby spot, where the next year it would grow up and bud new shoots. Once it was a year old, the cane that connected to the mother plant was cut. Vineyards in ancient Canaan that were planted like this probably resembled a veritable jungle of low-lying plants.

Overall, wine was red. Ancient writers refer to the purple color of wine or to red wine that sparkles (Prov. 23:31). Until recently experts believed that white wine was not invented until the third century BCE. New research from Egyptian tombs (see chapter 3) by Maria Rosa Guasch Jané suggests that white was made as early as the mid-second millennium BCE.

Those who squashed the grapes with their feet in the *gat,* or winepress, had ruby-stained garments (Isa. 63:2). The press was a square or ovoid enclosed area cut into the limestone rock common to the region. Once wine was trod in the *gat* (which was the only way to get grape juice until late in the first millennium BCE), the juice ran through a channel cut into the limestone to a smaller rock-cut cistern (*yeqeb*), where it would ferment. Larger installations often had an intermediate smaller cistern fitted with a filter to capture the stalks, grape skins, bugs, and such.

Filtering the wine seems to have been important to the Hebrews in Palestine, as it is mentioned frequently in the Mishnah, but that was written much later than most of the Bible. Small family producers used large pots called *pura,* into which the juice was poured for fermentation and settling as opposed to fermentation beginning in the large treading area of the *gat*. The Egyptians had a unique system: they pressed the pomace (the pulpy mash left over after treading) by wrapping it in a muslin bag. A person was stationed at each end of the bag. They twisted their ends in opposite directions to squeeze the last bit of juice from the pulp. Elsewhere in the Levant, pressing was done by treading until no juice was left. Beam presses weren't invented until the Hellenistic period, around the third century BCE.

The growing conditions in the Levant clearly favored red wine grapes, much as they do today. Iron-rich terra rossa is especially helpful for boosting the strength of the red pigments in the grape skins and for good drainage. By the eighth century BCE the Phoenicians, great seafarers, had perfected the Canaanite jar for storage and shipping. "The idea of a two-handled pottery container made especially for transport seems to have originated with the Canaanites, forefathers of the Phoenicians, in the coastal area of later Syria and Palestine." Often these amphoras were imprinted with the name of the vineyard, producer, year of production, and what kind of wine it was; earlier the Egyptians had made similar notations.

Descriptions of the earliest wines in Canaan are scarce, but we do know that wine from Ammon (Amman, Jordan) was prized, and the Prophet Hosea admires the "fragrant bouquet" of the wine of Lebanon, perhaps a muscat from Byblos. Helbon wine, mentioned by the Prophet Ezekiel and made in Syria, was also prized enough to be desired by the Persian kings. Some Talmudic texts written in the first century CE describe exilic times as well as more contemporary periods. The Talmud mentions about 70 wine varietals, so by the late first century BCE at least, a wine was available for every taste.

Most people drank *yayin*, wine that was barely a year old, but old wine was prized, though rarely was it older than three years; older wine was called *yayin yashan*, or *yayin meyushshan*. The Talmud mentions a fine array of wines that people enjoyed. Aluntit was a mix of old wine, clear water, and balsam, to drink after bathing. Kafrisin, caper wine, or Cyprus wine, was prized, while yen zimmukin was a raisin wine, and Inomillin was wine mixed with honey and pepper, just to name a few.

By the beginning of the Talmudic period (ca. second century BCE), wine was so sacred and important to the activity of the priests at the temple in

Jerusalem and elsewhere that a hierarchy of quality wines for that purpose was established: Hattulim and Keruthin, from the Jordan Valley northeast of Jerusalem, were considered the best; wines from Beth Luban, northwest of Jerusalem in the mountains, were less prized but still good. Wines from Petra, Tyre, Beirut, and Carmel were also considered to be of high enough quality for use in sacred rites. Wine from Canaan will figure strongly in the next stop on our journey, the story of Jacob and Joseph.

Three

JOSEPH AND THE CUPBEARER

*So the chief cupbearer told his dream to
Joseph, and said to him, "In my dream, behold, there
was a vine in front of me; and on the vine were
three branches. And as it was budding, its blossoms
came out, and its clusters produced ripe grapes.
"Now Pharaoh's cup was in my hand; so I took the
grapes and squeezed them into Pharaoh's cup, and I put the
cup into Pharaoh's hand."*

—Genesis 40:9–11

JACOB, JOSEPH, AND JOSEPH'S BROTHERS

The story of Joseph, the great grandson of Abraham and son of Jacob, provides a vivid chapter in the saga of wine. During this time (mid-second millennium BCE) the land of Canaan was a vital center of viticulture. After the earliest wild grape vines were domesticated, the grapes and technology of the earliest wines had migrated from the central Zagros Mountains of western Iran, as well as the Caucasus and Taurus Mountains in Turkey, throughout the ancient world.

Abraham, who shared in the legacy of these viticultural traditions, had transmitted this knowledge of wine to his son Isaac and his grandson Joseph. Now Isaac was old and about to die and ready to leave the family fortune to his eldest son while blessing him. When Jacob disguised himself as his first-born twin, Esau, in order to receive the patriarchal blessing, Isaac asked that his son bring him food. Although Isaac asked only for food, not wine, Jacob also "brought him wine, and he drank" (Gen. 27:25). Thinking that he was blessing Esau, the older twin, and clearly under the influence of wine, Isaac spoke the following benediction to Jacob: "May God give you of the dew of heaven, and of the fatness of the earth, and plenty of grain and wine" (Gen. 27:28).

Jacob's later purchase of land was a partial fulfillment of the blessing, as was his planting of vineyards and grain fields. This was in the hill country that Jacob would occupy, and this was where he would have time to plant grain and grapes, harvest them, and enjoy the end products, such as bread, beer, and wine. He also fulfilled the blessing by passing it down to one of his sons, ordinarily the oldest, even though Jacob himself, the second born, received it by tricking his father at his mother's behest.

When Esau discovered that Jacob had stolen this blessing, and earlier had tricked Esau out of his birthright for a bowl of lentil stew, he became angry and told his father, Isaac, "Have you not reserved a blessing for me?" Isaac responded: "I have already made him your lord, and I have given him all his brothers as servants, and with grain and wine I have sustained him" (Gen. 33:36–37). The blessing and birthright went hand in hand, and wine became key to the family blessing that would accompany Isaac's bequest.

Isaac's blessing of Jacob, who would later be named Israel, was symbolic of the profound place that wine held in the emerging Israelite religion as well as the cultural and economic significance of wine. Wine reveals the evolution of humanity from nomadism to a settled society. More profoundly, this blessing presages the evolution of a unique new culture, and a key instrument for humanity's continuing development is wine.

To fulfill his father's blessing Jacob must purchase land, occupy it, plant and harvest, ultimately drinking plenty of wine. Although he was from a family of nomadic wealth, Jacob settled in Succoth and built a house there (Gen. 33:17). The very next verse says, "Jacob came safely to the city of Shechem" (Gen. 33:18), where archaeologists found an ancient winepress (see chapter 2), and where people were engaged in "wine-making in abundance" (Judg. 9:27). The wealthier families in the Levant would no doubt have had access to wine, and some would have had vineyards. Jacob and his sons certainly would have been exposed to fine Canaanite wine and most probably planted a vineyard.

Although fathers in ancient patriarchal societies did give such blessings to the eldest son, favoritism ran rampant in Jacob's family system. Thus Joseph, the favored baby of the family, seems to have been the more likely candidate for learning the craft of wine making inherent in his grandfather's blessing. Jacob had twelve sons, and the narrative portrays Jacob's older sons as working out in the field for days on end, while Joseph, the youngest child and the only son of Jacob's favorite wife, Rachel, stayed at home. Joseph was Rachel's first child, and, Genesis reports, "Israel loved Joseph more than any other of his children, because he was the son of his old age" (Gen. 37:3). As the youngest, Joseph remained close to his father, while the others were out shepherding, mirroring the relationship of Jacob and Esau: "When the boys grew up, Esau was a skillful hunter, a man of the field, while Jacob was a quiet man, living in tents" (Gen. 25:27).

This partially explains the remark in Psalm 80:8 (80:9 Hebrew), "You brought a vine out of Egypt; you drove out the nations and planted it." The vine may be taken as a metaphor for Israel, but it is also a reflection of viti-culture. Because the vine is the most precious of Israel's royal plants (Judg. 9:7–15), the psalmist then depicts the vine as an emblem of God's people. The huge viticultural connection between Canaan and Israel makes the metaphor all the more powerful. Though living in Canaan, the Israelites were uniquely from Abraham's genealogical line, often referred to as "Hebrews." After wres-tling with a "man" later identified as "God," Jacob receives the blessing of being called "Israel" for the first time, which seems to demarcate Israelite viticulture by a new divine enactment of Isaac's earlier blessing to Jacob who would in-herit the land (Gen 32:24–32).

Perhaps the Canaanite vines originally brought to Egypt finally mark the death of Canaanite hegemony in viticulture when they died during times of famine, such as in the Joseph story, or times of war after vineyards were utterly destroyed. When these vines were taken back to Canaan after Joseph died, the Israelites would now claim the land according to Isaac's blessing of Jacob and supplant Canaanite viticulture with their own. By way of analogy, vines have been returned to their place of origin in modern times: France had to retrieve certain French varietals from California and Chile, among other places, after phylloxera—a microscopic yellowish insect, native to the United States, that feeds on the sap of vine roots, creating fungus-infected galls that gradually develop and strangle the roots, killing the vine—destroyed almost all French vineyards in the mid-nineteenth century.

By Joseph's time (ca. fifteenth to seventeenth centuries BCE) wines in Canaan were experiencing a heyday. By then wine had spread from the far north across the Levant, all the way down to Egypt, where most of the Joseph story takes place. Israel/Canaan became the chief supplier of wine to Egypt. When Joseph was in Egypt, Canaan was a major Egyptian province and exported wine to Egypt as a way of paying taxes. Yet Joseph's horizons in viticulture were about to expand.

Joseph's encounter with wine begins in Genesis 39, around the mid-second millennium BCE, when he meets a figure much like a sommelier. The narrative suggests that Joseph's brothers hate him and are jealous of him because their father loves him more than he loves them. When their father, Jacob, makes Joseph a special coat, the situation becomes worse. Joseph has dreams that seem to predict that his brothers and parents someday will bow down to him, causing them to loathe him all the more. While the brothers are in the fields, Joseph comes to see them. His envious brothers remove his coat and throw him in a hole. Then they sell him into slavery, smear blood on his fancy coat, and tell their father that Joseph has been killed by a wild animal. Jacob believes that his beloved son is dead. The slave merchants take Joseph down to Egypt and sell him to Potiphar, an Egyptian officer of the pharaoh. Potiphar finds he likes Joseph because he has integrity and promotes him to "overseer in his house and over all that he had" (Gen. 39:5).

Joseph is "very handsome in form and appearance" (39:6), and Potiphar's wife tries to seduce him. After Joseph rejects her advances, she grabs hold of his garment one day, but Joseph wriggles free, leaving his garment in her hand, and flees (Gen 39:12). Potiphar's wife screams, alerting the whole household, and claims that Joseph had come on to her. She shows Joseph's garment to her husband. Potiphar then becomes enraged and puts Joseph in the prison where the king of Egypt's prisoners are also confined.

THE CUPBEARER'S DREAM

In this same jailhouse, the chief cupbearer and chief baker are imprisoned alongside Joseph because the king of Egypt is angry with them. The baker most likely was in charge of the dual process of baking bread and brewing beer, the staples of both poor and wealthy Egyptians. The cupbearer is the expert wine taster. Both men's professions are right in line with Isaac's blessing for Jacob and his descendants: "May God give you . . . plenty of grain and wine" (Gen. 27:28). The narrative does not reveal why the baker and cupbearer are in jail. Perhaps the cupbearer served the pharaoh wine that did not satisfy his palate or the cupbearer became drunk on duty. Paintings in tombs depict banquet guests who are completely intoxicated. One even depicts an elegantly decked-out woman who is turning her head to the side in order to vomit. The chief baker probably committed the greater crime because he is eventually hanged. The only dialogue occurs when the cupbearer relates his dream first, and his testimony eventually vindicates Joseph. His testimony perhaps explains how wine eventually becomes the preferred beverage (over beer) in Egypt.

By the second millennium BCE Egypt had a sophisticated and centuries-old process of procuring, producing, and preserving delicious wines. By drinking the wine first, the cupbearer protected the pharoah from poisoning, but he also acted as a sommelier, in charge of choosing the best Egyptian wines and even the more prestigious wines from Israel.

The hieroglyph for *cupbearer* is 𓏙, which seems to be this person carrying wine on his head. As we know from archaeological evidence, the Egyptians purchased their wine jars and transplanted grape vines from Canaan. The cupbearer would know this and would welcome a Canaanite, especially someone like Joseph, described in the narrative as a wise man. He likely worked the family vineyard that provided his grandfather, Isaac, with the wine that accompanied his blessing to Jacob. Thus crafting and selecting wines would have counted as wisdom (Prov. 3:10; 9:2).

Mašqe, the Hebrew word for cupbearer, literally means "one who gives drink." A pottery jar unearthed at Ein Gev contains an inscription that says, "Belonging to the cupbearer" (*lémašqe*). Just as this *mašqe* would have served a social maintenance function of delivering the best wines to the Egyptian pharaohs, so an official performing the same function would have worked for the king in Israel. The king of Israel's cupbearer would have been the wine expert of his day, guaranteeing that the king and his guests would receive the best wine available—and free of poison. At minimum the *mašqe* in any culture would be able to discriminate between what was good and what was inferior wine. Yet this figure, whom Joseph met in the jail cell, was called the *sar hammašqîm* in Hebrew, a term that implied that he was the prince/chief/master of wine experts. If he served a bad wine, the king could put him in prison or even put him to death. This is what initially happened to the cupbearer (and the baker) in Genesis 39. By this time the wines in Israel/Canaan were among the best wines of the known world, and it's likely that Egyptian winemakers trained there. The discovery of many Canaanite-style wine amphoras in old Egyptian tombs, determined by molecular analysis of the amphoras' clay, suggests that the Egyptian wine experts were influenced by people who had long experience with wine making, Canaanites.

In the Joseph narrative the captain of the jailhouse guard puts Joseph in charge of the pharoah's top two experts in beer and wine. Both men have dreams related to their professions, and Joseph interprets them, beginning with those of the *mašqe:* So the chief cupbearer told his dream to Joseph, and said to him, "In my dream there was a vine before me, and on the vine there were three branches. As soon as it budded, its blossoms came out and the clusters ripened into grapes. Pharaoh's cup was in my hand; and I took the grapes and pressed them into Pharaoh's cup, and placed the cup in Pharaoh's hand." Then Joseph said to him, "This is its interpretation: the three branches are three days; within three days Pharaoh will lift up your head and restore you to your office; and you shall place Pharaoh's cup in his hand, just as you used to do when you were his cupbearer" (Gen 40:9–13).

The dream reveals the cupbearer's role in placing a cup of wine into the pharaoh's hand and maybe even more about ancient fermentation. Interpretation of the *mašqe's* dream by Joseph, an Israelite, would have been of great significance because Israel exported the best wines to Egypt, produced the finest wine jars, and provided shoots that would be transplanted in the northeastern Nile delta. These wine experts functioned in society early in Israelite and Egyptian history. Moreover the story sets up a hierarchy: the Israelite becomes the wise adviser to the foremost wine expert in Egypt.

The story does not end in the jail cell. The plot thickens when the pharaoh has a birthday party to which he invited all his officials and servants (Gen. 40:20). The writer says that the pharaoh "lifted up the head of the chief cupbearer and the head of the chief baker," which implies that he let them both out of jail. The pharaoh probably needed the top wine expert and the most excellent baker in the kingdom to make a splash at his birthday. Afterward the pharaoh "restored the chief cupbearer to his cup-bearing, and he placed the cup in Pharaoh's hand; but the chief baker he hanged, just as Joseph had interpreted to them" (Gen. 40:21–22).

Then, two years after the party, the pharaoh has a troubling dream that none of his wise men can interpret:

> Pharaoh dreamed that he was standing by the Nile, and there came up out of the Nile seven sleek and fat cows, and they grazed in the reed grass. Then seven other cows, ugly and thin, came up out of the Nile after them, and stood by the other cows on the bank of the Nile. The ugly and thin cows ate up the seven sleek and fat cows. And Pharaoh awoke. Then he fell asleep and dreamed a second time; seven ears of grain, plump and good, were growing on one stalk. Then seven ears, thin and blighted by the east wind, sprouted after them. The thin ears swallowed up the seven plump and full ears. Pharaoh awoke, and it was a dream. In the morning his spirit was troubled; so he sent and called for all the magicians of Egypt and all its wise men. Pharaoh told them his dream. (Gen. 41:1–8)

Pharoah's fear haunts him. The Nile Valley represents desirable grazing land, optimal agriculture, and a viable environment for viticulture. Yet nothingness swallows all this. The pharaoh may have his master of wine and a new chief baker/beer maker, but without grapes and grains these are nothing. Then the cupbearer remembers Joseph and tells the pharaoh about Joseph's ability to interpret dreams. Joseph interprets the pharaoh's dream, warning that there will be seven years of great abundance followed by seven years of famine. He then counsels the pharaoh to prepare for these bad years during the abundant years. Joseph advises the pharaoh to select a wise and discerning man and to put him in charge of the land of Egypt. He advises the pharaoh to appoint overseers to collect one-fifth of the produce of the land of Egypt during the seven plenteous years so that Egyptians will "not perish through the famine" (Gen. 41:46). The collection is to include food, grain, and wine.

The story has a happy ending, at least as long as Joseph lives. Pharaoh appoints Joseph to be his chief of staff, overseeing the efforts to put stores aside. And the prominence of Joseph's leadership to the cupbearer, whose testimony would not only vindicate Joseph but elevate him above himself, foreshadows God's election of Israel. In a sense Joseph's rise to power offers two metaphors;

the first, representing Canaan/Israel's wisdom and mastery of wine, and, second, Israel's eventual challenge, to rule Egypt spiritually, if not physically.

Jacob's 12 blessings that he speaks to each of his 12 sons in Genesis 49 extends the meaning of Israel's future destiny significantly with the blessing spoken to Joseph singling him out above the others, as "a fruitful bough" (Gen. 49:22). The promise of Israel and its bounty comes to Joseph (Gen. 49:26). A fruitful bough can be interpreted as a fruitful vine: "A young vine is Joseph." The gifts and blessings of viticulture that Joseph has bestowed on Egypt now go back to Israel. Psalm 80:8, "You brought a vine out of Egypt," realizes both the figurative and proper use of the word *vine*. Here, the divine path YHWH sets forth for Israel as his "chosen people" is uniquely summed by combining the metaphor of the vine as Joseph, its great importance and quality as a symbol of Canaan's wine-growing excellence, and how Joseph's excellent work embodied by expertise in winegrowing and other wise policies as well as his character, will ultimately come back from Egypt to Canaan (Israel) to build a better society there.

Joseph serves as an ambassador of wine. He is positioned throughout the narrative as adviser to the chief wine expert from the wine capital of the known world. Joseph's father has purchased and settled on land in an area where the Levantine wine industry is booming and the family blessing pertaining to Jacob's inheritance includes occupying that land and enjoying great harvest, with the end result of plenty of wine. Though Jacob is now dead, he leaves the land by blessing and not by an inheritance that he once owned. Joseph himself inherits the patriarchal blessing of wine stewardship and abundance and then oversees a thriving wine industry in a country whose nobility stored wines even into eternity.

EGYPTIAN WINE GROWING: FROM BEER
TO WINE FOR ROYAL EGYPT

Although ancient Egyptians were known for their beer, wine was the drink they offered their gods. The pharaohs used wine to placate the gods so that they would protect Egyptians and cause them to prosper. From an early time Osiris was the god of wine and the divine giver of viticulture. Herodotus even likened Osiris to Dionysus/Bacchus. By the Second Dynasty (early third millennium BCE), wine was the beverage most commonly offered to the gods. The Temple of Amon-Re, king of all gods, committed enough land for more than five hundred vineyards for the citizens of the temple. Many temple and tomb paintings depict pharaohs offering wine to the gods and wine-making scenes.

While Egyptian vineyards were originally planted in royal gardens near the delta and further south around the royal city of Memphis, by Joseph's time (ca. the fourteenth century BCE) the vineyards had spread southward to Fayum, about 50 miles southwest from Memphis. Viticulture later extended to the oases of Khargah and Dakhlah, Tanis, and Lake Mareotis. Amenhotep III (1390–1352 BCE) had a vineyard planted for the Temple of Luxor, and the legend surrounding this event suggests that the volume of wine produced exceeded the volume of water in the Nile. Erman suggests that after Joseph's time, Ramses III (d. 1156 BCE) planted vineyards in the northern and southern oases where foreigners worked. Foreign influence was important to the Egyptian wine industry, and Canaanites/Hebrews like Joseph would have been integral to that process.

Archaeology tells us much about Egyptian wine. Amphoras taken from Tutankhamun's tomb, for example, revealed through molecular analyses that one jar placed to the west of his sarcophagus was filled with red wine from the "Aten Temple in the Western Delta," while one to the east was filled with white sweet wine "from the 5th year of the Estate of Tutankhamun made by vintner Khaa."

Lists of distinct wines that clearly had been produced at the various Nile delta vineyards were found in tombs, too. By the end of the Old Kingdom (ca. 2150 BCE), five wines, all probably produced in the delta, were specifically for the afterlife; vineyards and wine remained under state control in Egypt. Tomb paintings depicted the lives of the ruling elite and may have reflected a hopeful imagination in how they portrayed the afterlife. Poor Egyptian farmers probably had no access to wine during Joseph's time. The presence of the vine in Canaan is mentioned in many Egyptian inscriptions. In letters of Sinuhe (Shanhat) the Egyptian, writing around 1800 BCE, he mentions Canaan this way: "it is a land blessed by the gods, where fig trees and vines flourish, and wine is more abundant than water." The Chronicles of the voyages and expeditions of Thutmoses III speaks about the dried and fresh grapes and the wine of Canaan, saying that even more important in Egypt are the Israeli wines with added honey.

The wild grape (*Vitis vinifera sylvestris*) never grew in ancient Egypt, but genetic testing shows that shoots were transplanted from the Levant to the wide alluvial plains of the Nile River delta between 3100 and 2700 BCE when the wine industry began to flourish. We know that wine jars of Canaanite origin existed from the end of the fourth millennium BCE as found in Scorpion I's tomb. By Joseph's time the Egyptians had refined and improved the jars, adding two lug handles to carry them and elongating the oval body to secure equal distribution of weight during transport. This new jar became common not only in Egypt but across the entire Mediterranean basin and came to be known as Canaanite jars. Further evidence for the influence of Canaanite wine on Egypt comes from the oldest ship carrying amphoras ever found, a Canaanite ship off the coast of Turkey, probably headed for Egypt in the fourteenth century BCE. If a Hebrew from a wealthy family like Joseph's had authority over all agriculture, was a friend with the chief cupbearer, and Egyptian wine experts recognized those jars as originating from his land, they would have heeded his wisdom, especially regarding wine.

Egyptian hieroglyphics found on older-style, handle-less jars depict a rather sophisticated system of wine for the time. Hieroglyphic signs for the "grape, vineyard, or wine" were stamped onto clay stoppers that fit into these elongated jars. Since wine continued to ferment in these jars, the wine makers would put a small hole in the stopper for gases to escape and then they would seal the hole after fermentation ceased. One of six wine jars in Tutankhamun's tomb burst because the stoppers were sealed too early.

Some hieroglyphs show vines growing on trellises that encouraged the vine to grow upright in lines so that cultivation, pruning, and harvest would be easier (𓇟). The full hieroglyph for wine would be 𓇋𓏤𓇟, or a very similar hieroglyph that substituted the two connected wine jars instead of the hieroglyph with the trained vine: 𓇋𓏤𓏤. These two connected wine jars, 𓏤𓏤, may signify both red and white wine, or a mechanism for carrying the jars by lashing them to poles and carrying them together on shoulders. The glyph also spoke of the initial wine and the good wine at the end. Other hieroglyphs represented the winepress.

As we noted earlier, ancient Egypt had a sophisticated labeling system, indicating place of production, vintage (by stating year of the specific pharaoh's reign), product name, estate name, winemaker's name, and quality. Only a drawing of a grapevine appeared on the jar for some everyday wines, but the label design for more special wines seemed to receive more attention. Hieroglyphs even provide names that would have either spoken of five major wine regions or even five wineries that may have been equivalent to the "First Growths" of Bordeaux because they were the most valued wines of Egypt: northern wine, abesh wine, sunu wine, hamu wine, and Imet wine.

Because the trading system of the ancient world was expanding, this rather precise labeling system no doubt would have influenced the later development of labels in Greece and Rome. The labels on amphoras in Tutankhamun's tomb named the vineyard and listed the vintage. Two of fifteen producers of the wines in his tomb bore Syrian names, either because the wines were imported or the Egyptians had brought experts down from the North to teach them wine making.

Other hieroglyphic labels even listed such specifics as "sweet wine" and "very fine wine." These would have been some of the best wines because only the best accompanied the pharaoh into eternity. A fine example from Tutankhamun's tomb is an amphora inscribed, "Year 5. Shedeh of very good quality of the Estate of Aten of the Western River. Chief Vintner Rer"—an ideal label even by modern standards.

Tomb paintings, such as the well-preserved depictions of harvest and pressing in the tomb of a royal official named Nakht at Thebes, dating to about 1400 BCE, depicts the sophisticated viticulture in ancient Egypt. Laborers gather grape clusters grown on vines trained on a pergola. An inspector, who would have been much like those Joseph advised the pharaoh to "appoint over the land" (Gen. 41:33), observes the flow of grape juice from the winepress into a vat, as workers tread the grapes. Another painting depicts Intef, a Royal Herald of the early Eighteenth Dynasty in the sixteenth century BCE, making wine in his own private winery for private consumption.

Yet another tomb painting depicts a mechanism for twisting a pomace bag to squeeze out grape juice, which was customary after the treading could produce no more juice. In this period such a winepress appears to have been particular to Egypt and nowhere else. Other paintings show potters making wine jars and sealing them after they have been filled with fermented liquid.

In telling the Joseph story the Bible describes the oldest form of wine making, by crushing grapes in a cup, as described in the chief cupbearer's dream (Gen. 40:11). But this passage includes a magically instantaneous fermentation. Just imagine picking grapes, putting them in a wine glass, and immediately drinking wine, not grape juice. The earliest intermediate development between fermentation in a drinking cup and the later winepress system was the cupmark, which consisted of a depression cut into the bedrock in the shape of a cup. Grapes would be crushed in the cupmark. This was the precursor of the winepress system that used two depressions cut into bedrock, usually in a rectangle but sometimes in a circle or semicircle (see chapter 2).

Egyptian hieroglyphics were invented in 3200 BCE, and one of the first was the sign for *winepress:* . This was pronounced *sheshmu* and was in the shape of a bowl with streams of grape juice flowing into it after the grapes were pressed from above. (Sheshmu was also a demon who tore the head off of a wrongdoer and then threw the head into a winepress to squeeze out the blood as if it were grape juice.)

Various Egyptian tomb paintings and hieroglyphics display a trellis grape vine heavy with grapes, tended and watered, and people treading grapes in a trough. These techniques are similar to those still used today in Portugal's wine-making Douro Valley, where the grape juice is left to ferment with the grape skins, seeds, and stalks to produce a delicious red wine. The Egyptians' tomb paintings and hieroglyphics tell us as much about ancient Israelite viticulture as Egyptian since we have little other information about wine making in Israel in this period.

WHAT WOULD PHARAOH DRINK?

Egyptian kings and nobility drank wine freely. A papyrus dating to the time of Seti I (1318–1292 BCE) lists wine among the rations given to soldiers. The nobility, and Egyptians who could afford wine, used utensils made of bronze, alabaster, ceramic, silver, and gold, including a shallow drinking bowl, a strainer, and a small jug into which they drew wine from the amphora.

So what would Pharaoh drink? Because 30-year-old wines, some of which Egyptians considered to be quite fine, were placed in King Tut's tomb, we know that pharaohs had a taste for well-aged wine. Egypt had both sweet and dry wines. Most were reds. Nevertheless paintings depict greenish wine, dark red wine, and even dark blue wines. For Egyptians wine was related to the color red, symbolically the blood of Osiris, "the first god that came back to life," killed by his brother Set and thrown into the Nile. Red also is the color of the Nile at flood season when it carries millions of tons of sediments downriver from the highlands. Thus red wine was related to the rebirth of the land and to immortality, which was why red wine was placed in royal tombs.

The pharaohs of the New Kingdom loved wines so much that they elevated the Egyptian wine trade in Thebes during the reign of Ramses II (early thirteenth century BCE). Egyptians also made date wine, fig wine, palm wine, and pomegranate wine, according to the Song of Songs (8:2). Paintings on walls of the Egyptian tombs show just how amphoras were brought to the storehouse of the pharaoh. The Egyptians did not mix their wine with water as did the Greeks, Romans, and, later, devout Jews. Since sweet wines were generally considered a separate category as compared to other wines because of their special designation (*irp ndm*), we can assume that the Egyptians mainly drank dry wines.

Therefore the Egyptian palate was more like the modern palate than those of the Greeks and Romans. Athenaeus (second century CE) describes a white wine from near Lake Mareotis that appears to have been dry: "Excellent, white, pleasant, fragrant, easily assimilated, thin, not likely to go to the head, and diuretic." This statement is not conclusive and comes from a later period, but the wine Athenaeus was discussing probably was a lot like the wine found in Tutankhamun's tomb. Athenaeus was describing a wine (Mareotis wine) from Mariut, located southwest of Alexandria in the Nile delta, and praised by Virgil himself a century earlier.

Egyptians drank wine from shallow bowls or goblets, so they certainly did not swirl their wine to aerate it. A mural at Tel el-Amarna depicts Queen Nefertiti pouring wine for her husband, King Akhenaton, from a small jug through a strainer into a shallow drinking glass. This indicates that either the wines were not strained before they were bottled or that they were drinking older wine that had sediment. Chapter 9 discusses modern Egypt's wines.

EGYPTIAN WISDOM: WINE AS MEDICINE
FOR THE BODY AND SOUL

Wine and medicine are intimately linked in the ancient world, especially in Egypt. From 3300 BCE until the Persian Empire in 525 BCE, Egyptian medical practice was highly advanced for its time, with physician-priests who practiced minor surgery, such as setting bones, using as anesthesia a wide range of pharmacopoeia with wine. Medicine was linked with belief in the supernatural and religious practices, and wine's natural traits were a logical tool. The Egyptians had a formidable and detailed pharmacopeia. Papyrus scrolls, some as old as the mid-Twelfth Dynasty (ca. 1850 BCE), provide information about the importance of medicinal wines to the Egyptian physician (*swnw*, the hieroglyphic word, is noted as early as the Third Dynasty, ca. 2650 BC).

Healers often steeped herbs in wine or water. The ailing person drank the mixture as an oral medicine. A wine jar dated to 5100 BCE contained traces of the herbal additives often mentioned in medical texts. Sample residue taken from a jar in Scorpion I's tomb (3150 BCE) showed that the grape wine it contained also was laced with various compounds of herbs and resin of Levantine origin that had therapeutic benefits and enhanced the taste.

Egypt, which rivaled the world in knowledge, was a leader in ancient medicine, and Egyptian physicians were world renowned for their expertise. The earliest known physician, Imhotep, came from Egypt. In later times Egyptians revered him as a hero and faultless physician. Later Egyptians deified him, calling him the "god of medicine" and "prince of peace." He was the prototype of Asclepius (Asklepiós), the Greek god of medicine. Imhotep used wine to heal. In the pharaonic Temple of Debod, one panel of a late mural portrays King Ptolemy presenting an offering of wine to Imhotep and the god Ptah.

Yet ancient Egyptian writing included caveats about wine. One papyrus mentions a number of problems that might arise, such as "He who drinks too much wine lies down in a stupor." Wine was taken medicinally in small doses, and it was used externally as well. Some remedies seem ridiculous today. To make a concoction to cure epilepsy they steeped the testicles of an ass in wine. The Egyptian treatment for asthma was far more palatable: one part honey, eight parts beer, and five parts wine.

Biomolecular studies of consumables left in pharaonic tombs maintain that alcoholic beverages were the universal drug until the advent of modern medicine. The health benefits were obvious—they relieved pain, stopped infection, and killed microorganisms and parasites in tainted water. Wine was also a social lubricator, easing the problems of daily life, and acted as the delivery system for mind-altering substances such as opiates, wormwood, and perhaps even ergot, a fungus with LSD-like properties for religious practices like the Eleusinian Mysteries. McGovern notes that "by using biomolecular archaeological techniques, humankind's first medical forays can be pushed back into prehistoric times."

Primarily, additives to wine for medicinal purposes appeared to have antibacterial as well as anti-cancer properties, according to one study. The resin too, had its medicinal role to play, as the ancients used resin so often both for mixing wine and coating their amphorae. The most interesting aspect of these findings was their seeming origin: the Jordan Valley and its surroundings, attested by the clay sealings found on the jars, confirming again the intimate connection to Levantine culture and land that Egypt maintained.

BRINGING NEW WINES TO THE LAND OF PLENTY

The vine was so highly treasured in Israel that its fruit not only made the heart glad (Ps. 104:15) but produced huge amounts of revenue: as Isaiah 7:23 notes, a "thousand vines [were] worth a thousand pieces of silver." Wine was an expensive commodity that needed to be protected: "When someone causes a field or vineyard to be grazed over, or lets livestock loose to graze in someone else's field, restitution shall be made from the best in the owner's field or vineyard" (Exodus 22:5). Because it was part of Jacob's/Israel's blessing, agriculture became a sacred institution in Israel, and wine too was sacred. Exodus 29:40 admonishes the Israelites in their "going out" from Egypt to provide food and wine offerings to their God: "With the first lamb one-tenth of a measure of choice flour mixed with one-fourth of a hin of beaten oil, and one-fourth of a hin of wine for a drink offering" (1 hin = approximately 6 liters). As in Egypt, wine offerings were part of Israelite religion. Leviticus describes the rations of wine allocated to the Levites, a tribe of rabbis and teachers, along with rules for wine consumption. An outgrowth of Isaac's blessing for Jacob is that

Leviticus enjoins Israel to provide the Levites with ample rations of grain and wine to accompany a burnt offering of lamb: "The grain offering with it shall be two-tenths of an ephah of choice flour mixed with oil, an offering by fire of pleasing odor to the LORD; and the drink offering with it shall be of wine, one-fourth of a hin" (Lev. 23:13). Leviticus also gives a stern warning about use and misuse of wine during sacerdotal rites: "Drink no wine or strong drink, neither you nor your sons, when you enter the tent of meeting, that you may not die; it is a statute forever throughout your generations" (Lev. 10:9). This is nearly identical to the admonishment that Mohammed makes to his followers regarding not drinking alcoholic beverages before prayer: "O you who believe! Draw not near unto prayer when you are drunken, till you know that which you utter" (Koran 4:43). This is an eminently sensible notion.

Numbers 20 suggests just how treasured vineyards and wine were. Moses asks the king of Edom if the Israelites can pass through his land. Moses even vows that they will not go through the king's vineyards or drink any water from his wells. Moses promises that the Israelites will remain on the king's highway. He recounts the events in Egypt to the king and describes Israel's deliverance from bondage. Yet the king of Edom does not allow the Israelites to pass through. The vines were precious, and vintners in those days could not risk any damage to them.

The Israelites may or may not have drunk wine while in the wilderness, but they learned the sacredness of wine while living in the fertile land of Bashan and working in the vineyards of Egypt, as well as during their earlier experiences in Canaan. Yet after they left Egypt, the book of Numbers tells them while "in the wilderness" to give their wine as an offering to God: "You shall offer one-fourth of a hin of wine as a drink offering with the burnt offering or the sacrifice, for each lamb" (Num. 15:5). Wine and lamb chops provided YHWH and priests with quite a meal. Numbers 6 also gives an injunction to a special holy class called Nazirites not to eat or drink anything that comes from a grape vine (it also tells them not to cut their hair or touch a dead body, even that of a family member).

In Numbers 13 Moses sends spies from the wilderness through the desert and into the Promised Land during "the season of the first ripe grapes" (13:20), telling them: "See what the land is like, and whether the people who

Mount Ararat towers over the surrounding plains near the Turkish-Armenian border, with vineyards located to the north of the mountain, seen here.

Inhabited since the Neolithic period, Catalyöhük lies to the south in central Kapadokya, with remains of habitation dating as far back as 7500 BCE, including carbonized hackberry pips, the fruit likely made into wine. Drinking cups have also been discovered here and at other nearby archaeological sites, attesting to southeast Anatolia's importance as a primary wine grape domestication area.

The Hittites were fond of wine, and spread its culture throughout their vast Empire. This beak wine jug with grape motif dates from the second millennium BCE.

Around three thousand years old, this wine press (gat) cut into the limestone rock in the Yatir Forest, south Jerusalem Hills, clearly delineates the square treading floor (gat) in middle distance, and the small and large yeqebs (cisterns) for filtering, then receiving the juice or partly fermented wine afterward in the foreground.

Part of a massive tribute frieze, this section on a wall at the palace complex at Luxor shows in the lower panel a man who appears to be presenting wine jars to pharaoh as tribute.

From Tyre, Phoenicians shipped a great amount of wine throughout the Mediterranean. This view shows the Mosaic Road with marble columns extending practically to the sea.

Roman Jerash's Forum, with the main street (Cardo) leading to the Triumphal arch in the distance, with the hills and modern city behind.

A fifth-century BCE red figure krater or mixing bowl for a symposion *reveals how guests reclined on benches while drinking and the importance of music to the proceedings as well.*

One of the most beautiful and symbolic mosaics from Zeugma in eastern Turkey, dating from the second century CE. Acratos (ruler) presents holy wine to Euprocyne (joyful, elater) in a golden krater *taken from a divine fountain with a cornucopia. The bell* krater *on the left is shown larger and above the figures, focusing on the importance that celebration and wine have for life, as well as wine's divine character.*

A beautiful silver set of utensils essential to hosting a convivium, including a sieve (left) to catch sediments before the wine is poured into the individual's kantharos (right) from the serving jug, which took wine from the convivium host's larger krater (center).

Clusters of Kalecik Karasi grapes ready for harvest in Kalecik Turkey, east of Ankara, the homeland for this wonderful indigenous Turkish variety.

Harvesting Kalecik's native variety just after sunrise at VinKara's rocky rolling vineyard near the Red River. Harvesting is done mostly by women, who hand-pick the clusters carefully into the small picking bins for transport to the nearby winery.

Olus Molu's family owns the small Vinolus winery and vineyard near Kayseri in Cappadocia. She stands in the midst of her bush-trained vines, growing on the poor volcanically derived rocky tufa-like soils at 900 meters.

Pendore's rolling hillsides at its vineyard in the Manisa area northeast of Izmir provide perfect conditions for growing fine native varieties like öküzgözü (seen here) as well as others like syrah. The soils are rich in iron and magnesium, giving the red color and composed of both limestone and volcanic material.

Harvest time in a beautiful vineyard near Elaziğ where the limestone, shale rocky soils produce textbook öküzgözü grapes, the indigenous, deliciously fruity variety.

At the sixth-century CE Alaverdi Monastery in Khaketi region, Georgia, Archbishop Davit and his winemaker are leading the revival of the ancient qvevri production of wines, using large ceramic jars, much like their ancestors did beginning six or seven millennia ago.

live in it are strong or weak, . . . whether the land they live in is good or bad, . . . whether the land is rich or poor, and whether there are trees in it or not. Be bold, and bring some of the fruit of the land" (Num. 13:17–20).

A similar journey today, coming from the Dead Sea and Jordan Valley, would likely lead past Tel Arad, which is just west of Masada in the north-eastern edge of the Negev, then up into the hill country that leads to the Yatir Forest. The forest, Israel's largest, is noted for many winepresses from the Canaanite era, as well as vineyards belonging to the present Yatir Winery.

Numbers 13:23–24 suggests that these spies went to a valley where grapes grew in clusters so large that they had to sling one on a pole between two men to get them back to Moses. This area was the Wadi Eshcol (Valley of Grape Cluster; see chapter 2). Two of Moses' generals, Caleb and Joshua, were sent there as spies and came back with a good report: "They told Moses, 'We came to the land to which you sent us; it flows with milk and honey, and this is its fruit" (Num. 13:27). Caleb wanted to occupy this land that had amazing viticulture, just as Isaac's blessing for Jacob had suggested. These spies found vineyards in the hill country to be much more lush than in Egypt.

However, other spies returned with a bad report, suggesting that giants who lived there would devour Israel, which would be a mere hors d'oeuvre of grasshoppers to them. All the children of Israel wept, complained to Moses, and even threatened to kill Moses, Caleb, and Joshua. YHWH spoke to Moses, threatening to "strike them with pestilence and disinherit them," thus revoking the blessing of Israel (Num. 14:12). Moses responded by reminding YHWH that "he is slow to anger, and abound[s] in steadfast love" (Num. 14:18) and points out that if YHWH commits this act, the Egyptians and other peoples will hear about it and say, "It is because YHWH was not able to bring this people into the land he swore to give them that he has slaughtered them in the wilderness" (Num. 14:16).

Therefore YHWH allows the Israelites to live but commands that only Caleb and Joshua will inherit the Promised Land, which flows with milk and honey and has amazing vineyards. For the Israelites' failure to believe in both Moses and YHWH, YHWH declares a curse that will cause the Israelites to wander for 40 more years in the wilderness, thus nullifying Jacob's blessing and the promise of wine. However, Deuteronomy alludes to the idea that the children of Israel did not drink wine in the wilderness in order to see clearly: "You have not eaten bread, and you have not drunk wine or strong drink—so that you may know that I am the LORD your God" (Deut. 29:6).

Deuteronomy, written later than Numbers, describes what life will be like for the children of the Israelites who left the wilderness and entered the Promised Land, and it connects this experience with the blessing of Jacob, who was later called Israel. The extension of this blessing resounds multiple times throughout Deuteronomy; for example, "He will love you, bless you, and multiply you; he will bless the fruit of your womb and the fruit of your ground, your grain and your wine and your oil, the increase of your cattle and the issue of your flock, in the land that he swore to your ancestors to give you" (Deut. 7:13).

Egyptian offerings of wine to the gods for protection influenced Israelite sacerdotal rights to YHWH. Leviticus lists wine as a sacrifice, discussing how much to use at different festivals; Pesach, Shavuot, Succoth, etc. (Lev. 23; 13; 18; 37). The most important aspect of sacrifices, wine offerings, were given at the end.

Analogous to the birthday party that the Pharaoh threw for his servants, the writer of Deuteronomy (the Deuteronomist) enjoins the Israelites after leaving Egypt to have a seven-day feast. However, the Israelites do not stay in a fancy palace but leave their abodes and to set up their own tents after harvest and wine production. "You shall keep the festival of booths for seven days, when you have gathered in the produce from your threshing floor and your wine press. Rejoice during your festival, you and your sons and your daughters, your male and female slaves, as well as the Levites, the strangers, the orphans, and the widows resident in your towns" (Deut. 16:13–14).

Unlike Egyptian parties, this harvest party includes all members of society and wine becomes available for all social classes. This forms the "origin" of Succoth, the Jewish harvest festival, commemorating both the end of hard work and celebrating God's beneficence and the Israelite's freedom from Egypt.

The book of Deuteronomy lists blessings for those who keep the covenant and curses those who do not. The greatest curse would be found in vineyards that did not produce fruit or wine to drink: "You shall plant vineyards and dress them, but you shall neither drink the wine nor gather the grapes, for the worm shall eat them" (Deut. 28:39). Curses even result in vile wine: "Their vine comes from the vine-stock of Sodom, from the vineyards of Gomorrah; their grapes are grapes of poison, their clusters are bitter; their wine is the poison of serpents, the cruel venom of asps" (Deut. 32:32–33). Their failure to learn from their journey leads them to incur the curses of bad viticulture, suggesting a link between moral and earthly levels of poor viticultural choices.

Yet part of the blessings of the Deuteronomist and blessing over Jacob lay in Israel's consumption of wine described in the Song of Moses (Deut 32, verse 14): "you drank fine wine from the blood of grapes" (wəḏam-ēnāb tišteʰ-ḥámer). The image, "blood of grapes," seems to imply the production of fine wine (*Hemer*). This Hebrew word, *hemer,* is a word that only appears once in the Hebrew Bible. Using *hemer* instead of the usual *yayin* seems to be intentional, especially since it is paired with a personified "blood of grapes." Most commentaries completely avoid this word and do not even acknowledge it.

The word *hemer* is not referring to ordinary wine. We believe that the phrase "blood of grapes" is more than a mere poetic metaphor here, but actually personifies viticulture with the very life that is in the blood. This imagery repeatedly appears in other spiritual imagery; that of Dionysus, Mithras, and eventually, Christianity. Without a microscope to detect the natural yeasts on the grape skins, the ancient world thought that the grape's ability to transform into wine on its own proved that it was living and magic.

Yet *hemer* here probably speaks of a wine that is naturally carbonated during a specific point in the process of fermentation. The verb ḥámar appears in Psalm 75:8 to speak of a wine that foams: "For a cup is in the hand of the LORD, and the wine foams . . ." (our translation). All wine "foams" during the fermentation stage. The phrase "blood of grapes" tells us that this sparkling wine is red, so it's possible that the Israelites, long before Dom Pérignon in Champagne, had their own version of sparkling wine that was so rare that its descriptive *hemer* is truly a unique word in the Old Testament. Especially if the phenomenon was difficult to recreate and control, then *hemer* itself would be rare.

The brilliance of Egyptian viticulture was an important milestone on the Bible wine trail. Although Canaanites undoubtedly influenced it, Egyptian viticulture in its own right influenced Levantine and ultimately Greco-Roman wine making. The Egyptians invented a sophisticated labeling system and even improved on the Canaanite amphoras and transport of wine. They stored some wines for many years and produced a product that would satisfy many modern palates. Modern scientific research has found that ancient Egyptian medicine relied heavily on alcoholic beverages to deliver medicines and ease pain.

Egyptian improvements in viticulture passed back to Israel in a manner that intensified viticulture in Israel, and the next chapter will show how this prevails during the time of the judges and the monarchy in the early first millennium BCE. Canaanite wines were among the most prized in the ancient world and Israel stepped into a viticultural gold mine, while inheriting their blessing.

Speaking of viticultural sharing between two nations that improved wines, perhaps the psalmists' words are not just metaphor: "You brought a vine out of Egypt; you drove out the nations and planted it" (Ps. 80:8).

Four

WINE UNDER SIEGE

Biblical Wars on Wine

The Lord will bring a nation from far away, to swoop down on you like an eagle, a grim-faced nation showing no respect to the old or favor to the young. It shall consume fruit of your ground until you are destroyed, leaving you neither grain, wine, and oil, until it has made you perish.

—Deuteronomy 28:49–50

Wine and war have been entwined throughout the ages. The prized *hellenico* grape that once produced renowned Greek wines disappeared from Greek soils under Muslim rule, Ottoman occupation, and war. Now any vestige of this superb variety, aglianico, exists only in southern Italy, brought through Greek colonization between the sixth and fourth centuries BCE. Similarly war triumphed over wine in Israel, which today does not produce indigenous grapes, one result of a millennium of occupation by Muslims. The same happened in biblical times.

During the period that Israel occupied the land of Canaan, from the period of the Judges (the group of "divinely" inspired leaders beginning with Joshua and ending with Samuel, who attempted to preserve the Israelites' culture and territory against the local kings) through the monarchic period (from Saul and David until the destruction of Jerusalem by the Babylonians, thirteenth to sixth centuries BCE), it had an agricultural society that depended on vineyards, olive orchards, and grain fields as the foundations for all life.

Viticulture was grounded in inheritance, traditional blessings, and the covenant that YHWH made with Israel. Jacob's one blessing rested on a twofold basis of grain and wine (Gen. 27:28). This presupposes that the Israelites would occupy the land, grow vineyards, and drink the wine. Because of its high economic value, wine production and vineyards were strongly affected by war. So the emotions that accompanied war and the destruction of the vineyard are perfectly understandable: "Joy and gladness are taken away from the fruitful field; and in the vineyards no songs are sung, no shouts are raised; no treader treads out wine in the presses; the vintage-shout is hushed" (Isa. 16:10).

Wine was also important to warriors during battle, giving them courage to fight. When the effects of wine wore off, their courage often evaporated. Soldiers wanting wine "cry to their mothers, 'Where is bread and wine?' as they faint like the wounded in the streets of the city" (Lam. 2:12). Israelite soldiers stored wine in bunkers: "He made the fortresses strong, and put commanders in them, and stores of food, oil, and wine" (2 Chron. 11:11). Before they go into battle, the soldiers are told to enjoy the fruit of the vine in case they die (Deut. 20:6).

The psalmist depicts "a warrior shouting because of wine" (Ps. 78:65). This fermented fruit even prepares an elephant to do battle: "They offered the elephants the juice of grapes and mulberries, to arouse them for battle" (1 Ma. 6:34). Wine even served as a currency for soldiers, priests, and monks. And after a successful battle wine became a means of celebration (Zech. 10:5–7).

Biblical writers use destruction of vineyards and the after-effects to evoke emotions: "And daughter Zion is left like a booth in a vineyard, like a shelter in a cucumber field, like a besieged city" (Isa. 1:8). A prophet likens the war-torn state of Judah to a watered-down wine: "'Your silver has become dross, your wine is mixed with water'" (Isa. 1:22). Wine even symbolizes a blood bath during battle: "They shall drink their blood like wine, and be full like a bowl, drenched like the corners of the altar" (Zech. 9:15).

WINE WARS IN THE NEWLY
INHABITED PROMISED LAND

Wineries have been found at the site of one early Israelite conquest at the Philistine beach town of Ashkelon (Judg. 1:18). The battles happened near winepresses. An angel appeared to Gideon (one of the Judges who reluctantly took up YHWH's command to free the people of "Israel" from other tribal oppression. He requested proof of YHWH's will through three miracles (one involving an angel, the other two a fleece), and called him a "mighty warrior" while he secretly beat wheat in a winepress so that the Midianites, a neighboring tribe descended from Abraham's eponymously named son, living southeast of Israel in what is now the Sinai Peninsula near the Gulf of Aqaba, would not see him (Judg. 6:11–12). Yet the angel aroused him to battle at the winepress, where he ultimately won the war (Judg. 7:25).

The Ephraimites, a "tribe" of Israel descended from Ephraim, a son of Joseph, "contended with [Gideon] fiercely" because he did not call upon them to fight against Midian (Judg. 8:2). Essentially, Ephraim wanted to help Gideon defeat Midian because they wanted the vineyards and wine. Ephraim had more people than Gideon's clan, placing Gideon at a disadvantage.

So Gideon responded with a proverb, which is one way of using wisdom to gain leverage: "Is not the gleaning of Ephraim better than the vintage of Abiezer?" The operative terms here are *Ephraim* and *Abiezer,* which transform the meaning of *gleaning* (ʿōləlôṯ) and *vintage* (bāṣîr). Throughout their semantic range, ʿōləlôṯ is usually a negative term and bāṣîr is usually a positive. What the biblical writer is saying is that the worst of Ephraim is still better than the best of Abiezer.

Ephraim may have produced better wine, but it's also possible that Gideon was using flattery to prevent Ephraim from pummeling him and taking the vineyards. The passage shows that in the time of the Judges (thirteenth to tenth century BCE), each society was able to rate the quality of the wine and the grapes that generated it. The destruction of vineyards during war becomes a common biblical theme, and the watchtower built at the edge of a vineyard to look for warriors, thieves, or gleaners, those who enter a field after harvest and pick the remainder left behind, often helped owners to protect their assets (Isa. 5:2; Matt. 21:33).

Later in Classical Greece, we find similar sentiments expressed by the great comic poet Aristophanes in his comedy, *Peace:* "Peace, the Goddess best and greatest, vineyard-lovingest of all!" As in ancient Canaan, vineyards in fifth century BCE Greece were very important to the economy and were considered a serious loss when destroyed by war.

During this period the Philistines, who invaded and settled cities in coastal Israel, were the strongest group in the Levant. They had iron weapons and chariots that gave them an advantage, while all other armies still fought with bronze weapons. The stories about the Judges serve in part to describe how Israel could regain control of its lands from the Philistines particularly, but other nearby opponents, too. Samson assaults the Philistine vineyards. Judges describes one especially clever, if ruthless, act: "So Samson went and caught three hundred foxes, and took some torches; and he turned the foxes tail to tail, and put a torch between each pair of tails. When he had set fire to the torches, he let the foxes go into the standing grain of the Philistines, and burned up the shocks and the standing grain, as well as the vineyards and olive groves" (Judg. 15:4–5).

Conveniently, Sampson not only destroys the enemy's vineyards but also kills the pests that ate grapes on his own land, where he presumably had trapped them. Three hundred foxes tied together with torches now become weapons that create a major economic setback to Philistine commerce. These smoldering vineyards will not produce enough fruit to make wine for at least four years. (Recently a grower in the Jerusalem Hills named Ya'acov Ben-Dor, whom we met at Yatir Winery, showed us electrified fencing to keep jackals, foxes, gazelles, and even hyenas from eating the grapes before harvest.)

WINE SKIRMISHES IN ROYAL FAMILIES

From the twelfth to tenth centuries BCE, the value of viticulture did not diminish. Warfare shifted from battles with foreign enemies to wine skirmishes within the families and clans. Judges 9 tells of one such family war—that of Abimelech. No king yet sat on the throne of Israel but usurper kings, like Abimelech, eliminated rivals to the throne. Abimelech killed all 70 of his brothers—except Jotham, who hid from him—and became a self-appointed king.

Jotham uses a parable to try to dissuade the clan from confirming Abimelech king: The olive tree, fig tree, and the vine are offered kingship, they all remain devoted to their natural functions, which for the vine was to produce new wine (*tîrôš*) that "cheer[s] gods (*'ĕlōhîm*) and mortals," demonstrating the importance of wine. Why would you give away something worth so much to be king? The parable likens Abimelech to a bramble, which the author Nogah Hareuvni suggests is a plant that has shallow roots and chokes out everything around it. Later, "lords of Shechem" pick grapes, have a party, and rebel against this self-appointed king: "They went out into the field and gathered the grapes from their vineyards, trod them, and celebrated. Then they went into the temple of their god, ate and drank, and ridiculed Abimelech" (Judg. 9:27).

The narrative does not reveal how many days this process of picking grapes, pressing them, and making wine took, but they likely drank new wine. This drinking occurred at a feast in the temple and may have been part of a sacred act of stirring up the gods against Abimelech. Perhaps this festival succeeded. Abimelech, who was never an Israelite king, had a short-lived small-clan kingship. His last attempt at attacking cities and burning down their towers ended when a woman dropped a millstone onto his head from a tower.

In David's time, around the beginning of the eleventh century BCE, the Israelites experienced less warfare (2 Sam. 7:1), but sibling rivalry and wine played a significant role in a fratricide. David's oldest son, Amnon, raped his half-sister Tamar (2 Sam. 25:8–19), and David's second son, Absalom, was furious. So when David's sons convened for a sheep-shearing feast, Absalom commanded his servants, "Watch when Amnon's heart is merry with wine, and when I say to you, 'Strike Amnon,' then kill him" (2 Sam. 13:28). The next verses describe Amnon's death at the hands of Absalom's men. Absalom originally planned a family feast, but after his father declined the invitation (2 Sam. 13:25), the family feast became a family slaying with wine as a weapon. In a twofold purpose, wine plays a role where Absalom avenges his sister Tamar and removes Amnon, who is his rival heir apparent.

WINE WARS AGAINST PEASANTS AND THE POOR

During the period we have been discussing, changes in the economic structures of Israel and surrounding kingdoms caused by incessant warfare created a situation whereby small farmers and the peasantry were increasingly being expelled from their holdings, or worse yet, killed by the warring tribal kings and their armies. Land was confiscated and turned over to wealthy retainers or allied merchants, even if those lands belonged to their own peoples, as a reward for subservience and service to a king's cause.

Prophetic invectives against the rich are many: "Ah, the proud garland of the drunkards of Ephraim, and the fading flower of its glorious beauty, which is on the head of those bloated with rich food, of those overcome with wine!" (Isa. 28:1). The prophet Amos insults the rich by calling them "cows of Bashan" for "oppressing the poor." The rich "say to their husbands, 'Bring [wine] now, that we may drink it!' (Amos 4). In another passage "those who are at ease in Zion . . . [and] secure on Mount Samaria . . . drink wine from bowls, and anoint themselves with the finest oils, but are not grieved over the ruin of Joseph!" (Amos 6:1, 6). The images here are of crapulous gluttons who drink so much wine that they stagger. These images convey the view of a society increasingly polarized between rich and poor, landed versus homeless.

Isaiah 5 is a song about a vineyard; the song depicts the destruction caused by Judah's ruling elite, which waged war on the peasants by giving them loans that they could not pay back and sent their vineyards into foreclosure. Isaiah 5:1–2 is a parable that describes judgment, indictment, sentence, and a summary (see 2 Sam. 12).

The parable begins: "Let me sing for my beloved my love-song concerning his vineyard: My beloved had a vineyard on a very fertile hill. He dug it and cleared it of stones and planted it with choice vines; he built a watchtower in the midst of it and hewed out a wine vat in it; he expected it to yield grapes, but it yielded sour grapes" (our translation).

To interpret this we need to refer to an earlier passage that was removed from this context, where it originally belonged, Isaiah 3:13–14: "The LORD rises to argue his case; he stands to judge the peoples. The LORD enters into judgment with the elders and princes of his people: It is you who have devoured the vineyard; the spoil of the poor is in your houses." This comment leads to an indictment of the rich and mighty: "What do you mean by crushing my people, by grinding the face of the poor? says the Lord GOD of hosts. And now, inhabitants of Jerusalem and people of Judah, judge between me and my vineyard. What more was there to do for my vineyard that I have not done in it? When I expected it to yield grapes, why did it yield wild grapes?" (Isa. 3:15, 5:3–4).

The book of Isaiah clearly and harshly pronounces the sentence for this behavior: "And now I will tell you what I will do to my vineyard. I will remove its hedge, and it shall be devoured; I will break down its wall, and it shall be trampled down. I will make it a waste; it shall not be pruned or hoed, and it shall be overgrown with briers and thorns; I will also command the clouds that they rain no rain upon it" (Isa. 5:5–6).

In the end Isaiah writes a summary appraisal of the judgment: "For the vineyard of the LORD of hosts is the house of Israel, and the people of Judah are his pleasant planting; he expected justice, but saw bloodshed; righteousness, but heard an outcry!" (Isa. 5:7).

Ultimately this assigns guilt to the ruling elite of Israel for waging wine wars on the poor by taxing them and foreclosing on their vineyards. In the agrarian political economy, Israelite wine was an export and commodity. Assyrian kings had their own vineyards farther north in Syria, Lebanon, and southern Turkey, where grapes grew in such abundance that prices fell and the broader spectrum of society gained access to wine. But Israelite wines were superior, and rapid agricultural intensification in the eighth century BCE permitted the elite minority to prop up the royal establishment at the expense of farmers. Vineyard ownership decreased because the ruling elite imposed taxes on owners, taxes they could not pay. The burden of heavy taxes led to mass foreclosures. This forced many family vintners to sell off their land, or it was seized by the wealthy; owners became laborers.

Wine provided currency for the elite to buy imported military materiel and luxury items, all at the expense of the peasant majority. Amos comments on the political and social disruption caused by this shift in agricultural ownership: "Therefore because you trample on the poor and take from them levies of grain, you have built houses of hewn stone, but you shall not live in them; you have planted pleasant vineyards, but you shall not drink their wine" (Amos 5:11). By taking the land from the rightful owners, selling the produce and dispossessing them, Amos' verse condemns the rich and powerful to never enjoying YHWH's blessings in the future because they have acted immorally.

As wine production increased in the hill country, growers made more use of terracing, built watchtowers for fermenting and storing wine, and royal vineyards. Let's look again at Isaiah 5:2 to better understand what and why the prophets were railing against the rich, and the importance of wine: "He dug it and cleared it of stones, and planted it with choice vines; he built a watchtower in the midst of it, and hewed out a wine vat in it; he expected it to yield grapes, but it yielded sour grapes." In the Hebrew, the wordplay on *grapes* and *sour grapes* and sound-play, *ṣedāqāʰ* (righteousness) and *ṣeʾāqāʰ* (outcry), reflect polar opposites: "He expected justice, but saw bloodshed; righteousness, but heard a cry!" The rich waged war on the poor by stealing their heritage. The prophet announces judgment against the ruling elite.

Another story (1 Kings 21) further illustrates how kings pump up the royal coffers at the expense of farmers. Naboth's vineyard was next to King Ahab's palace. The king offered Naboth money or a better vineyard to convert this land into a vegetable garden (1 Kings 21:2). Naboth refused to take money or a better vineyard. So Ahab went home dejected. Jezebel, Ahab's wife, retaliated by bringing a false charge against Naboth, claiming that he had "cursed God and the king." She then ordered officials to stone him and told Ahab, "Go, take possession of the vineyard of Naboth the Jezreelite, which he refused to give you for money; for Naboth is not alive, but dead" (1Kings 21:15).

Elijah the prophet ran into Ahab in the vineyard and told him: "Thus says the LORD: In the place where dogs licked up the blood of Naboth, dogs will also lick up your blood" (1 Kings 21:19). Elijah even says that YHWH will judge Ahab as harshly as the most evil king of Israel.

Since Jezebel appears to have been responsible for Naboth's murder, what wrong did Ahab do besides seizing the vineyard after Naboth was killed? Ahab is rather polite. He does not meet Samuel's low expectations for a king: "[Someone who] will take the best of your fields and vineyards and olive orchards and give them to his courtiers" (1 Sam. 8:14). Other kings, such as David (2 Sam. 24:18–24; 1 Chron. 21:18–24), set a price that they would pay for land, but Ahab allowed Naboth a choice, to name his own price or to barter for a better vineyard.

The vineyard was not Naboth's to sell; his forefathers had left it as an eternal inheritance (*naḥălāʰ*). "May YHWH forbid that I should give you the inheritance of my fathers." The words "May YHWH forbid" (*ḥālîlāʰ llî myhwh*) carry the meaning of profaning the covenant or acting in a manner repulsive to YHWH by selling the vineyard. Deuteronomy 28:30 uses the same word, *hll* (profane), to suggest a curse if someone plants a vineyard and someone else "uses its fruit" (*hll*): "You shall plant a vineyard, but not enjoy its fruit." The double meaning of *hll* implies that if another "uses the fruit" than the one who planted the vineyard, he/she "profanes" it.

In the Naboth story the act of tearing up a God-intended vineyard to grow vegetables was the grave sin. The writers of the books Genesis to Kings carefully used the word *garden;* they mention one only twice between Genesis 3 and 1 Kings. The first is in a comparison of the lushness of Sodom and Gomorrah and the gardens of YHWH (Eden; see Gen. 13:10). The second is a vegetable garden in Egypt (Deut. 11:10). Both cases relate a garden to some sort of exodus or banishment from Eden. When a garden finally appears in the Bible again, Ahab wants to replace Naboth's vineyard with a vegetable garden, effectively banishing Ahab from YHWH's grace.

The garden theme runs from Eden through Exodus. Ultimately, with the destruction of Judah's vineyards, the last king is banished from Mount Zion leaving through a garden—a representation of banishment. Ahab broke the covenant of inheritance, hence reaping similar consequences to Adam and Eve when they were banished from the garden. Beginning with Noah the first winemaker followed by the Jacobean blessing of fatness of land and abundance of grain and wine, the vineyard now replaces the garden of Eden as the Divine garden/paradise, especially the vineyard on Mt. Zion (Isa. 5).

NEHEMIAH, THE FIRST SOMMELIER

After the Persian conquest of Nebuchadnezzar, the Babylonian king, who in the mid-sixth century BCE captured Jerusalem in 586 BCE and destroyed the first Temple, taking captive and exiling the Jews to Babylonia, the same viticultural problems persisted. There were not enough people to work the larger sites, destroyed vineyards, vineyards seized and exploited by the rich for their own good, and all within the context of the larger destruction wrought by the conquest. Nehemiah was a captive Jewish boy exiled into Persia, and he eventually rose to the high-ranking position of cupbearer to Artaxerxes, the new king of Persia. Nehemiah then learned of the viticultural problems first hand. When men from Judah told him that the Jews who had escaped captivity now wanted to rebuild the walls of Jerusalem that Nebuchadnezzar had destroyed, Nehemiah became sad. Rebuilding Jerusalem would help those who had returned to plant new vineyards have both a safer home, and, ostensibly, a market to sell their produce, as the Jerusalem area was noted for its fine wines. While Nehemiah was serving wine to Artaxerxes, the king observed

Nehemiah's sadness and granted him the right to return to Judah as governor to rebuild the walls of Jerusalem (Neh. 2:1–9).

As sommelier to the Persian king, Nehemiah was an expert on wine who now was concerned with viticulture back home. When he got back to Judah, Nehemiah saw people using their houses and vineyards as collateral to pay the king's tax. Slowly taxes and loans outweighed production. Peasants lost their vineyards (Neh. 5:3–4). Former governors had laid heavy burdens on the people and had taken their food and wine (Neh. 5:15).

Angry that "vineyards now belong to others" (Neh. 5:5–6), Nehemiah made charges against the rich nobility (Neh. 5:7). As governor, he provided some wine and food to the dispossessed instead of demanding these as taxes (Neh.5:18; 8:9–10). He gave loans without interest and demanded that the nobility restore the properties to their rightful owners (Neh. 5:11), allocating wine as part of the tithes and offerings that are given to priests, singers, and gatekeepers (Neh. 10:37; 13:5, 12). His actions paved the way for a revival of wine making and a return of land to the Israelites, who were allowed back in Israel after the Babylonian exile.

WINE AS A SYMBOL OF JUDGMENT

The biblical writers frequently liken war to a state of intoxication (Zech. 12:2). They describe Israel as a vine and YHWH's act of working vines in a winepress as an image of YHWH's judgment about his people (Lam. 1:15). Jeremiah likens judgment to viticulture gone wrong, where poor harvest decisions result in sour wines or grapes that do not have the sugar level to make good wine: "In those days they shall no longer say: 'The parents have eaten sour grapes, and the children's teeth are set on edge.' But all shall die for their own sins; the teeth of everyone who eats sour grapes shall be set on edge" (Jer. 31:29–30).

The prophet Joel laments the devastation of the vineyards with cosmic language: "The fields are devastated, the ground mourns; for the grain is destroyed, the wine dries up, the oil fails" (Joel 1:10). "The vine withers, the fig tree droops. Pomegranate, palm, and apple—all the trees of the field are dried up; surely, joy withers away among the people" (Joel 1:12). In the book of Isaiah, Assyria, which is God's "rod of anger" and "club of punishment," brings down first Israel and later Judah: "On that day every place where there used to

remark by Herodotus tells us that vineyards in Babylonia were less important than in Egypt.

The typical wine garden in ancient Mesopotamia was in an orchard, which makes it difficult to evaluate how extensive the vineyards were. A tablet lists vineyards that have two thousand to twenty-nine thousand vines. As early as the Third Dynasty of Ur (third millennium BCE), records from the Ur excavations record that these gardeners may have set "six acres of vines below nurmu (pomegranate) trees among which are 91 full-grown palm trees . . . 1.5 acres of vineyard below nurmu trees, among which are 36 full-grown . . . palm trees."

Still another entry describes vineyards and barley planted next to each other, though this was not the norm. The vines would climb in the woods from tree to tree and would hang in the air between the trees. This agricultural arrangement both conserves water—by not having vines in a separate place where water would be wasted—and shades the vines to prevent sunburn and withering, thus providing another means of conserving water. What would a Hebrew have learned from the Babylonians about viticulture?

The Judean Hills have enough water through rain (16–27 inches/400–700 mm), with a similar climate to today, and aquifers that the Hebrews could have produced wine by dry farming. One could grow enough grapes to produce great wine in Israel's mountains and coastal plains without irrigation. The Golan and Galilee get about as much rain as Portland, Oregon, and Seattle, Washington (35–47 inches/900–1200 mm). The Judean Hills and Jerusalem Hills have as much annual rainfall as Carneros in southern Napa (16–23 inches/400–600 mm). However, the desert near the Dead Sea and the Negev could not produce wine. The Babylonians may have taught sophisticated irrigation techniques to the winemakers during the Exile. Perhaps this would explain the many places in Isaiah that mention fecundity in the desert: "And her wilderness He will make like Eden, And her desert like the garden of the LORD; Joy and gladness will be found in her" (Isa. 51:3). Irrigation would explain where all that lushness came from. Certainly we know that by the fourth century BCE the Nabateans had designed elaborate irrigation systems in the desert, as seen at Petra and Arad.

One notes as well that as prophets like Isaiah wrote about the fecundity of the desert, it is probable that during the early post-Exilic period, there may have been milder, more humid conditions prevailing in the desert areas.

Written testimony about large amounts of rainfall and evidence of aragonite, a carbonate formed especially when there is a lot of precipitation, were both discovered in the Qumran Caves by the Dead Sea at 330m below sea level. From this data it appears that the level of the Sea was as high as the caves, and precipitation was about 40 percent more than today, suggesting that the nearby desert areas like the Negev were more hospitable to crops and vineyards then. Paleoclimatologists also have noted that rapid climate change events (RCC), occurring in fifty- to one hundred-year intervals since the end of the last Ice Age about ten thousand years ago, indicate that a cool, wetter period likely happened during at least part of the post-Exilic period.

"Babylon was a golden cup in YHWH's hand," according to Jeremiah (51:7a). The Babylonian Empire brought some choice wine down the Euphrates. The Babylonians imported Levantine wines. They advanced the industry by bringing serious wines from the North, where some of the best were being made.

But the golden cup holding Babylon's wine industry became corrupted. It turned into rusty iron by their "making all the earth drunken; the nations drank of her [Babylon's] wine, and so the nations went mad" (Jer. 51:7b). Babylon became drunk on its own sense of greatness and made slaves out of Israelite vintners. It demolished prized vineyards of the kings of Judah. After destroying the Assyrian Empire, Babylon found it no longer needed Israel as an ally.

Instead Babylon became dominant over Judah and destroyed it. Yet some Judeans did not go into exile but remained in Judah under a Babylonian governor, Gedaliah—a good guy working for the bad guy (the Babylonian king), who tells them to "gather wine in great abundance" (Jer. 40:8, 10, 12).

Although the Judeans learned tricks from the Babylonians about irrigation and planting, only under Persian rule would Israelite viticulture experience a revival. The metaphor of wine would delineate rebirth for Israel. But Israel would remain under the Babylonian kings' control so long as they reaped the wealth of their empire, including the bounty of Israel's vineyards and the massive wealth captured from the Temple in Jerusalem.

Belshazzar (Balthazar), the son of Nabonidus, the last king of Babylon, threw a great party "for a thousand of his lords, and he was drinking wine in the presence of the thousand" (Dan. 5:1). Several biblical writers describe parties similar to the internationally observed *marzēaḥ* festival that takes place between the fourteenth century BCE and the Roman period. The *marzēaḥ* represents a type of drinking banquet dedicated to the gods, and it crossed many cultures throughout the Fertile Crescent; evidence of its celebration has been found in ancient Israel, Ugarit, Phoenicia, and Babylonia, and it is featured in rabbinic literature. It originated in Ugarit, which was famous for its wine and supported a wine-god cult, and it was associated with Ugarit's chief god, El, aspects of whom would later migrate west to Greece as Dionysus.

Over time, as the *marzēaḥ* festival moved into other eastern cultures, it became associated as well with commemorating the dead of the *marzēaḥ*'s host; people would imitate the gods by drinking themselves into a stupor. Given the excess of such a feast, its juxtaposition of celebration and death, one can understand the Israelite prophets' distaste for any feast held by the wealthy that smacked of this behavior. The Hebrew Bible mentions it twice: "Alas for those who lie on beds of ivory, and lounge on their couches, and eat lambs from the flock, and calves from the stall; who sing idle songs to the sound of the harp, and like David improvise on instruments of music; who drink wine from bowls, and anoint themselves with the finest oils, but are not grieved over the ruin of Joseph! Therefore they shall now be the first to go into exile, and the mirzaḥ of the loungers shall pass away" (Amos 6:4–7).

"For thus says YHWH, 'Do not enter a house of *marzēaḥ*, or go to lament or to console them; for I have withdrawn my peace from this people,' declares the LORD, 'My loving kindness and compassion'" (Jer. 16:5).

During the eighth century BCE (the period in which Amos was written), not only did the rich have a festival that the poor could not afford, but the wealthy profaned sacred objects. The *marzēaḥ* festival later had aspects similar to the agape feast, which was really a feast with and for the dead; in Corinth it excluded the poor.

Belshazzar's feast was like an *agape* feast on a grandiose scale. However, it was small compared to a feast that Ashurnasirpal had thrown approximately five hundred years earlier that was attended by almost seventy thousand people who consumed, among other things, ten thousand jars of beer and ten thousand skins of wine.

"Under the influence of the wine, Belshazzar commanded that they bring in the vessels of gold and silver that his father Nebuchadnezzar had taken out of the temple in Jerusalem so that the king and his lords, his wives, and his concubines might drink from them," the book of Daniel (5:2) relates. The wine stirred up religious sentiments: "They drank the wine and praised the gods of gold and silver, bronze, iron, wood, and stone." During the frolic "the fingers of a human hand appeared and began writing on the plaster of the wall of the royal palace" (5:5): "MENE, MENE, TEKEL, and PARSIN" (5:25). The king could not read the language in which it was written and asked his wise men to give an interpretation, offering them great rewards and the rank of third in the kingdom, but none could do so except Daniel.

What he told the king could not have been comforting: YHWH had numbered the days of his kingdom—it was over. The king's life and behavior had been found deficient, and the kingdom would be divided and "given over" to the Medes, a northwestern Iranian culture that preceded the Persians, absorbed into the Persian Empire by Cyrus the Great in 550 BCE, and the Persians.

Ironically Daniel's role in Babylon mirrored Joseph's in Egypt. Daniel told Belshazzar that he had placed himself above YHWH. His father had stolen the gold vessels from the Jerusalem temple, but Belshazzar's wives, concubines, officials, and he himself drank wine from them. His court had praised the gods of silver and gold and did not honor God (Dan. 5:23). Drinking from the holy vessels of the Israelites added insult to injury for the generations in exile from Israel and their own vineyards, and YHWH's punishment was the death of Belshazzar, the destruction of Babylon by the Persians, and the exiles' subsequent return to Israel.

YOU BET SHIR-AZ THE PERSIANS GAVE THEM WINE

After their captivity in Babylon the Judeans returned home with distaste for their captors but an affection for the Persian Empire and hailed the Achaemenid king Cyrus as a savior. Isaiah 45:1 refers to Cyrus as "his [YHWH's] messiah" because he set the exiles free, rebuilt the city of Jerusalem and its temple, and funded the replanting of vineyards. He was a patron of early Judaism. Legend has it that he marched into Babylon, encountered no resistance, and set the exiles free. The Cyrus cylinder discovered in 1878 CE makes specific reference to the Jews who were brought to Babylon and seems to reflect the religious tolerance he showed them. At the time of Cyrus's reign, not only did he fund the

MYTH OF SHIRAZ

Legend has it that the term *syrah* is a local French rendering of the name of a city in Iran called Shiraz that produced the well-known Shirazi wine. This legend recounts that the red syrah grape really originated in Shiraz and then was brought to the Rhône area by way of Marseilles, a city founded approximately in 600 BCE by Phoenicians, or Phoenician Greeks. A grape that sounds much like syrah was grown in the Rhone Valley, where it was called *Vitis allobrogica*, Pliny's *vinum picatum*, or pitched wine. Another wrinkle in the legend was that Gaspard de Stérimberg, a crusader, brought the variety to Rhône. But the famous Shirazi wine was white; no one made a vine/grape analysis of the grapes from Shiraz; and the Crusades were focused on the Holy Land, and the theory does not consider why a crusader would have journeyed as far east as Persia.

Jancis Robinson speculates that the term *shiraz* is in fact a so-called strinization of *syrah* by way of *sycra*, the Aramaic word for bright red (Clos de Gat in Israel uses this name for its syrah). *Shiraz* and *hermitage* gradually replaced *sycra* in Australia from the mid-nineteenth century, and British sources that go back to at least the 1830s document the spelling *shiraz*. In 1999, however, DNA testing found syrah to be the offspring of two obscure grapes from southeastern France, dureza and mondeuse blanche. *Vitis sylvestris* grapes did not originate in the hills of Shiraz, but early vintners transplanted them there from the North. Persians did not make wine from the syrah grape that Australians now call the shiraz. Recent genetic studies reveal that it is likely that syrah's ancestral origins are in Georgia, along with pinot noir and nebbiolo.

replanting of vineyards in Judah but more wines were imported from Persia. Some believe that Cyrus ordered his head be placed in a wineskin filled with human blood after his death—mordant humor from a king!

Ironically, today Iran deems wine making illegal in the very place where archaeologists have provided chemical evidence for some the earliest bona fide grape wine, which has been dated to approximately 3500 BCE.

Cyrus the Great emerged from the cool high plateaus of Shiraz, where viticulture flourished. He commenced his reign over a small kingdom whose capital was Anshan, identified today as Tepe Malyan, an archaeological mound set in the oak-covered highlands northwest of Shiraz. Excavations show that Tepe Malyan benefited from beer and wine that may have come from Godin Tepe. The Kaftari period cylinder seals show men and women of Shiraz holding up small cups and drinking wine in a posture similar to those displayed in the later depictions of the Greek *symposion* or Roman *convivium.* Persia produced its vintages in Shiraz and Bactria not only for local consumption but to supply a considerable export market.

Persian vines were so large that they were classified as trees and not bushes, perhaps the derivation of Pliny the Elder's similar classification of vines in his *Natural History,* book 14. Vines could be trained upward and into pergolas much like those used in Egyptian viticulture. Such big vines may not have produced the best grapes, but they produced lots of wine. Exiles returning home, like Nehemiah the cupbearer, would have brought with them experience in Persian drinking customs and understanding of viticulture. Persian wine was in demand, and Susa (Shushan in the Old Testament, located in the lower Zagros mountains) was a central market for shipping wine. Yet the residents of Susa were smart enough not to trade away all their wine but kept some in reserve for themselves, for libations to the gods and personal consumption.

The Persian Empire brought wine consumption to new heights. The fifth-century Greek historian Herodotus tells us that the Persians loved wine and that they made important decisions in the following manner. First they became drunk, since they believed that only when you are drunk do you tell the truth. Then they reconsidered the matter the next day when they were sober. Pliny suggests that wine was also mixed with drugs, specifically a drug called *achaemenis,* for collecting information. It had the following effect: "When it is drunk in wine, criminals confess to everything." We find ironic how little of this historical behavior is in evidence in modern-day Persia/Iran and that in 636 CE Arabic armies conquered Persia and dumped all its wine.

Some Persians once told King Xerxes I (486–465 BCE) that his father, Darius, was the richest man in the world because Pythius had given him "the golden vine," a description that evokes Jeremiah 51:7's description of Babylon. In Esther 1:7, during a weeklong wine fest in Susa, "drinks were served in golden goblets." There were no restraints on how much anyone drank; every man was expected to follow his own desires (1:8).

Throughout the book of Esther, King Ahasuerus (likely Xerxes I) demonstrates passion for his wife, the queen, on every occasion that wine is mentioned. But while "Queen Vashti gave a banquet for the women in the king's palace" (1:9), the inebriated king sent eunuchs to retrieve Vashti so that he could show her off (Esther 1:10). Vashti refused. Perhaps she just wanted to stay at her own party with the women she had invited, but some surmise that the phrase "display her beauty" was a euphemism for the king's intention that Vashti parade naked before the male crowd. In the narrative Ahasuerus replaces Vashti as queen with a Jewish woman named Esther.

During this period Darius the Great (550–486 BCE) was beginning his efforts to conquer Greece, bringing together a mass of viticulture in a way that civilization had not experienced since Greece colonized Asia Minor. The earlier Bronze Age (late second millennium BCE) Mycenaean culture in Greece's Peloponnese had brought together trade between Greece, Phoenicia, Ugarit, Israel, and Egypt. In his *Agesilaus* (9.3), an encomium to his friend the Spartan king, the Greek writer Xenophon refers to Persian kings' sending vintners to scour every land for new or exotic wines. Xenophon suggests that in Babylon wine was made from dates. From eastern Turkey, at the headwaters of the Euphrates, came old wines with fine aromas. The Persian wine world would now share in the viticultural traditions that dated to Homer, who wrote about an "eleven year old wine" or a Pramnian raisin wine with honey, cheese, and barley groats added. The Persians also would have had access four centuries after Homer (ca. ninth century BCE) to a later Pramnian wine from Ikaria that in their time was more delicate and dry.

After Artaxerxes succeeded Xerxes, the Persian Empire continued to interact with Judah, connecting both the empire and the kingdom with a much larger world of viticulture. Having served wine in the Persian courts, a cupbearer like Nehemiah who went back home to Judah would have brought with him an extensive knowledge of wine, viticulture, and wines from everywhere in the empire that were potentially fit for a king. With the expansion of the Persian Empire, Nehemiah probably would have drunk great wines from Greece, Turkey, Syria, Palestine, Armenia, Cappadocia, and even Egypt. The Persians would have also taught him to drink from a horn-shaped drinking vessel known as a rhyton. The Persian court offered the elaborate feasts or banquets that the Greeks later knew. The existence of rhytons and the mention of wine filters in the ancient literature from Persia suggest that wine expertise would have influenced Judean exiles. Nehemiah provides a perfect example of those who brought knowledge of Persian wine culture back to Judah. The Persian Empire connected the ancient wine world all the way to China by way of the Silk Road.

CHAMPAGNE BOTTLE SIZES

Why are splendid biblical names—jeroboam (3 liters), rehoboam (4.5 liters), methuselah (6 liters), salmanazar (9 liters), balthazar (12 liters), nebuchadnezzar (15 liters), melchior (18 liters), solomon (21 liters), sovereign (25 liters), primat (27 liters), and melchizedek (30 liters)—used for the largest bottle sizes of champagne? Bottles larger than the magnum (1.5 liters) are relatively recent in origin, probably no earlier than the 1920s. The oldest use for any biblical name for a wine bottle was jeroboam in Bordeaux. It may go back to at least the eighteenth century, according to Tom Stevenson, author of *The World Encyclopedia of Champagne and Other Sparkling Wines*. We surmise that biblical names were chosen partly to reflect the tremendous size of the bottles and even age-worthiness of the wine. Wine in large format bottles (magnums are ideal) is thought to age longer and stay fresher (hence the use of methusaleh?). Another possibility is that *champagne* producers are superb marketers, promoting their sparkling wine as the drink of celebration. Several bottles, such as the belshazzar, are named for party-throwing kings, others for debauched or wicked ones. Solomon was wise but not ascetic. Perhaps those who decided on these names knew the biblical personalities.

When the really large bottles were created, however, the technology to ferment wine in bottles larger than the jeroboam, or perhaps the rehoboam, did not exist, and even today no one does it. Virtually all large-format bottles are filled by decanting from smaller ones under pressure, and thus should not be aged long, as the wine inside will have suffered some oxidation during the transfer process. The originators of big bottle sizes knew this. Thus the bottles, while grand and impressive, are flawed, much like the people for whom they were named.

Tourelles in France's Rhone Valley (see chapter 12). Much later, large multi-level complexes, with multiple treading floors, filter basins, and collecting vats, and one or two presses, were built, such as at Castra near Haifa. These developments meant more wine could be produced for export.

By the fourth century BCE the Greeks had increased the use of amphoras, called *pithoi* by Greeks and *dolia* in the Roman era, for fermentation and storage of wine. These held the equivalent of 20 to 70 amphoras (140 to 500 gallons). The amphoras then were buried in the floor of the wine operation, and the thermal conditions kept the juice cooler while fermenting. This tradition is more than seven thousand years old in places like Georgia, where many producers continue to make ancient-style wines in large jars called *qvevri*. Vintners in Italy, France, and Slovenia are now attempting to make wines like this (see chapter 12).

The expansion of wine production in the Levant coincided with increased trade to Greece, Asia Minor, and, over time, Rome. Phoenicians established large grape-growing farms in northern Africa and as far west as Spain, likely taking the same grapes of the Levantine area with them. The Phoenicians adopted new growing practices, including more rationalized vineyards: row cultivation of bush vines (Theophrastus), and low-trained "vine trees." The Greeks, who adopted similar techniques, settled southern Italy and Sicily by the mid-eighth century BCE, while Phocaean Greeks from Asia Minor settled Massilia (Marseilles) around 600 BCE, bringing their wines and vine cuttings, which were much appreciated by the more rustic Gaulish tribes.

Phoenicians did the most to spread viticulture across the Mediterranean. Phoenicians led the Etruscans, who had developed an extraordinary culture based in central Italy (Tuscany), forward into a new wine culture; amphoras found near the French coast suggests that the Etruscans were the "principal exporters of wine to southern France by 600 BCE."

ANCIENT TRADE IN WINE: AMPHORAS

The first evidence that wine was exported from Canaan is the Canaanite wine jars found in Abydos, Egypt, that date to about 3150 BCE. The eventual destruction of the kingdoms of both Israel and Judah by invading forces eventually caused the lucrative wine trade to collapse in the sixth century BCE.

The use of wine amphoras expanded immensely in the post-Exilic period and was directly related to Greek influence in the Mediterranean. Several Greek city-states of Asia Minor and the Aegean islands (Rhodes, Chios, Samos) crafted unique styles for their clayware, adopting Egyptian and Phoenician practices for designating the origin, producer, style of wine, and even vintage.

Depending on period and origin, jars were stoppered with clay balls or disks. Small holes on the upper flank of the jar or in the balls allowed gases to exit as the wine fermented, then were sealed off when the wine was finished and ready to be drunk. Amphora design was informed by function first, then form: bottoms that became more pointed, waists that became more slender, narrower bottoms, two handles. Design signified the amphoras' origins, and to some degree the wine inside; Chian amphoras had long handles and long necks.

While amphoras' capacity varied, the popular Rhodian amphora held about 26 liters (7 gallons) when filled to just under the brim. Attesting to the demand for wine are the thousands of amphoras made in Judea (the Roman name for the section of their province of "Palestine," centered around Jerusalem) and filled with Judean wine that have been found in shipwrecks all around the Mediterranean basin.

Various islands, including Chios and Rhodes, and Phoenician towns as far afield as Carthage were especially noted for their amphoras. A lot of wine from the Hellenistic world was imported to Palestine from these places. Chemical analyses of the clay, and the residue within, have revealed where the jars were made and what kind of wine they contained.

Amphoras were also recycled for use by local producers. The Greek historian Herodotus reported the large-scale employment of secondhand wine jars for carrying water from Egypt to serve travelers along the desert road to Syria. He was astonished to see no empty wine jars lying about in Egypt even though it received continual shipments of Greek and Phoenician wine, which were shipped out again to Syria in the mid-fifth century BCE.

Because the wine trade was growing, late Hellenistic era wine amphoras bore information about the origin, date, size, and the quality of the wine inside; this also helped tax collectors to tax and regulate the production of wines. The island of Thásos, famous for its high-quality *vins de paserillés* (dried grape/raisin wines), kept quite close control of production and sale, and one can still find the wine laws on marble slabs there.

NEW WINE STYLES AND DRINKING
HABITS: THE GREEK INFLUENCE

First described in Hesiod's delightful *Works and Days* (ca. 700 BCE), sweet wines made from grapes left to dry for ten days and nights, then crushed and pressed, remained popular. But dry wines from Asia Minor and Cyprus, among other places, were also desirable though less common, as were white wines until the third century BCE. Athenians, though, found these dry wines objectionable. They "liked not the hard, stiff poets any more than they liked Pramnian wines, which contract the eyebrows as well as the bowels," Athenaeus reports. Influenced by the Greeks, the wealthy Jews and pagans in Palestine in particular came to enjoy scented and spiced wines, especially those with myrrh, thyme, cinnamon, and floral scents. Observant Jews could drink honeyed wine, as it was considered permissible on the Sabbath. The Mishna notes a typical mix was four parts wine to one part honey. Myrrh-enhanced wine was a Greek specialty but considered dangerous as a drug. In Mark's gospel Roman guards offered Jesus myrrh-enhanced wine that he refused; perhaps the guards had compassion for the man they were about to nail to the cross and felt the drug would anesthetize him for what was coming (Mark 15:23).

Wines flavored with seawater, or *oinos thalassikos,* as the Greeks called it, became popular in biblical lands under Hellenistic influence. "Wine is sweet when sea-water is poured into it," says Athenaeus, who was writing in the second century CE. Kos had a history of making *oinos thalassikos,* particularly a white wine, as did Clazomenae on the Aegean coast of Turkey, where fine wine is again being made at Urla today.

Seawater in wine seems repulsive and downright dangerous today. Drinking seawater will make a person quite ill; large amounts will kill. Remember, however, that most wine was sweet and strong. Ancient winemakers used seawater like a sterilant to clean out jars. If the jars were not rinsed with freshwater, the salt became impregnated in their pores. Lucius Junius Moderata Columella, author of *De re rustica,* says of Roman wine: "Every sort of vintage in every district ought to be salted . . . for this prevents there being any mouldy taste in the wine."

Furthermore seawater may have removed some of the bitterness introduced when using resin (see the discussion of Turriculae wine in chapter 12).

As recently as the 1960s California vintners would first season or rinse new American oak whiskey barrels with a brine solution to try to remove the worst of the tannins from the barrels, then would rinse them with freshwater. Finally diluting a rich sweet wine lowered its alcohol content and added an extra layer of flavor, according to ancient writers and our own experience.

Two things happen when mixing salty and sweet flavors in wine. First, they combine deliciously; think sauternes and blue cheese. Second, seawater would mask the off flavors of a bad wine, as well as contribute some cleansing aspects. And the ancient Greco-Roman tastes in food were different. Romans added their favorite fermented fish sauce, *garum,* to just about everything; it lent savory flavors and perhaps disguised rancid meat.

Greeks considered drinking undiluted wine barbarous, so they usually cut their wine with water; a ratio of 4:1 was typical but sometimes they used less water. By the time the Talmudic period begins in Israel from the second century BCE (while written in the first to fourth centuries CE, the Talmud refers back to BCE) the Jews were drinking a wine called *mazug,* wine mixed with water in a 3:1 ratio (water to wine), illustrating the degree to which Palestine under Ptolemaic-Greek rule had accepted Hellenistic customs. By the second century BCE, even the Shabbat wine was mixed with water before the *barucha* (blessing) was given (berakhot 7:5—a book in the Midrash).

As production methods changed, more wine made in different styles emerged as grapes were brought to new lands and tastes evolved, even in Palestine. In Cato the Elder's time (234–149 BCE), the concept of dedicated vineyards with rows, or blocks, of trained pergola–style vineyards gained favor.

Drinking habits in the Greek world became more egalitarian, as wine became affordable across a wider range of socioeconomic levels. The common wine was probably no fancy *cru*—wine with a unique personality and high quality from a particular vineyard, village or region, such as in modern Burgundy—but a coarse blend made from mixing pomace with water to make a sharp, thin wine. At the same time the upper echelons of Greek society relaxed, learned, and philosophized at the *symposion,* a drinking party only for men that under the right conditions provided an opportunity to enjoy a light meal with friends, discuss ideas, play games, listen to female flute players, and drink a lot. The hierarchy of the *symposion* required the leader, the *symposiarch,* to determine the quality/type of wine to be drunk, the percentage of water

went to him and bandaged his wounds, having poured oil and wine on them. Then he put him on his own animal, brought him to an inn, and took care of him" (Luke 10:34).

During the centuries rabbis learned to combine wine with herbs and spices to alleviate pain or cure diseases, developing prescriptions from Egyptian and Greek pharmacopeia. A patch soaked in wine and placed over an inflamed eye was said to reduce the pain and swelling. One of our favorite cures is for impotence: "Drink three quarters of a log [roughly two pints] of wine cooked with ground forest saffron." The sagely Rabbi Yohanan swore that "these treatments restored my youth." Assuming that the forest saffron is what we know today as *Elaeodendron croceum* or a similar species, the good rabbi was lucky to live, let alone have his impotence cured. Preparations of the root or bark are fatal to humans.

Judaic culture noted wine's aphrodisiac capacity. According to the German writer Julius Preuss, "the Talmud recognizes the aphrodisiac properties of wine, especially in regard to women . . . but also to men. A wine famous for its aphrodisiac nature was the Ammonite wine." On the other hand, later Greek writers like Athenaeus recognized excess consumption of wine led to sexual problems, citing Alexander the Great's great indulgence in wine and lack of enthusiasm in the bedroom.

Overall, Jews practiced temperance. They rarely drank to excess, even at festivals like Purim or the *marzēaḥ*. "Perhaps one of the reasons is that our sages have recommended moderation in all things: 'There are eight things in which excess is harmful, and in which moderation is to be observed: travelling, sexual relations, wealth, labour, food and drink, sleep, hot baths and letting blood.'" Punishments for drunkards were harsh, and warnings in the Bible attest to the results of chronic abuse: "And they shall say to the elders of his city, 'This son of ours is stubborn and rebellious, he will not obey us, he is a glutton and a drunkard.' Then all the men of his city shall stone him to death; so you shall remove the evil from your midst, and all Israel shall hear of it and fear" (Deut. 21:20–21). In post-Exilic Judaism, being drunk was criminal behavior. For other early Levantine cultures, the Greeks and later the Romans, drinking to excess was condemned as uncouth and uncivilized but was not in itself a crime.

Proverbs 23:29–34 provides a vivid description of what befalls those who overindulge: "Your eyes will see strange things, And your mind will utter perverse things. And you will be like one who lies down in the middle of the sea, Or like one who lies down on the top of a mast."

For the Greeks wine served as medicine and was a key component of living well and long. The father of modern medicine, Hippocrates, was born on the island of Kos. There people worshiped the god of healing, Asclepius, at a great sanctuary and hospital. Hippocrates learned his craft there. He prescribed regular consumption of moderate amounts of wine for good health (red wine, no doubt). A follower of his at the temple wrote an inscription: "The doctor is the giver of wine." By studying the effects of wine on patients, he came to see that red wines and cooked wines (boiled down) were best for intestinal ailments, while white wines succeeded with bladder problems and should be used to clean and disinfect wounds. Finally, as Pliny notes, even vinegar "is often beneficial in combination with other substances," controlling coughs and suppressing nausea.

THE FIRST JEWISH WINES: INTRODUCING KOSHER

Kosher wine in early Judaism begins with the promise to the Jews that never again will the Lord allow oppressive foreigners to drink their wine that God promised them (Isa. 62:8). Nehemiah, the cupbearer and instrument of spiritual reform, stipulates that the purity of wine cannot be preserved if it violates Sabbath laws: "In those days I saw in Judah people treading wine presses on the Sabbath, and bringing in . . . wine, grapes, figs, and all kinds of burdens, which they brought into Jerusalem on the sabbath day; and I warned them at that time against selling food" (Neh. 13:15). Nehemiah reminds the Judeans that part of the reason God sent their ancestors into exile was that they had profaned the Sabbath (Neh. 13:18) and undermined purification laws (Neh. 13:22).

Jewish wine now becomes sacred; "unclean" non-Jews will not be able to drink it. Wine now becomes a symbol of purity. According to Jewish law, the contents of imported amphoras were impure. Early in the time of Second-Temple Judaism, long after Nebuchadnezzar had destroyed the first holy place and the second one was just being built, the prophet Haggai used the concept of "unclean" to foreshadow the question of "why the vine yields nothing" (2:19).

A QUICK GUIDE TO KOSHER

Wine as the symbol of Israel "had to be kosher [*kashrut*] like meat." The later-written Talmud forbade Gentiles to touch wine that had not been securely sealed and corked. It also forbade Jews to drink wine with Gentiles, told Jews to avoid intermarriage, and instructed them to avoid idolatry and idol worshipers. Preparation of a gat (wine press) for receiving grapes included ritual washing of the plaster used to coat the gat's surfaces and make them impermeable to the liquid. Harvested grapes that touched the ground could not be used, but the poor could come into vineyards after the harvest and take any remaining fruit (Num. 18:13).

Here, we won't talk *tref* (whatever is unclean or unfit according to Jewish law; the opposite of kosher), as one of our grandmothers used to admonish us as kids. Virtually all wine today is made with the same procedures and techniques, whether by kosher or nonkosher wineries. But to be certified as kosher,

Grapes from new vines cannot be used until four years after planting.

No other crops can be grown between vine rows.

After the first harvest the vineyard must lie fallow every seventh year; this practice is known as *shnat shmita*.

Only exceptionally religiously observant male Jews (usually called *haredim*) can be involved in the wine-making process once the grapes arrive at the winery.

All equipment for harvesting, and that used in the winery and other facilities, must be kosher; this means they must be cleaned three times with steam, scalding water, and even fire.

All barrels must be new or used only for making kosher wines.

Only observant male Jews may touch the equipment during wine making. This requirement excludes most Israeli winemakers, leading to frustration at times.

No animal protein products, such as gelatin or egg white, can come in contact with the wine. And any products used in wine making, such as yeasts, must be kosher.

Wine certified as kosher for Passover also cannot come in contact with any cereal products, such as bread.

Lastly, a small symbolic amount of wine (usually 1 to 2 percent) must be siphoned from tanks or barrels. This supposedly represents the tithe once paid to the temple in Jerusalem.

One special difference applies to wines called *mevushal:* they must be pasteurized. This is done today by flash-heating the juice before fermentation to 80–90°C/176–194°F for about 45 seconds and then quickly chilling it down to 15°C/59° F. In ancient times the wine was boiled, a practice that was not uncommon in the production of many ancient Greek and Roman wines. Either way, this process stunts the development potential of the wine, but it also makes it possible for non-Jews to handle the wine once it reaches the market. This is an important issue for observant Jewish communities and for service in restaurants or by caterers, most of whose employees are not observant or Jewish.

Unclean practices, such as those of Samaritans, blocked blessings. The book of Daniel, chapter 1, probably written in the second century BCE but set in the post-Exilic period, foreshadows the prototypical role of the rabbis regarding the increasing codification of laws regarding diet, dress and other aspects of a distinctly Jewish nature. When Daniel refuses to eat what King Belshazzar does, the verses underline the growing awareness of differences in diet between Jew and Gentile.

ABSTINENCE AND WINE

One of the great blind spots of some conservative biblical interpretations today results from an extremism that focuses only on passages about abstinence from alcohol but not on ones that celebrate wine. Until now we have discussed how important and positive Israelites and other cultures in the biblical world considered wine to be. It created joy, promoted conversation, appeased the gods, and allowed people to relax and forget their hard lives, at least for a little while. Far more biblical passages refer positively to wine than negatively. Yet the negative aspects cannot be ignored. But putting them in the proper context is important.

While the focus of keeping kosher is purity, the focus of asceticism (for example, that of the Nazirites) is abstinence. Judges 13 says that the unnamed wife of Manoah was pregnant with Samson. She indulged in no wine, fermented drink, or anything unclean (13:4) because the child in her womb

Six

THE ROMAN WINE EMPIRE
AND THE NEW TESTAMENT

And let the wine be the same for all guests—where is it laid down that the banquet's host should get drunk on wine with a fine bouquet while I must burst my belly on new stuff?

—Lucan, *Saturnalia*, 22

THE ROMAN WINE EMPIRE

Rome's rise to dominance near the end of the second century BCE led to a new wine era in the Mediterranean world, from Mesopotamia to Gibraltar.

Effectively, the Roman imperial system created an international market in which wine was a principal commodity. The market was based on a relatively efficient Mediterranean transportation network and laws that promoted taxation, instead of extortion or violence, to promote economic growth. For much of the early Roman Empire (until the first century CE), upper-class Romans imported the top wines of Greece and fine vintages from Palestine, Asia Minor, and Egypt. They had little confidence in their own wine-making potential until the vintage of 121 BCE during the consulship of Lucius Opimius. Romans were good adopters, imitating key production techniques and anything else that would increase their wealth. This famous Opimian vintage was apparently the first year with ideal growing conditions, yielding a wine that even two centuries later tasted very sweet and concentrated; Pliny the Elder suggested that it improved other wines when added to them.

Making amphoras, adopting Syrian glass-blowing techniques, and absorbing smart farmworkers into their system helped Romans create a serious wine industry in Italy. Their northern neighbors, the Etruscans, had been practicing viticulture since approximately the eighth century BCE; the Etruscans probably learned about wine in their home country, which probably was Lydia, and from Phoenician traders. Etruscans loved wine and good living, and their god Fufluns would eventually become identified with Dionysus/Bacchus. From the seventh century BCE, perhaps earlier, Etruscans organized wine exports to southern Gaul (France) and adopted wine styles, grapes, perhaps including the ansonica (inzolia) and amphoras from their Greco-Phoenician "teachers."

Once the civil wars of the first century BCE ended, the empire under Augustus expanded its control and stabilized the entire region. Rome became the focal point for a huge wine trade. Fine wines from top *crus* in Greece continued to arrive in Italy, as did a growing number of prestigious wines from Italy whose names still excite: Falernum, Caecubum, Mamertinum, Aminaeum, and others. Competition came from vineyards in old Phoenician regions conquered by Rome, such as Carthage and southern Spain. These provided the average wines that a growing population required. The amounts were staggering, even by modern standards, with a million inhabitants in Rome who were consuming as much as 23 million gallons yearly by the first century CE (assuming an average consumption of about 100 gallons per year per adult, though this could be the diluted quantity). Rome would have needed even more wine than that, given the thirst of the Roman army: a five-thousand-man legion alone would need approximately half a million gallons year, and Rome fielded about 30 legions.

The population of the empire in the mid-first century CE probably reached between 50 and 65 million, based upon certain censuses, including that taken under the Emperor Claudius. If even 15 percent were adult males (the principal drinkers), consumption would have been on the order of 800 to 900 million gallons of wine a year empire-wide. In comparison the 300 million people in the United States in 2011 consumed 746 million gallons of wine.

Urban immigration, consolidation of land holdings under wealthy landowners, and increasing consumption of wine in taverns as more people inhabited cities and public celebrations with concomitant free food and wine were among the reasons for the massive Roman wine empire, the largest wine year revolves, shall draw a well-pitched cork forth from a jar." An amphora in Beaune's Musée de Vin de Bourgogne was found in a wrecked ship that had been carrying wine from Pompeii to France and in its neck is a sizable gray black cork. Because corks did not fit perfectly, they were covered over with an airtight layer of lime-based mortar. A buyer could insist on sampling a wine jar before purchase, but this was only a precaution against outright fraud. Since contamination and degradation could occur during the transport of the jar, it was nearly impossible to prosecute *vinarii* (wine dealers) directly.

Columella and others worried about wine quality and hygiene, given how much wine was shipped all over their world. Problems arose from the penchant of Roman wine producers or shippers to fiddle around with the wine after the fact, opening amphoras and adding spices, honey, or herbs, all of which meant the wine was aerating and potentially oxidizing with resulting spoilage.

Pliny recommended adding tree resins to the wine as a preservative in case it was opened, though the preferred practice was to coat amphoras and *dolia* with pitch before their first use; other methods were to use a seawater rinse and add myrrh to sweeten the wine. While the use of oak barrels became quite common for storing and shipping wine later in the empire, it was rare during the biblical period of the first century CE, and generally used only in the cooler northern vineyards of Gaul and northern Italy. Though oak barrels could not be used to age wine, they were economical to use for shipping wine short distances, such as to a wine tavern, for immediate consumption.

The shift to large-scale wine production created a broader consumer base of millions. At the same time appreciation for the top wines, made in smaller volumes, continued. Roman advances in large-scale glass production helped promote the shift to mass production. The ability to create inexpensive glass serving and drinking vessels, often in the same regions as the wines themselves, provided a lighter, less expensive means of serving, storing, and consuming wine and a more visually pleasing drinking experience.

A REPUBLIC OF WINE AND IMPERIAL GRAND *CRUS*

The Roman Empire had no shortage of wine drinkers, but there was also no such thing as a wine expert in the sense of a critic. In the Romans' world custom, wealth, political fashion, health issues, and proximity to source, as

Raeticum

Raeticum

Ratavinum
Adrianum

Mutinense

Faventinum

Praetutium

Picens
Spolentinum
Caere Sabinum

Nomentanum

Setinum Vaticanum
ROME Albanum

Caecubum
Falernum
Faustianum

Tarentinum

Surrentinum
Pompeiianum Buxentinum

Thurinum

Cosentinum

Reginum

Mamertinum
Mesopotamium Tauromenitanum

0 ——— 100
miles

Major
Ancient
Wine
Centers

Important Roman Vineyards, 1st Century CE

well as price, dictated what one drank. Yet the Roman system produced the conditions necessary to make available everything from the cheapest swill of North Africa to the finest *crus* of Italy, Greece, and elsewhere. Political conservatism, combined with empirical observation (Pliny, Columella), influenced imperial era writers' judgment of quality, vineyard practices, and why certain wines were ordinary or not. Galen observed wine with an eye to its medicinal benefits and precise taste, while Athenaeus was more interested in recounting how the ancients (Greeks, early Romans, even the gods) enjoyed and perceived good wine. These later writers are more concerned with high quality, differentiation of grapes and wine than Cato ever was back in the third century BCE.

The *cru* concept did not start with the French, as many believe. The Romans adopted from the Egyptians and Greeks the notion that certain vineyards (*cru* or growth) or well-defined vineyard regions produce special wines of quality. Pliny comments: "Indeed, some vines have so great an attachment to certain localities that their reputation is indissolubly linked to them and they cannot be transplanted anywhere else without inferior results." Relatively safe living conditions throughout the vast Roman Empire allowed the development of an acquisitive and large class of people who appreciated the best wines and talked about them. By the mid-first century BCE this led to a wider range of regional appellations, as well as the important distinction between noble vines and cheap wine production.

Where were *grand crus* found? What were they like? Pliny mentions 87 famous wines in his era, two-thirds of them in Italy. Oddly, ancient writers mention many wines but rarely say if they were white or red. We can presume that many prized Roman wines, especially Italian, were whites. If we go by the biblical descriptions, the Greeks and Levantines generally preferred red wines. Romans usually liked their wines sweet and rich, quite different from today's preferences.

Anyone living in Rome at this time would have been drawn to the cult wines grown near Rome and south into Campania, including Naples, Vesuvius, and the Sorrento Peninsula. Here, the most respected wines of the early first century CE were produced. Wealthy Romans or senators no doubt invested in their own wine farms in this region; the most popular wines were Setinum, Caecubum, and Falernum.

Caesar Augustus preferred Rhaeticum from Verona, then setinum because it was better for his digestion. Caecubum, made on the Tyrrhenian seacoast, was the most generous (sweet?) wine in flavor until the mid-first century CE. It was grown on marshy land in a warm area, not unlike the Sauternes region of Bordeaux, and André Tchernia and his coauthor, Jean-Pierre Brun, believe that the noble rot (*Botrytis cinerea*) may have easily developed. In fact the vineyard disappeared because of the owners' neglect; perhaps the terroir was too marshy for it to survive, as Pliny notes.

Thus Falernum, made on the slopes of Monte Massico, came to be the second most highly prized wine after Caecubum by the mid-first century CE. It was made in three styles of white and red—dry, sweet, and light. According to Pliny, it was "the only wine that takes light when a flame is applied to it," implying that it had high alcohol content.

"The third prize attained by various degrees is from Alban wines, the grape Eugenia, a refugee from Taormina in Sicily which are very sweet, though occasionally dry, as well as those of Sorrento, only grown in 'vineyards' [rows], and recommended for their thinness and health-giving qualities," Pliny informs. The most famous wine today in the Colli Albani is the soft, fragrant, and delicious white wine called frascati.

Pliny considered Surrentinum (from Sorrento) wines excellent for their thinness and health-giving qualities, but the emperor Tiberius thought it was "generous vinegar." From these comments we can surmise that Sorrento's wines likely were drier white wines. Today fresh wines with firm structures are made from the fiano, greco, and falanghina grapes still grown around Sorrento. Pliny noted that Caesar thought highly of the lively, light, sweet, and probably white Mamertinum wines from the Messina area.

Praetutium, a fine white wine with "sweet scent" from the Adriatic coast near Rimini, was highly regarded by Augustus's daughter, Julia Augusta. Today's aromatic verdicchio white wines are produced nearby, with good results. Rhaeticum from the Valtellina and Verona areas was also well thought of at the beginning of the first century CE. Rhaeticum likely was made from both white and red grapes, much like today's recioto di soave and recioto di valpolicella. Grapes were picked ripe, then hung up to dry into raisins through the cool autumn months before they were crushed to make a strong, sweet wine. Romans called wines made from raisins *passi*.

Pliny discusses the best wine of France: "A vine has now been discovered that of itself produces a flavor of pitch in the [red] wine; this vine gives celebrity to the territory of Vienne [near Côte Rôtie in the Rhone Valley south of Lyon]." Could this be the ancestor of today's syrah grape, which is grown on the same steeply terraced slopes?

At least two wines, Eugeneum and Aminaeum, achieved wider fame. Aminaeum was mentioned alongside Greek wines in the sumptuary legislation of the early first century BCE in Rome, which limited the sale of so-called luxury wines above a certain price per gallon, and only one cup of Greek wine could be served at a dinner party per guest! The aminaeum grape was grown throughout southern Italy, often trained up a tree. Pliny also notes that the "vines of Aminaea are in the top category because of their body and their character, which clearly improve with age." Some today think aminaeum's ancestor is the greco grape, grown in much of Campania and in Puglia as well.

Also favorably noted by ancient wine writers was the apianis (bee vine—the insects loved its sweetness). It grew well around the Vesuvius area but also did well in Tuscany. It was probably a muscat-type grape; Columella notes it was not as popular as others—it began sweet but became rougher with age. Today's growers in Campania believe their fiano derives from the apianis. Next in order of quality were the nomentanum vines, which produce less wine than other varieties. One red grape that continued to make excellent wine in southern Italy was the ellenicum (in Greek the *hellenico*), brought into the area by the Greeks centuries before. Today's aglianico variety is probably its descendant, producing fine wines in the Irpinian hills near Vesuvius, and found only rarely in Greece.

Roman writers could be damning about what they didn't like. Martial summed up Corsican wines this way: "We drink the black poison of a Corsican Jar." He also thought poorly of Tuscan wines. Pliny the Elder damns with faint praise the wines from the Pompeiianum, the vineyards around Pompeii; these wines were largely made from the murgentina grape of eastern Sicily. They grow well on Vesuvius's fertile slopes but should be aged no longer than ten years, "gaining nothing further and are 'unwholesome' because of a headache which lasts till noon the following day."

Pliny and Columella are generally in agreement on the best wines in the empire outside Italy and Sicily. Asia Minor's best white wine, and one of the empire's best in Pliny's day, came from Clazomenae (Urla today) west of Izmir; it was prized because it had lower amount of seawater mixed in compared to the usual 4:1 ratio for wines noted in previous chapters. From Chios and Thásos came Greek wines comparable in quality to the aminaean vintages. Pliny praised the most highly regarded Homeric wines, dark Maronean from Thrace, and Lesbos white wines "with a natural taste of the sea." Many also praised the medicinal wine of Kos, made as a *passum* aged in casks in the sun and then mixed with seawater.

Pliny thought many of the Greek wines, whatever their color or style, needed about seven years to reach moderate maturity. Most interesting for a Roman, the first century CE poet Horace praised the good wines of Palestine. Strabo the geographer, writing in the late first century BCE (*Geography* Book XIV), called the wines of Ephesus "very good." An indication of how tastes and standards changed in the Romans' day is that Pliny dryly remarks a century later that Ephesian wine is second rate.

In Athenaeus's *Deipnosophistai,* Galen the Physician comments on the good and bad aspects of certain famous old wines: "Falernian wine is good to drink after 10 years and best after 15–20 years. After that it causes headaches and affects the nerves." A guest at a party given by Athenaeus praises the wine from the Greek island of Skiathos for its refreshing effervescence. Could this wine have been a primitive sparkling wine? Mario Fregoni, a prominent Italian professor of viticulture, raises this same issue with regard to a passage in Propertius's *Elegies:* "Let the table swim even more liberally with floods of Falernian, let it bubble more lusciously in your golden goblet."

People throughout the empire drank wine mixed with herbs, flowers, and spices. They used these additives not only for flavor but in some cases for their ability to alter reality. And given contemporary knowledge, people were aware of the consequences, pleasant or not, of mixing certain things into their wine, such as myrrh and opium from poppies.

Likewise, *Artemisia absinthium,* known as common wormwood, was frequently used as a medicine to quell anxiety and distress, but it was clearly understood in the classical world that its active ingredient, thujone, taken in wine, released inhibitions, increased the imaginative powers, and inspired writers and poets. A passage in Revelation (8:11) indicates the ancient Jews understood the power of this root, including the negative consequences of using too much: "And the name of the star is called Wormwood; and a third of the waters became wormwood; and many men died from the waters, because they were made bitter." Although Romans adulterated wine a lot, frequently to cover up flaws, Columella acknowledges: "We regard as the best wine any kind which can keep without any preservative, nor should anything at all be mixed with it by which its pleasure by its own natural savor would be obscured; for that wine is most excellent which has given pleasure by its own natural quality."

What remains clear is that for at least three centuries wines and vineyards in the Roman world satisfied the most discerning palates. Also, the empire produced more than enough wine to allow most people to enjoy it on a regular basis at a tolerable price.

CORINTHIAN BACCHANALIANS HAVE AN AGAPE FEAST

Early in Christianity, devotees celebrated an agape feast, which may have been the foundation for the Eucharist, or Lord's Supper. What distinguished it from other feasts was that the Words of Institution were spoken, which echo those of Jesus at the Last Supper consecrating the bread and wine, the Eucharist (1 Cor. 11:23–27).

Since wine was often expensive in the ancient world, it was a marker of social classes during the writing of the New Testament, despite the injunction that "there is neither Jew nor gentile, slave nor free" (Gal. 3:28)—that is, no social divisions. When early Christians gathered to celebrate the Eucharist in Corinth, the rich ate big meals in private and got drunk on the communion wine instead of sharing in a community meal and heeding the biblical command that says, "This is my body for you *all.*" Paul even referred to the wealthy as those who owned houses in which they could eat food, and their behavior was in fact quite similar to that of wealthy Romans at a *symposion* or *convivium* (feast) rather than a Christian love feast.

A major difference between the *symposion* and the *convivium* was that at the *symposion* wine and water were mixed in a large *krater* for all to share. The participants drew the first cup of wine from the *krater* to praise the gods. Pythia, the Delphic priestess, advised people to call on Dionysus to give them health. According to the poet Eubolos, Dionysus said: "For those who think well, I mix wine in three bowls [*kraters*]: the first one to drink for health, the second one for the pleasures of love and the third one for sleep. When that is emptied wise guests walk home. The fourth cup is no longer mine, but is insult [hubris] and violence. The fifth one is for uproar, the sixth for drunken revel; a seventh cup is for black eyes; the eighth for calling the guards and the ninth for bilious bitterness. The tenth is for rage and fury and throwing things. Too much wine poured in small vessels knocks the legs from under those drinking it."

This *symposion/convivium* provided the educated upper class with a way to have intellectual discussions while drinking and an opportunity to indulge in excessive eating and drinking. Pliny suggests that alkanet (forget-me-not), "the plant that cheers," would be added to the wine during these events. The *convivium* had music, and participants would discuss the specifics of proper wine ingestion, such as the dilution ratio of water to wine. Food festivities were central, whereas at a *symposion* food was eaten separately and the focus was on drinking. The evolution of the *symposion/convivium* to the agape feast no doubt occurred organically, as new Christian communities, especially more wealthy individuals, adapted more ancient practices to suit the conditions of their newly adopted religion.

Wealthy Corinthians may have confused the purposes of the Lord's Supper with the *convivium*. Just as the rich excluded the poor from the *symposion* and *convivium*, they excluded the poor from the love feast at which the Eucharist took place. First-century churches met in homes. In Corinth people ate and drank by social classes. The wealthy used the rear *triclinium* (dining area) to entertain company; hosts and guests would recline on pillows while feasting. Various *tricliniaria* held love feasts around the themes of wine, food, and love. The scandal of Corinth was that the rich remained in the *triclinium,* eating and drinking, where the poor could not enter. The wealthy profaned the Lord's Supper by celebrating this rite as a feast and excluding the poor.

Paul's question—"Have you not houses to eat and drink in?" (1 Cor. 11:22a)—admonishes wealthy Corinthians to reserve feasts for the wealthy such as the *symposion* and *convivium* for private occasions in their own homes and to not hold them in conjunction with the Lord's Supper in a house where everyone gathered to celebrate the Eucharist together. Celebration of the Lord's Supper should be a love feast and not exclude anyone on the basis of social status: "There is no longer Jew or Greek, there is no longer slave or free, there is no longer male and female; for all of you are one in Christ Jesus" (Gal. 3:28).

WINO WINE GODS

Ancient cultures had their own versions of a wine god/goddess who has given the gift of wine to their devotees and causes the rains to fall and the grapes to grow. From being relatively unimportant, the deities of wine and the vine gradually came to the forefront of religious consciousness, as symbols concerned with rebirth and the life hereafter. Where these gods were of less importance, such as in Mesopotamia and Egypt, their lower status probably was connected to the difficulties of cultivating vines in these regions, as well as the critical importance of water to the survival of their societies.

Although he was a son of Zeus, Dionysus wasn't considered Olympian; early on he was considered a wild primitive god, often portrayed as a living vine with branches hanging heavily with fruit. But his more exuberant side— the irrational nature he represented—captured people's attention and ultimately made his cult more popular throughout the Greco-Roman world than the cults of all others.

The Hebrew wine god was often identified as the Israelite YHWH and appeared early in certain passages in Genesis (14:13; 18:1–15). Deities who appeared to Abraham, like Mamre and Eshcol (meaning Grape Cluster), had sacred shrines near Hebron where wines were famous. Evidence of a Palestinian wine god that may have been an old Dionysian god exists in the Near East. When the Maccabees introduced their festival of Hanukkah, they included some Dionysian elements, such as the procession with the *thrysus,* the god's symbolic staff covered with vine leaves and grape clusters (2 Macc. 6:7; 14:33; 3 Macc. 2:29). Bet She'an, Ashkelon, Tyre, and Sidon were major centers of Dionysian worship, while grape and chalice symbols found on Jewish coins as early as the fourth century BCE suggest YHWH had some Dionysian origins.

The ancients considered wine to be golden nectar, the drink of the gods, which symbolized immortality and ensured victory over death to all who drank it. As a result of Dionysus's increased popularity, by 186 BCE the cult of Bacchus in Rome threatened to become more popular than the cults of the state gods, with their call to piety. The Romans adopted the name Bacchus for Dionysus. By 139 BCE Jews in Rome worshiped YHWH as Bacchus, who was more recognizable to their neighbors, keeping them from getting antsy about Judaism. Any cult that promised personal redemption, including the cults of

Bacchus, Isis, Jesus, and others, ran counter to traditional pagan values. By the mid-first century BCE, worship of Bacchus/Dionysus was practiced openly, with the symbolic festooning of buildings and statues with *thrysi,* vine garlands, and masks. In Jerusalem his cult was so popular that a large golden vine was draped over the entrance to Herod's temple in the late first century BCE and "from [it] hung grape clusters as tall as a man"—in honor of Dionysus, not YHWH. Only in the fourth century CE did many Dionysian symbols and rituals disappear, when they were absorbed into the Eucharist.

Even the way one chose, prepared, and served wine had sacred meaning. Therefore Pliny suggested: "And since life is upheld by religion, it is considered sinful to pour libations to the gods, not only with wines made from a vine that has not been pruned, but from one that has been struck by lightning, or one in the neighborhood of which a man has been hanged, or wine made from grapes that have been trodden out by someone with sore feet, or squeezed from grape-skins that have been cut round or have been soiled by something not quite clean dropping on them from above; and likewise Greek wines must not be used for libations, because they contain water."

Jesus in a sense replaces the wine god. Roman pagans truly found it difficult to separate the Bacchic and Christian cults from one another because they shared themes of forgiveness and resurrection from the dead and offered ceremonies and prayers to a supreme deity.

A parallel to the virgin birth of Jesus is the mythical birth of Dionysus. Zeus impregnated the princess Semele. Zeus reveals himself in all his divine glory, but no mortal could survive such an encounter. As Semele lies dead, Zeus rescues the fetus from her womb and sews it into his thigh—and a few months later the fully developed baby Dionysus is born from Zeus's leg. This and other, similar myths of semidivine beings made the gospel story of the virgin birth easier for a Hellenistic audience to accept.

At Cana in Galilee (John 2:1–11) Jesus arrived at a marriage feast where the wine had run out, and he changed water into wine. Scholars long maintained that the Cana story had a Dionysian background. John 2:3 says, "When the wine gave out, the mother of Jesus said to him, 'They have no wine.'" Addressing her respectfully with "woman," Jesus responds by telling her that his hour has not yet come, meaning his glorification or universal kingship has not yet taken place and that this first miracle, of turning water into wine, would open up that kingly reign. After his mother tells the servants to do whatever Jesus says, he tells the servants to fill with water six jars that hold 20 or 30 gallons each. When the steward, who is unaware of the source of the wine, tastes the water that has become wine, and did not know from where it came, though the servants who had drawn the water knew, the steward calls the bridegroom over and says to him, "Everyone serves the good wine first, and then the inferior wine after the guests have become drunk. But you have kept the good wine until now" (John 2:9–10).

Catholics pray to Mary to ask her to intercede on their behalf partially because Jesus turned the water into wine at her request. Mary appears at two points in John's gospel; one is here, in John 2, and the other is at Calvary, where Christ died on the cross. Mary connects the two as prophecy of the marriage supper of the lamb when Christ takes the Church as his bride. She is present at Cana and serves as the communicator of the miracle of water made into wine and foreshadows the miracle of transubstantiation, where bread and wine at the Eucharist change their substance to Christ's body and blood.

Therefore we should not be surprised when art portrays Mary as the virgin of the grapes, even, in a sense, as a wine goddess. Massaccio's Pisa Altarpiece (1426), the *Madonna and child with Angels,* now in London's National Gallery, hints at this relationship, where the baby Jesus is sitting on his mother's lap, eating grapes she has offered him, no doubt symbolic of his blood, and the Communion wine.

The wine at Cana probably was white because the wine steward still thought it was water until he tasted it. Some, however, prefer to interpret it as red because of the symbolism of the blood of Christ. Just as water converts to wine in Cana, wine used during the Eucharist transubstantiates to Christ's blood. Hence, Catholics understand that it is Christ's blood "not in appearance and accidence but in substance."

Jesus's words—"I am the bread of life" (John 6:35) and "those who eat my flesh and drink my blood have eternal life" (John 6:54)—speak of the Eucharist. Wine becomes the very blood that "flows within Emmanuel's veins," as the old hymn says, by referring to Jesus as Emmanuel in messianic fulfillment of Isaiah 7:14. Wine bears witness to the eternal salvation purchased with the blood of Jesus Christ. During the Eucharist the Christian hears the words "This is my body . . . this is my blood," while receiving sacramental grace when eating the bread and drinking from the "cup of salvation."

Just as wine was precious in the ancient world for reasons of commerce and pleasure, wine was all the more so in the Christian church for spiritual reasons. "Eat of my flesh, drink of my blood" is similar to words and commands issued by Osiris, Dionysus, Zagreus (an identity of Dionysus as worshiped by followers of Orpheus, the mythical poet who descended to Hades and returned), and Mithras to their followers. The ancients saw the grape as mystical and extraordinary, the only known substance that could by itself change from a solid to liquid form.

The myths often picture Dionysus as a drunk; the gospel narratives describe how Jesus enjoyed his wine: "For John the Baptist has come eating no bread and drinking no wine, and you say, 'He has a demon'; the Son of Man has come eating and drinking, and you say, 'Look, a glutton and a drunkard, a friend of tax collectors and sinners!' Nevertheless, wisdom is vindicated by all her children'" (Luke 7:33–35; Matt. 11:19). Hence, Jesus had the reputation of being a wine drinker.

However, the gospels according to Matthew (26:29), Mark (14:25), and Luke (22:18) suggest a different eschatological ("end time") relationship with wine: "For I [Jesus] tell you that from now on I will not drink of the fruit of the vine until the kingdom of God comes."

Before they put him on the cross, the Roman guards offered Jesus myrrh-enhanced wine; perhaps someone had compassion and thought the drug would anesthetize him (Mark 15:23). Jesus refused and spent hours suffering on the cross before he received a drink called *posca,* a wine vinegar often enhanced with medicinal herbs into which people dipped bread in ancient times (for example, ḥōmeṣ as in Ruth 2:14). Yet John's gospel suggests, "When Jesus had received the wine, he said, 'It is finished.' Then he bowed his head and gave up his spirit" (John 19:30). Although dogmatic theologians argue otherwise, this final act parallels the role of a wine god. In his last hours Jesus succumbs to the wild, dangerous, and mystical side of drinking wine and thereby finds a means of final reconciliation and passage to heaven.

BEHAVIOR WITH ALCOHOL IN THE CHURCH

Jesus's act of turning water into wine after the wedding guests were already intoxicated clearly celebrates wine as a festive gift from God and does not make a judgment about the morality of drinking. Yet Paul suggests that "it is good not to eat meat or drink wine or do anything that makes your brother or sister stumble" (Rom. 14:21). Ephesians 5:18 takes this a step further, cautioning readers: "Do not get drunk with wine, for that is debauchery; but be filled with the Spirit." Ironically, when the first Christians gathered on the day of Pentecost, they were so "filled with the spirit that others sneered and said, 'They are filled with new wine,'" which implies that spiritual ecstasy and tipsiness may produce similar behaviors (Acts 2:13).

Another passage exhorts readers to drink wine as therapy and to purify water: "No longer drink only water, but take a little wine for your stomach's sake and your frequent ailments" (1 Tim. 5:23). The same writer suggests that deacons must not indulge in much wine (1 Tim. 3:8). A bishop must not be addicted to wine (Titus 1:7). The New Testament teaches moderation, not abstinence, and allows for the occasional excess to celebrate a great event, such as the wedding at Cana, where the best wine was served last after the wedding guests were already drunk (*methuō* in Greek).

WINE, WATER, AND BLOOD

The First Epistle of John speaks of the sacraments of baptism and communion in this way: "This is the one who came by water and blood, Jesus Christ, not with the water only but with the water and the blood. And the Spirit is the one that testifies, for the Spirit is the truth. There are three that bear witness: the Spirit and the water and the blood, and these three agree" (1 John 5:7–8).

This passage refers to the passion of Christ and how his dead body became a prophecy of the sacraments: "Instead, one of the soldiers pierced his side with a spear, and at once blood and water came out" (John 19:34). This reflects more ancient resurrectional aspects of Osiris, Mithras, and Dionysus, where the elements of water and wine over which the Spirit bears witness infuses the sacred Christian life. The blood here is the sacramental wine used during the Eucharist, which Jesus says "IS my body," in contrast to a mere symbol of his body.

The words of Jesus confused and probably alarmed the people of his day: "Very truly, I tell you, unless you eat the flesh of the Son of Man and drink his blood, you have no life in you. Those who eat my flesh and drink my blood have eternal life, and I will raise them up on the last day" (John 6:53–54). This gospel writer does not say that the bread and wine *symbolize* the body of Jesus and his blood. No, they *are* his body and blood. This became the early Church's understanding of transubstantiation. Wine becomes sacred as it transubstantiates into the very blood of Jesus Christ, thus bearing witness to the eternal forgiveness provided through his sacrifice on the cross.

THE WINE CUP AS SYMBOL

The cup (the Eucharist) has multiple meanings. It often speaks metaphorically of the violence that was done to Jesus Christ yet is called the cup of blessing because it signifies the shedding of blood for the remission of sins (1 Cor. 10:16). Paul compares the cup of the Lord and the cup of demons (1 Cor. 10:21). In the Apocalypse the cup also represents the wrath of God provoked by all sinfulness.

The significance of a chalice of wine at Roman, Greek, and Jewish meals was different. In *The Odyssey* Homer recounts that a cup is placed before each guest "to drink as much as he wants," and in *The Iliad* he reports, "The mixing bowls are filled to the brim" as an omen of good luck. The stewards are to "serve wine to everyone in the halls." The best receive special honors with full cups. For Greeks and Romans fine art adorning the cups used for a *symposion* added to their value and emphasized the prestige and importance of the banquet; such decoration also honored the god for whom they had gathered.

Hippolochus of Macedonia describes all his great drinking banquets: "Proteas jumped from his couch and asked for a six-pint bowl (*skypphos*), filled it with wine from *Thasos* (sprinkling on a dash of water in it) and drank it all, saying: 'Whoever drinks most will have the greatest pleasure.' Katano then said: 'You were the first to drink so you will be the first to get the bowl as a gift; this will be the reward of all who drink well.' At these words all of us stood up to grab a bowl, trying to outreach each other."

For Hippolochus the cup represents hedonism. As with the modern Court of Master Sommeliers, proper service was essential. Sappho praises her brother Larikhos for pouring wine in the town hall of Mytilene: "Among the Romans, the noblest of youth did this service at public sponsored ceremonies. Such was the level of comfort in older times that in their sumptuous feasts they had not only wine-pourers but also wine inspectors, or superintendents." The process of serving and drinking wine had other implications for scholars. According to Aristophanes (in *Lysistrata*), the cup had significance for religion and health: "I believe that you shall drink a cup to the goddess of Health . . . using a more powerful wine-pourer" (the wine steward who will mix a less diluted wine). To the intellectual class a cup of wine meant divination and health.

Jewish feasts offer another lens through which to interpret the purpose of wine drinking. The Torah commands the recitation of the kiddush (blessing) before the meal on the eve of Shabbat and Jewish holidays. Also, Jews recite the kiddush before the evening meal on Shabbat and other holy days as a religious obligation, because the words spoken for the Shabbat have a special meaning intertwined with wine. The following provides an English translation of the kiddush said before the Shabbat eve: "Blessed are You, LORD our God, King of the universe, who created the fruit of the vine. Amen." After the kiddush (as for any other blessing) those present say amen, which means "truly" or "may it be true." Similarly, the words of the Lord's Supper give meaning to the eating of bread and drinking of wine (1 Cor. 11:23–26).

The language of the psalmist at times suggests a blessing is associated with the drinking of wine (Ps. 16:5; 23:5; 116:13) and at others that YHWH "will rain coals of fire and sulfur on the wicked; a scorching wind shall be the portion of their cup" (Ps. 11:6; see also Ps. 75:8). Second Isaiah associates the chalice of wine with the end of divine wrath: "Stand up, O Jerusalem, you who have drunk at the hand of the LORD the cup of his wrath, who have drunk to the dregs the bowl of staggering" (Isa. 51:17, 22).

Yet the cup of wine symbolizes wrath in the New Testament book of Revelation (Rev. 14:8; 14:10; 18:3). The winepress represents the shedding of blood: "From his mouth comes a sharp sword with which to strike down the nations, and he will rule them with a rod of iron; he will tread the wine press of the fury of the wrath of God the Almighty" (Rev. 19:15).

The angelic being, who must be present in all apocalyptic literature to mediate a vision that brings heaven to earth, uses the grapes, winepress, and juice flowing out of it to depict the judgment of shedding blood: "Then another angel came out from the altar, the angel who has authority over fire, and he called with a loud voice to him who had the sharp sickle, 'Use your sharp sickle and gather the clusters of the vine of the earth, for its grapes are ripe.' So the angel swung his sickle over the earth and gathered the vintage of the earth, and he threw it into the great wine press of the wrath of God. And the wine press was trodden outside the city, and blood flowed from the wine press, as high as a horse's bridle, for a distance of about two hundred miles" (Rev. 14:18–20).

A different angel describes "judgment of the great whore . . . with whom the kings of the earth have committed fornication, and with the wine of whose fornication the inhabitants of the earth have become drunk" (Rev. 17:2). The cup here is the "golden cup full of abominations and the impurities of her fornication" (Rev. 17:4). Even at the Last Supper the drinking of wine signified unpleasant portents, such as when Jesus dipped bread, possibly in wine, and gave it to Judas as a sign that Judas would betray him.

Throughout the ages people have offered a toast to give purpose for eating and drinking, and in this way the wine chalice became an important symbol for early Christians' religious beliefs and traditions. Words said over the cup of wine give purpose, whether they are said within or outside spiritual settings, or with benevolent or sinister intent.

THE CHURCH: THE TRUE VINE

Just as Israel is the vine in the Old Testament (Hos. 10:1–2; Jer. 2:21; Ez. 15:1–8; 17:1–10), the Church becomes the vine in New Testament traditions. Jesus says that true followers must produce fruit: "You will know them by their fruits. Are grapes gathered from thorns, or figs from thistles?" (Matt. 7:16; Luke 6:44). Paul refers to the fruit of the Spirit (Gal. 5:22–23). In this instance and others, talk of grape vines, fig trees, and olive trees infuses many descriptions about the early Christian church. In one instance Jesus insists that "new wine must be put into fresh wineskins" (Luke 5:38) or the old wineskins will burst. The spirit of the Gospel cannot harmonize with the spirit of pharisaic legalism, the rigid and traditional viewpoint that characterized the prevailing Jewish leadership of the time.

Another parable tells of a newly planted vineyard that, after its owners have waited the four years required by Jewish law, has begun to produce its first wine. Viticulture is and was labor intensive, requiring in early Roman times three times the workers as olive production. The tenant farmers of the vineyard in this story not only refused to hand over the produce of the vineyard to the owner but mistreated and killed the servants, as well as the son of the owner. The death of the son in this instance foreshadows the death of Christ, and the tenant farmers foreshadow the rigid Jewish leaders who guided and shaped the destiny of Israel before and during Jesus' time (first half of the first century CE). Followers of Jesus now can be the new tenants sharing in the inheritance of the vineyard that is bearing new fruit.

According to John's gospel, the death of Christ bears much fruit and the Church assumes the role of the new Israel as the vine that abides in Christ and partakes in sacramental grace via Baptism and Lord's Supper.

CHRISTIANITY AS THE NEW JUDAISM

As the vine transfers from Israel to the Church it becomes clear that Christianity is rooted in Judaism. Christians boldly assert that the Church was the fulfillment of Israel's hope and that a new Israel emerges from the old. Paul speaks of a holy olive root, branches, and branches cut off, meaning those who have rejected the gospel. Yet Paul warns Christians not to become arrogant about being the new Israel because they are merely wild shoots grafted into the true root of Israel, which supports them as secondary branches (Rom. 11:24). In the same manner the church in John's gospel is the vine that Christ "appointed . . . to go and bear fruit, fruit that will last" (John 15:16).

Wine becomes sacred in a new way, evolving from its purpose in the seder meal to actually attesting to the death of the Christian Messiah, who takes on the role of suffering servant. Christianity was a sect within Judaism, not a new religion, and grafted from other cultures every aspect of Christian life as the Church encountered them.

Wine's fundamental importance as a key protagonist for the evolution of society from rootless and nomadic to settled, spiritual, and cultured informed our writing of this book. In our judgment wine is the heart, soul, and body of Western civilization; it magnifies our best virtues and noblest ideas, yet its excessive use equally diminishes our humanity and dignity.

The resurrection is bound up in one event: "Very truly, I tell you, unless a grain of wheat falls into the earth and dies, it remains just a single grain; but if it dies, it bears much fruit" (John 12:24). When the wine of the Eucharist transubstantiates into the blood of Christ, it grounds the Church as the new Israel, the new vine through the death, burial, and resurrection of Jesus Christ.

John's gospel supplies the metaphor of the Church's becoming the vine, with its members the branches: "I am the true vine, and my Father is the vine-grower (γεωργός)" (John 15:1). How the Church abides in Christ—the Eucharist(John 6:56)—expresses the relationship between the shoots and the main stock of the vine, which depend on each other to bear fruit (John 15:4): "I am the vine, you are the branches. Those who abide in me and I in them bear much fruit, because apart from me you can do nothing" (John 15:5).

Christ here evokes the portrayal of Dionysus as a living vine, his shoots flowing out, becoming Maenads (female worshipers of Dionysus who were incited to religious frenzy) and thus his followers and converts. The language of the Eucharist is so evocative in John's gospel, we should not fail to imagine that the fruit borne here becomes the sacramental wine that provides mystery. The fruit of that vine becomes the blood of Jesus Christ. The Church then is the vine as it partakes in sacramental grace.

Judaism singles out wine for its own blessing uniquely among the Abrahamic religions, reflecting its centrality to the religious and cultural identification and development of the Jewish people on one level, but also to that of humankind on a more original one.

Wine in the Bible and the entire ancient world fulfills a social, economic, symbolic, and spiritual function, whether in Judaism, Christianity, or Dionysian cults. This rich heritage still looms presently in the life of growers, wine makers, and lovers of wine. By understanding how wine has evolved from the beginning of time to the present helps us to understand how the Bible Wine Trail still is fertile and again producing fine wines today.

Part 2

THE MODERN DIVINE WINE TRAIL

And the threshing floors will be full of grain, And the Vats shall overflow with new wine and oil.

—Joel 2:24

We have traveled a long way by following the ancient biblical wine trail. Now we embark on the modern wine trail through areas that biblical characters populated so vividly centuries ago. In researching this book we organized many of our journeys in Turkey, Greece, Israel, and elsewhere to follow as much of the route that Paul took on his third missionary journey as we could. We wanted to see what he saw in a huge swath of the eastern Roman Empire, visit places he would have visited, and naturally drink the local wines. He traveled in areas that contained some of the empire's finest wines and are again producing fine wines today.

Ancient wines have given way to delicious modern wines as these countries experience a long overdue renaissance of their fine wine heritage. Increasing numbers of producers in countries not known for their wines, including Israel and Greece, are establishing wine exports as a key component of their trading mix.

Contemporary wines reflect local pride, tradition, indigenous character, and ancient and modern techniques. They also illustrate a new global perspective. Many are produced within the famous wine regions of antiquity, whereas others are found in newly planted areas. Already, consumers and wine journalists have proclaimed abundant praise that evokes what was said thousands of years ago about their ancestors' wines.

This section is divided into chapters devoted to the exploration of each country's modern wine lands, along with brief discussions of the geology, key vineyard regions, and appellation system, if any. We will also provide our perspective on some of the finest current producers and their vanguard wines, identifying our favorites. Our modern journey will follow the ancient one, beginning where wine originated, then proceeding to those countries south and west, just as the spread of wine culture did thousands of years ago.

Lastly, in chapter 12, we taste through a range of wines that are made using ancient wine-making practices or concepts, including "recipes" from Columella, that provide a lens through which to focus on the question of "What wines would Jesus drink?" His wine world was quite different from ours, with completely foreign tastes, as we learned. Tasting wines made today that resemble those described in the first half of the book, many not from the eastern Mediterranean, is immensely useful to our understanding of how difficult it was then to make fine wines and provides an often delightful window into the tastes of a long-lost world.

All the wines we single out for mention as our favorites are bottled wines. While we tasted many wines in barrel or tank that were excellent and show great promise, it is not fair to discuss them, as last-minute blending decisions and the complexity of the bottling process may result in significant changes to the wine in progress. Nor can we name all we tasted; we have limited our favorites to one or two wines for each producer, based partly on the absolute number of wines tasted, and on overall quality, according to our judgment.

Space does not allow us to write in detail about each winery we visited, which we truly regret, given the generous time many gave us. Therefore at the end of each chapter, and sometimes at the end of a section about a particular geographic area, we have a section with brief entries about these producers. We hope to fully include these and others in a future book.

Enjoy the journey.

TOURING AND TASTING ALONG THE ROUTE OF PAUL'S THIRD MISSIONARY JOURNEY (52–57 CE)

Not that Paul particularly enjoyed wine, or even that he drank much, but certainly, as a Jew and a follower of Christ, Paul would have celebrated the Sabbath, and probably the Eucharist in an elementary form, wherever he could. But many of the more austere remarks about wine attributed to Paul were written by his more severe disciples (Eph. 5:18; 1 Tim. 5:23; Titus 1:7). His own words were not so dour: "But the fruit of the Spirit is love, joy, peace, patience, kindness, goodness, faithfulness, gentleness, self-control; against such things there is no law" (Gal. 5:22–23). Here perhaps he recognizes the blessing wine represents ("the fruit of the Spirit") as a physical or metaphorical symbol of Christ's bond with humanity and the lifeblood that flows from God to humanity and that shows that his love can never be blocked.

If Paul were alive today, what would quench his thirst? We did not travel everywhere that Paul did (Patara, Philippi, Chios), but in all those places that both we and Paul visited, we found a diverse range of excellent wines. Make the journey and taste for yourself.

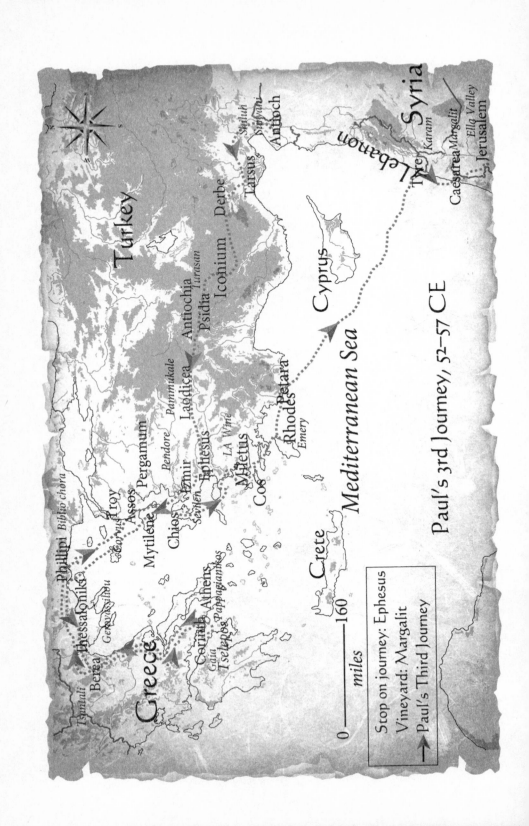

Paul's 3rd Journey, 52–57 CE

Stop on journey: Ephesus
Vineyard: Margalit
Paul's Third Journey

0 ———— 160
miles

Mediterranean Sea

Greece

Turkey

Syria

Lebanon

Cyprus

Crete

Jerusalem
Ella Valley
Caesarea Margalit
Karam
Tyre

Antioch
Stephani
Shiluh
Tarsus

Derbe
Iconium
Psidia
Antiochia Turasan

Pendore
Pammukale
Laodicea
Pergamum
Izmir
Sevhen
Ephesus
LA Wne
Miletus
Cos

Rhodes
Patara
Emery

Assos
Troy
Corupe
Mytilene
Chios

Phillipi Biblio chora
Thessaloniki
Berea
Tsintali
Gerovassiliou

Athens
Corinth
Gaia
Tselepos Pappagianhos

Seven

TURKEY

Now in the seventh month, on the seventeenth day of the month, the ark came to rest on the mountains of Ararat.

—Genesis 8:4

We begin our Ancient World wine country tour with Turkey, where Noah is said to have landed the ark and planted his vineyard near Mount Ararat. The Ararat region is not far from the oldest excavated winery, which dates from 4100 BCE. Famous Greek-Turkish wines figure prominently in the literature of Pliny and others, while the biblical passages, particularly in the New Testament, often describe places that were noted for their wine, such as Pergamum and Ephesus, where Paul visited.

Turkey, however, has been ruled by Muslims for more than a thousand years, and their prohibitions on alcohol have hampered the growth of its wine industry. But Muslim restrictions on alcohol were not always as strict as they are today, and until the early twentieth century, Greek, Armenian, and Syriac Christians who maintained wine traditions influenced Turkey greatly.

MODERN TURKEY: A SHORT VINOUS HISTORY

Until the end of World War I, Turkish vineyards produced wines that were sold throughout the Ottoman Empire. In the late nineteenth century they supplied millions of liters of wine to France and Italy, whose industries had been

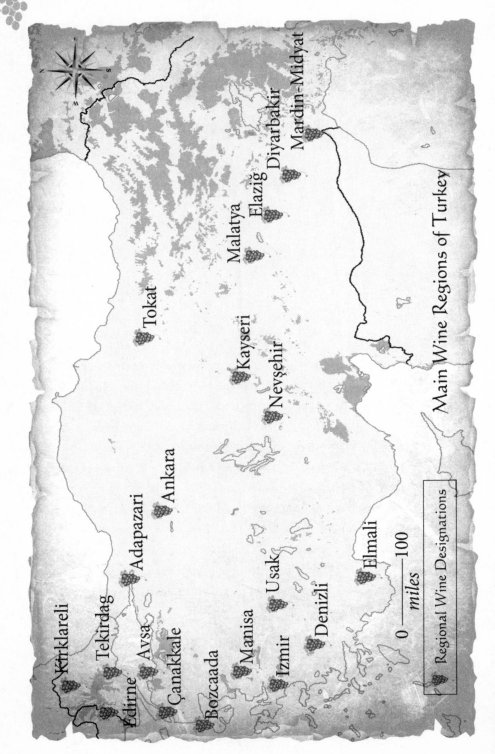

Main Wine Regions of Turkey

Regional Wine Designations

Mardin-Midyat
Diyarbakir
Elazig
Malatya
Tokat
Kayseri
Nevşehir
Ankara
Adapazari
Elmali
Kirklareli
Tekirdag
Avsa
Çanakkale
Edirne
Bozcaada
Manisa
Izmir
Usak
Denizli

0 — 100
miles

devastated by the phylloxera invasion that began in the 1870s. Even more remarkable, a century ago areas in western Turkey, which are now only beginning
to reassert their capability for fine wine production, produced large amounts
of well-made, flavorful, and moderately priced wine for export, including to
the great markets of Smyrna. But during the great exchange of populations between Turkey and Greece in the 1920s, Turkish Greeks were forced to leave for
Greece, Armenians were excluded from Turkey, and many Turks left Greece,
Bulgaria, and Albania to return home. Most of the population that appreciated
wine, and knew how to grow and make it, disappeared.

Modern Turkey's wine production really begins in the mid-twentieth
century. Some of the largest producers today, such as Kavaklidere, Kayra, and
Sevilen, started as raki distillers and grape growers in the 1930s and 1940s
when vineyards, like other farmland, were a series of parcels owned by many
small farmers. (Raki is a distilled spirit flavored with anise; it is similar to ouzo
and pastis.)

Grapes were just another crop, to be grown as inexpensively as possible
and sold at the highest price the growers could get. Wine was sold in casks
to merchants, some of whom were known to doctor it with hashish or other
substances. The government lacked regulatory control but, concerned about
health risks, finally mandated in 1946 that all wine be sold by the producer in
bottles.

The Muslim majority meant wine was no longer a key economic or cultural factor. A second exodus of Greeks and Christians in the 1960s virtually
guaranteed that any knowledge of higher-quality wine production, especially
the cultivation of grapes, disappeared from Turkey.

Even today traditional grape growers consider high-volume production
more important than quality because they are paid by the kilogram ($600 per
ton average). But attitudes have changed since the turn of the century. Growers
now receive bonuses to strive for the lower yields that produce better wine.
Today Turkey experiences impressive economic growth and relative stability;
its government is a parliamentary system that is supported by a military that
strives to maintain the secular model that Kemal Ataturk (1923–38) inaugu-
rated. Leaving politics aside, 15 years of economic growth have increased the
consumption of luxury goods, tourism in fabled cities and ruins as well as
seaside resorts and the number of cosmopolitan residents. Prosperous Turks

and visitors are now drinking Turkish wines, although they can be expensive because of high taxes. Estate-style wineries, launched since the turn of the century, are not only creating excellent wines but pioneering wine tourism by building beautiful wineries with tasting rooms, tours, and, soon, cellar-door restaurants.

In 2009 Turkey ranked sixth worldwide in grape production, producing 3.85 million tons of grapes on 1.2 million acres (486,000 ha). Yet only two percent of the total vineyard acreage yields wine grapes; about 77,000 tons in the 2009 harvest. Turkey has about 40 wineries but most of the production is centered on the five largest producers.

GEOGRAPHY, GEOLOGY, AND GRAPES

Ancient Turkey produced fine wines primarily along the Aegean and Mediterranean coasts. Outposts of quality wines can be found in Kapadokya (Cappadocia) and near famous southern and eastern cities like Zeugma on the Euphrates and areas around Antakya (ancient Antioch). Compare an ancient map of Turkey that shows wine regions with a modern map of grape-growing areas, and you will find a high degree of correlation. Turkey does not yet have a formal appellation system for their wine regions. Yet there are a number of areas that are effectively considered as such, like Tokat or Güney/Denizli. We will refer to them regularly in our discussion.

As in France, the fine wine regions of Turkey are spread the length and breadth of the country. While researching this book, we drove more than 4,300 miles (7,000 km) from the Greek border to Iran's, and from near the Black Sea to the Syrian frontier. West of Istanbul and along the Aegean seacoast, the climate is Mediterranean and moderate. Moving eastward the climate becomes colder, and harsh continental conditions prevail in the interior Anatolian regions, from Ankara in the northwest to Diyarbakir and Mardin in the southeast. Highland regions around Güney/Denizli, east of Izmir, are Mediterranean at the lower elevations and semicontinental at the higher elevations—hot summers, cold winters, and little rainfall.

While western Turkey's vineyards have limestone-rich soils, central Anatolia typically has volcanic soils. Many areas feature terra rossa, the iron-laden gritty soils with fine sand that were created from the erosion of iron-rich, ancient limestone seabeds. Virtually all the better Turkish vineyards are located several hundred feet above sea level and have poor soils with excellent drainage, which can be stressful to the vines in hotter years.

Although Western wine connoisseurs often seek out amazing indigenous varieties, with tongue-twisting names and deliciously unique flavors, Turks have been isolated from fine wines for decades and are enamored of French varieties like cabernet and syrah. Turkey now plants these grapes in large amounts, and these wines are sold in high-end restaurants.

Turkey has twelve hundred to fifteen hundred grape varieties, six to eight hundred of which are genetically different. Producers now focus on three indigenous white wine grapes: emir, narince, and bornova misketi. Originally from central Kapadokya, emir produces a crisp, lively, dry white wine with herbal, green melon, or apple flavors; with age it takes on a buttery note like chardonnay. Emir is traditionally grown as a bush vine; it lies low to the ground and is not trellised. Some vines are a hundred years old.

Narince, originally from the Tokat region in north-central Turkey near the Black Sea, is similar to a composite of sauvignon blanc, the rare Italian variety arneis, and Spanish albariño. We find citrus, pink grapefruit, herbal and mineral or chalky flavors with excellent fresh acidity and crisp finish.

The grapey bornova misketi is an ancient muscat variety from the Izmir area, and Turks are using it to make quite aromatic, perfumed, and floral dry and lightly sweet wines. These are especially good when served well chilled with mild Turkish cheeses or fresh fruit on a warm summer day at the beach.

The best of these three grapes are grown in cooler areas, such as Güney, east of Izmir; Thrace; and the higher areas of Kapadokya in central Anatolia. These areas offer the best terroir, the combination of soil, climate, variety, and human tradition that distinguishes a unique growing area and style for these varieties.

The ancient origins of the indigenous red varieties of Turkey are interesting to modern wine drinkers. Three important varieties are kalecik karasi, oküzgözü, and boğazkere. Kalecik karasi (the black grape from Kalecik) originated in the Ankara region and ripens late; it is extremely aromatic yet thin skinned. It prefers cool climates but often doesn't ripen well. These characteristics reflect its similarity to pinot noir, but kalecik karasi has a more haunting floral (rose, violet), tar, or mineral character with fine tannins. For those readers familiar with less common wines, think of nerello mascalese from Mount Etna combined with nebbiolo from Piedmont, Italy, and pinot noir. Kalecik karasi is among the most exotic, intriguing, yet exasperating wines produced in Turkey.

Öküzgözü (ox eye) is a deeply pigmented variety that produces rich, sweet-tasting fruit with large berries and quite fleshy pulp. Originally attributed to the Elaziğ growing region in Anatolia, it makes a deep-colored black cherry–raspberry-scented wine with soft tannins, plush fruit, and lively acidity that is reminiscent of the more full-bodied barbera from northern Italy.

Boğazkere originated in the southeastern Anatolian region of Diyarbakir, which is warmer than Elaziğ to the north. A mid- to late ripening variety notable for its deep color, historical records allude to its ancient origins. Its combination of high color, rich blackberry-tar-fruit flavors, moderate acidity, and elevated tannins make this complex grape highly desirable for eating as well as wine making. Think syrah married to nebbiolo. Boğazkere presents a great wine-making challenge; many producers blend boğazkere with öküzgözü to soften the astringency of boğazkere and to add a more gentle red-fruit character. Boğazkere has good aging potential, provided that the winemaker manages the tannins; when done well it is a revelation.

The most successful western European varieties grown in Turkey are, not surprisingly, syrah and cabernet sauvignon, but less popular ones such as petit verdot, montepulciano, and malbec show strong potential there.

TOP PRODUCERS BY REGION

Let's begin our Turkish journey in the northwest, Thrace, and wend our way eastward and south. Readers should be aware that many of the larger producers source fruit from all over Turkey, in order to have sufficient volume of some wines that can be sold nationwide in larger stores and supermarkets for moderate prices.

THRACE/TRAKYA

(Including the regions of Edirne, Kirklareli, Tekirdağ,
Şarköy, and the Gallipoli Peninsula)

Thrace borders Greece and Bulgaria and has made fine wines at least since the fourth century BCE. Today it is home to a number of fine small producers intent on reviving that tradition.

Arcadia Winery, Hamitabat (www.arcadiavineyards.com)

A new winery established in 2004 on about 87 acres (35 ha), Arcadia represents the new Turkey. The property was originally planted with wine grapes in the nineteenth century by Frenchmen. In recognition of that legacy, Arcadia's owner, Aras Özhan, has signed Michel Salgues, formerly of Roederer in Champagne, as his consulting winemaker. This part of Thrace, not quite halfway between the western border of Greece and Istanbul to the east, has rolling hills and plateaus where grapes were common two thousand years ago. Old maps show a town named Vineyard and a wine road. More curious yet, Özhan points out that the grape-growing and wine-making force in the area includes the Alevis, an old Muslim sect that doesn't prohibit alcohol consumption, especially wine. Indeed he notes that most townspeople who farm vineyards in the area are wine-drinking Muslims.

Alevis believe in including a bit of alcohol consumption in rituals to create a merry environment in which people can be themselves. Their sect was well respected during the foundation of the Ottoman Empire.

Özhan's wines reflect a desire to make elegant and aromatic vintages. He uses modern wine-making techniques, and the vineyards are farmed organically. Because this part of Thrace was once under a sea, the soils are limestone with a fair amount of sand, pebbles, and pure rock in some parcels.

Favorite wines: 2010 Rosé (12.6%); 2009 Red Blend (13.7%)

Umurbey Winery, Yazirköy, Tekirdağ (www.umurbeyvineyards.com)

"So let me get this straight. You lived and studied in Phoenix, Arizona, for many years. You are a mechanical engineer. Why did you come back to Turkey and become a wine grower?" Umur Ariner shrugged. "Our family has about 120 hectares of land [almost 300 acres] here outside of Tekirdağ, mostly for general farming. I wanted to come home, and knew that this area has been famous for its wines since ancient times. We are right next to the Sea of Marmara on the coastline."

Ariner's first vintage was 1997, all French varieties. The red wines of Umurbey, an established winery that makes only about eight thousand cases a year, are generally finer than its whites. Ariner acknowledges that Turkish consumers prefer his reds, which are pretty bold, showing the intensity of new oak and showcasing a New World sensibility. Maybe Umur Ariner's time in Arizona had more influence on him than even he realizes.

Favorite wine: 2007 Cabernet Sauvignon (67%)/Merlot (13.5 %)

Barbare Vineyards, Tekirdağ, Thrace (www.barbarewines.com)

Barbare's winery has a spectacular view across the Sea of Marmara and 57 acres (23 ha) of vineyard specially planted in Rhone varieties to take advantage of its mild climate and moderately high latitude (41 degrees). With his first vintage in 2009 winemaker Akin Gürbüz and his team produced wines with a real sense of place and excellent style. Owner Can Topsakal planted his first vineyard in 2003. Wisely, he enlisted the help of an ace viticultural consultant from Chateauneuf-du-Pape, Xavier Vignon, to create a dream vineyard and then worked with Gürbüz to fine-tune the organic farming, producing a modest six thousand cases of well-structured wines that are not too oaky.

Favorite wines: 2010 Mourvèdre and Merlot Rosé, Tekirdağ (14%);
Elegance 2009, Tekirdağ (14.3%)

Doluca Winery, Çerkezköy, Thrace (www.doluca.com)

Doluca is one of the two largest and oldest wineries in Turkey, founded in 1926 by Nihat Kutman. He started by primarily making wine from indigenous varieties, establishing the winery's reputation early on. Kutman realized that the area around Mürefte on the Sea of Marmara provided an excellent climate for European varieties and was the first to bring grapes like semillon, Riesling, and cinsaut to Turkey. His son, Ahmet Kutman, studied at the University of California, Davis, and came back full of new ideas. In southern Thrace, on the Gallipoli Peninsula, Kutman began the Sarafin Vineyard project in 1990, followed by Alçitepe Vineyard in 2004. Sarafin produced the first *mono-cépage* (single-variety) cabernet and merlot in Turkey, a revolutionary blend for the time, first released in 1998.

Now a brother and sister from the third generation, Ali Kutman and Sibel Kutman Orel, are intimately involved in running the company. Doluca makes wines from grapes grown in all major Turkish appellations. The winery is still based in Thrace, but all fruit is made into wine at its new state-of-the-art facility in Çerkezköy, which produces almost 700,000 cases annually. Overall quality at Doluca is consistent across its wide-ranging wines from different regions, showing how some varieties provide an excellent lesson for Turkey's terroirs, showcasing the winery's skill at maintaining individuality while also being affordable.

Favorite wines: 2010 Sarafin Sauvignon Blanc, Gallipoli Peninsula, Thrace (12.7%)

> *This sauvignon blanc, even from a difficult warm vintage year, expresses tremendous personality. The herbal, capsicum-jalapeño, and grapefruit aromas and strong mineral flavors with a zesty lemony acidity are compelling, a cross between a New Zealand style and Loire Valley Sancerre.*

2009 Kav Tuğra Öküzgözü, Gallipoli/Denizli (15%)

Gülor Winery, Şarköy (www.gulorwine.com)

The first winery to produce a Bordeaux blend in Turkey (1998), Gülor is located in Şarköy, a key old growing region on the coast of the Sea of Marmara. Owned by a wealthy Turkish family and under the strong leadership of Adnam Erem, this small producer has about 52 acres (21 ha) of vineyards and makes about thirteen thousand cases of rich, fruity, and distinctive wines each year.

Favorite wines: 2005 Gülor G-Silver cabernet sauvignon-merlot (14.1% alcohol); 2010 Gülor G-Silver öküzgözö-boğazkere (13.3% alcohol), a 65%–35% blend

Irem Camlica Winery, Büyük Karistiran

Owner Mustafa Camlica is about as animated and enthusiastic a wine grower as one can imagine. His young enologist, Asli Bayhan, crafts the wines from 150 acres (60 ha) of plots scattered throughout northern Thrace. One of the few producers of pinot noir in Turkey, Camlica has a cool site near the Black Sea and is planning to soon revive the dark local grape variety called papaskarasi. The first promising wines will be from the 2010 vintage.

Büyülübağ Winery, Avşa Island, Sea of Marmara (www.buyulubag.com)

Owner Alp Törüner created Turkey's first gravity flow winery on this lovely island in the Sea of Marmara in 2005. Although it is only 22 miles (13.6 km) from the Thracian coast near Şarköy, the climate is quite different. As a result Törüner harvests one week later than wineries in Şarköy.

He farms sustainably 124 acres (50 ha), handling the grapes gently with labor-intensive practices. He also revives vineyards on the ancient Çesme Peninsula. The wines have fine texture and promise, with deep fruit and balanced oak.

Favorite wine: 2007 Büyülübağ Cabernet Sauvignon Reserve, Çesme Peninsula (14.5%)

WESTERN ANATOLIA

(Including Çannakale, Boscaada Island, Izmir, Manisa, and Denizli/Güney)

Corvus Şaraplari (Winery), Bozcaada Island, Aegean Sea

Bozcaada (pronounced Bohz-ja-adah) Island is a charming island off the Turkish coast, not far from the entrance to the Dardenelles or from ancient Troy. The island was known as Tenedos in ancient times, and wine has been made here for thousands of years, when it was probably a raisin wine not dissimilar to the Pramnian style made nearby. Coins minted on the island in the second to sixth centuries BCE often highlight one or two clusters of grapes demonstrating how important wine was to the island's economy. In *The Iliad* Homer notes that Hekamede, the woman the hero Nestor won during the Myceneans' sacking of Tenedos, prepared a drink for him: "In this cup the woman, like unto the goddesses, mixed a mess for them, with Pramnian wine, and therein grated cheese of goats' milk, with a grater of bronze, and scattered white barley there-over, and bade them drink."

Today a mecca for weekenders from Istanbul and other towns, the island offers funky, comfortable guest houses and excellent seafood restaurants in a charming port. Then there is the wine.

The architect Reşit Soley, who started Corvus in 2002 to revive the island's economy, says, "For 20 years, I saw the vineyards disintegrating, falling into disuse, or, worse, being physically uprooted. I wanted to say 'Stop!' to this fast-spreading collapse of long wine-growing tradition before it disappeared completely to tourist developments." Soley's first vintage in his small winery (2004) received immediate acclaim in Turkey. Moreover, Soley replanted traditional old varieties like çavuş, vasilaki, kuntra, and karalahna (the last thought to be the same as Greece's xinomavro), and European grapes. Today he has 100 densely planted acres (40 ha).

Corvus means crow in Latin. Soley drily notes, "Unfortunately, our crows on Bozcaada are very sociable, if raucous, and they do like the grapes. But as residents of our island before us, what can you do?"

Because he had studied enology in Italy, he didn't want a French winemaker—"They follow the rules!"—and he understands Italian culture and language. The Italians respect tradition, which he wished to do on the island, so Soley works with a Piedmontese consultant.

His main vineyard consists of loamy sands, red soils, and big chunks of rock, primarily limestone, and it resembles a huge bowl, exposed to a direct wind channel between the Aegean Sea and the Sea of Marmara. The north wind often blows hard in summer and fall, which retards phenolic maturation of the fruit, but Soley uses irrigation to prevent dehydration and raisining.

Favorite wine: 2007 Cru Turk, cabernet sauvignon (14%)

Pamukkale Winery, Güney Denizli (www.pamukkalesarap.com)

Pamukkale is an older winery, started by the Tokat family in 1962 on hundreds of acres on the high plateau above the steeply sloped hillside in the town of Güney. Güney, according to many producers, is considered the finest place in Turkey to grow grapes because of the climate (cool, moderate rainfall, warm summers), high altitude (2,460 to 2,952 feet, or 750 to 900 m), soils (limestone terra rossa, free-draining soils), and adaptability (newer varieties like cabernet and syrah have thrived here). The combination makes the Güney plateau a superior source of fine wines, prompting many top wineries in Turkey to plant or contract for vineyards.

Pamukkale is a relatively large producer that encourages and aids local growers to plant better stock, providing agricultural guidance. Most vineyards owned and controlled by Pamukkale are planted with classic French varieties, since Güney's reputation demands only high quality wine, which Turks most associate with French varieties. Thus Pamukkale's choice of grapes runs strongly to indigenous and foreign varieties that are flavorful and dynamic.

Favorite wine: 2009 Pamukkale Senfoni Dry Red, Güney (13.5%)

Pendore Vineyard and Winery, Kemaliye, Manisa Province (www.pendorebaglari.com)

Pendore Vineyard is the largest contiguous estate in Turkey; nearly 470 acres (200 ha) spread across beautifully rolling hills of 820 to 1,476 feet (250 to 450 m) in Manisa Province. Greek wine growing goes back at least twenty-five hundred years and began not far from the famed Lycian city of Sardis. Sardis coins and a sarcopahagus at the Manisa Museum are embellished with grape clusters. According to the historian Ersin Döğer, these images depict the origins of the indigenous çavuş and rezaki grapes still grown here.

Pendore's winemaker is a determined, talented woman named Asli Odman. The vineyard was first planted in 2002 on hillsides. Because the Boz Dağ mountains to the west block much of the hot winds blowing off the Aegean in the summer, Pendore is much milder than its relatively low elevation would indicate and has low rainfall with refreshing winds. The vineyards planted at lower altitudes are on limestone, while the ones at higher altitudes have more volcanic soils and are farmed organically.

Relatively low yields (2.2 tons per acre/37.5 hl/ha), fruit thinning, and gentle handling (gravity flow movement) in the new, modern winery have paid off for Pendore. A wide range of indigenous and uncommon imported varieties, such as mourvèdre, tempranillo, carignan, and grenache, thrive at Pendore, producing quite intensely flavorful and distinctive wines.

Favorite wines: 2008 Pendore Boğazkere (13%)

> *Boğazkere is all tannin and power, often found in wines from its homeland area of Diyarbakir in southeastern Anatolia. Here the grape is typically dark colored and meaty, with a black fruit bouquet. The aggressive tannins and sharp acidity of less balanced versions are not present. Polished, finely grained tannins are harmoniously integrated in the Pendore Boğazkere—by no measure is it a rustic wine.*

2008 Pendore Öküzgözü (13.5%)

Urla Şarapçilik Winery, Urla, Izmir Province (www.urlawinery.com)

The town of Urla was founded about 3000 BCE on the Karaburun Peninsula about 19 miles (30 km) from Izmir, a city of more than 1.8 million people. The region, also called Urla, has been an important wine, olive, and fig zone ever since. Originally called Clazomenae, Pliny the Elder considered it one of the most famous wine areas, producing a light wine prized for being "sparingly flavored with sea water." While he was planting a nursery, Can (Jean) Ortobaş found ancient vineyard terraces covering nearby land and formed the Urla Şarapçilik winery to redevelop the viticulture that had been neglected on the peninsula since the 1920s.

He says, "We have decided on organic/biodynamic viticultural practices to restore the land and maintain an ecologically sound environment in keeping with our practices at the palm nursery." His modern winery operates sustainably, using gravity, and its consumption of electricity is only 15 percent of the amount usual for a winery of its size. The winery is housed in a beautiful building on lovely grounds surrounded by 37 acres (15 ha) of vineyards; it is located about 8 miles (5 km) inland at an elevation of 656 feet (200 m). In contrast a neighboring vineyard is planted on soils with high percentages of minerals and is even cooler at nearly 3,280 feet above sea level (1,000 m). Ortobaş's research showed that, because of its prevailing winds and temperate winters, his vineyard's mesoclimate is similar to that of regions 300 miles (500 km) farther north. This has allowed him to plant cooler-climate varieties, such as sauvignon blanc.

First planted in 1997, Urla now makes about 12,500 cases of wine annually. As an experiment, Ortobaş has planted unusual varieties such as nero d'avola and montepulciano and hopes to revive a long-lost local variety, urla karasi (urla black), propagated from three surviving vines (DNA testing supports the variety designation).

Favorite wines: 2010 Urla Nero d'Avola-Urla Karasi (14%)

> *Ortobaş adores nero d'avola, an old variety from southwestern Sicily that yields deep red wines capable of aging for as long as a decade. His 2010 Urla Nero d'Avola–Urla Karasi is a blend with only 3% urla karasi because of a shortage; Ortobaş is confident it contributes unique resiny, black fig flavors. The wine is aged 40% in oak barrels, and its color is a deep ruby purple. Its flavors and*

aroma are rich with strong mixed berry character. A sweet, fresh fruit finish,
augmented by bitter chocolate notes and firm tannins, persists and will improve
by 2014–2015, when the wine will have reached its peak.

2009 Urla Boğazkere (13%)

Sevilen Vineyards and Winery, Ortaklar, Aydin Province (www.sevilengroup.com)

Why would one of Turkey's oldest and most prestigious wineries, the first to be founded in Izmir in 1942, move from its original, lovely site outside Izmir, where a fine restaurant is set on nearly 400 acres (160 ha) of vineyards, to a brand-new but distant industrial park in a construction zone? During our first visit to the state-of-the-art winery during the final weeks of the 2011 harvest, masons were still plastering in the reception area, and workers were installing fine wood fixtures.

Perhaps if we had been more aware of our surroundings, the answer from owner Enis Güner would have been obvious. We had just come a few miles from the lovely ruins of the ancient city of Magnesia, once famous for its wines.

"We chose Ortaklar," Güner said, "as it is near Magnesia, on the way to Ephesus as well as Bodrum, and within easy reach of our important vineyards in Denizli and Güney in western Anatolia. If you are a tourist, we will have a perfect place to stop for tasting and light meals, and the new winery location allows us to make even better wines as transport time between harvest and processing is reduced."

While the new facility is quite large, it is not the only winery. Sevilen also owns an old Greek winery in the Thrace region at Mürefte on the Sea of Marmara; there it crushes fruit from the Thrace area, especially semillon and gamay. Yet the recent improvements to the vineyards in the Izmir area, and the superb new vineyards at Güney, at an elevation of nearly 3,000 feet (900 m), have Sevilen excited about the future. The warmer Izmir area, with a Mediterranean maritime climate and limestone soils, has about 208 acres (85 ha).

Sevilen, while large, impresses us for the overall range and quality of its wines. Its wine-making team has the advantage of employing the consultant Florent Dumeau from Bordeaux to refine and guide Sevilen's production of stylish, complex wines. Dumeau has pushed Sevilen to concentrate on understanding the terroir of particular sites, refining the wine making to maximize site potential. Sevilen uses rigorous viticulture practices, new sorting tables, more strict berry and lot selection along with high-quality barrels.

Favorite wines: 2010 Kalecik Karasi, Güney (14%)

> *From its Güney vineyards Sevilen has produced a prime example of kalecik kar-asi, the aromatic, complex, and difficult variety that was originally from around Ankara. Because of Güney's warmer climate kalecik karasi is fruitier here than elsewhere. Its color is the bright, medium-intense violet ruby characteristic of kalecik karasi. Because it is not aged in oak, its lovely dark cherry, floral-rose, black pepper-and-violet bouquet has been allowed full expression. The flavors are fresh, minerally, with lots of cherry fruit mixed with graphite and a roasted meat character. It was good when we tasted it and will be much better at its prime in 2014.*

2009 "900" Fumé Blanc, Güney (12.1%)

Selendi Winery, Akhisar, Manisa Province (www.selendi.com.tr)

The Selendi Winery was created in 2000 and planted with French varieties by Pelin Zaimoğlu, its young and energetic owner. Andrea Paoletti (formerly of Antinori and now also a consultant to Ornellaia) consults. Zaimoğlu expected to plant her first indigenous variety, narince, in 2012. Paoletti was enthusiastic about joining Zaimoğlu's project after seeing the soil was a fine mix of limestone, sand, gravel, and fossils, which reminded him of Tuscany. Selendi's wines unabashedly showcase varietal intensity and rich fruit.

Favorite wine: 2009 Selendi Red (13.5%)

Yazgan Winery, Izmir, Izmir Province (www.yazganwine.com)

Hüseyin Yazgan, who was born in Greece, established one of Turkey's oldest and largest wineries in Izmir in 1943. He moved there during the great exchange of populations between Turkey and Greece in the 1920s and 1930s. Until recently the company focused on quantity rather than quality. The French winemaker Antoine Bastide d'Izard changed things by replanting the vineyards with fine French wine varieties in an effort to produce higher-quality wine. The recent efforts to repurpose an old brand appear successful: Yazgan now produces indigenous and foreign wines that are juicy, forward, without pretenses, and simply good to drink.

Favorite wines: 2010 Yazgan Syrah, Çepindere Turgutlu (Manisa) Vineyard (13.5%); 2010 Mahra Boğazkere/Öküzgözü, Denizli (12.5%)

Urlice Vineyards, Urla, Izmir Province (www.urlice.com)

Urlice is the property of Reha Ögünlü and his wife, Bilge, who lived in Michigan for many years. His years in the United States are reflected in his idiosyncratic English, familiarity with American music, and enthusiasm for California wines. Reha Ögünlü returned to Urla and met with Can Ortabaş of Urla Şarapçilik, who convinced Ögünlü that he should become a wine grower and help revive the area's reputation. Ögünlü planted only red Bordeaux varieties and chardonnay, producing wines typically more powerful than his neighbor's because Urlice's climate is about five degrees warmer, according to Ögünlü. The rich and exuberant wines reflect Ögünlü's cultural mix.

Favorite wines: 2011 Urlice Chardonnay (13%); 2009 Urlice Cabernet Sauvignon Reserve (14%)

LA Winery, Torbali, Izmir Province (www.lawines.com.tr)

If any young Turkish winery has advanced and changed its philosophy more rapidly than LA, we aren't aware of it. In 2005 the new owner hired one of the best viticultural scientists in the world, Attilio Scienza, a professor at the University of Milan, to help analyze the winery's soils. His work led to planting 250 acres (100 ha) on alluvial soils in a windy, and therefore cool, site that had been famous in ancient times for its wines. The owner, Lucien Arkus Idol, recently hired LA's new winemaker, Brett Hetherrington, who has wide international experience and allows a slightly larger crop level than previously in order to maintain vine balance on the fertile soils, meaning the tannins in the red grapes are not as bitter. Emre Utku, the general manager, has moved LA into organic wine growing, and the new wines are much richer and better balanced, with fewer rustic hard edges than previously. This is a winery to watch.

Favorite wines: 2010 LA Mon Reve Chardonnay–Chenin Blanc, Izmir (13%); 2010 LA Mon Reve Tempranillo, Izmir (13.5%)

CENTRAL ANATOLIA AND CAPPADOCIA

Ankara, Turkey's capital and the gateway to Turkey's ancient Anatolian wine heritage, lies 220 miles (350 km) southeast of Istanbul. Turks speak of Anatolia as the all-encompassing heart of their country. Civilizations have risen and fallen here for more than eight thousand years, and some of the first wine, including Noah's, probably was made in eastern Anatolia. In the second millennium BCE Hittite kings ruled from their capital of Hattuşa, which was about 130 miles (200 km) from Ankara, an empire that extended from Europe east to Persia and south to Egypt.

As we traveled through this vast landscape, we could see why Anatolia is a cradle of wine growing: its altitudes and relatively low rainfall. The climate is continental, so the cool nights of its higher altitudes, 2,000 to 3,900 feet (600 to 1,200 m), temper the propensity toward hot summer daytime temperatures. The low rainfall helps alleviate strong fungal pressure on vines and forces them to work harder by growing deeper roots to seek water. Throughout Anatolia, including Vinkara's location an hour east of Ankara, strong northern winds cool things down and retard vine maturation. Yet summers are harshly hot and winters deadly cold, with icy winds and snow.

Vinkara Winery, Kalecik, Ankara Province (www.vinkara.com)

Kalecik, home to this winery, is at a slightly lower altitude and is warmer than Ankara, because it is surrounded by mountains to the west that rise 6,500 feet (2,000 m). Its weather also is moderated by its proximity to the Red River. Much of southern Anatolia has volcanic origins, but in these northern areas the land was under water in ancient times, which accounts for its limestone, including large cobbles in vineyards at lower altitudes.

Vinkara was born in 2003 in the homeland of the kalecik karasi grape, and the first experimental vintage in 2006 promised much. The winery's enologist, Çağlar Gük, planted on the rolling hills surrounding the Red River, which irrigates the region and flows southeast into Cappadocia. With more than 420 acres (170 ha) now planted, Vinkara produces about eighty thousand cases of wine annually, mostly from its own vineyards.

Newer plantations at higher altitudes are on basaltic volcanic and more clayish rhyolite. These soils are fairly acidic and have high clay content, thanks to the strong Anatolian winds that brought in deposits (loess).

The most prominent grape in Kalecik is its namesake, kalecik karasi. Kalecik has a color issue and small clusters that, like zinfandel, generally do not set in a homogeneous way. In the 1960s phylloxera killed virtually all the Kalecik vineyards. In Vinkara's experimental blocks, Gök uses mass selection techniques to see if he can rediscover better clones for planting. Vinkara allocates half its vineyards to kalecik karasi grapes but plants other Anatolian grapes, including öküzgözü and narince, as well as imports. Yields are fairly low, from 2.5 to 3.2 tons per acre, and the fruit is harvested by hand.

Mario Monchiero, Vinkara's Italian consulting agronomist, notes that "if a variety of grape is named after the region, it shows that the region is seeded in tradition and culture. As a result what got my curiosity and intrigued me, convincing me to work here, was that a vineyard was linked to wine-making tradition. In Italy, we call these regions 'the land blessed by God.' This region is a place that needs to be promoted as it is the homeland of a rooted culture."

> *Favorite wines: 2009 Vinkara Kalecik Karasi Reserve, Kalecik (14.3%)*
>
>> *This flavorful wine is aged in oak barrels for 14 months, but less than 30% new, the color is the medium ruby violet typical of this variety. The bouquet reflects kalecik karasi's ancient ancestry, with scents of wild meat, sour cherry, violet, and plum. Dry, dark cherry and licorice accented flavors, combined with elements of black pepper and vanilla, lead to a lovely hint of dried roses, and firm, but fine tannins in the finish. Voluptuous yet delicate, this should be at its best in 2014–17. Vinkara's Reserve wine defines the potential for Turkey's finest indigenous ancient grapes in a modern setting.*
>
> *2010 Vinkara Doruk Narince, Tokat (13%)*

Vinolus Winery, Kayseri, Cappodocia (www.vinolus.com)

Oluş Molu, Vinolus's charming proprietor, and her family have owned a large farm outside Kayseri (ancient Eusebia/Caesarea) in the Cappodocia region for decades. Oluş, a biologist, took charge around the turn of this century, working with her brother, Aziz. Today she has about 50 acres (20 ha) planted in the native kalecik karasi and narince, but she was one of the first Turks to experiment with roussanne and tempranillo. Her land is high, dry, rocky, and damn cold in winter, with volcanic basalt subsoil, likely formed from eruptions by the high, nearby volcano Mount Erciyes. This is the main reason she has planted the vineyard traditionally with bush-trained vines. Small production and great dedication, along with a fresh perspective, augur well for Vinolus's future.

> *Favorite wines: 2010 Kalecik Karasi–Tempranillo, Kayseri (14%); 2009 Syrah, Güney (14.5%)*

Kocabağ Wines, Yesilyurt, Uçhisar, Cappodocia (www.kocabag.com)

Kocabağ Wines, founded in 1972 by Mehmet Erdoğan in his ancestral town of Yesilyurt, is a pioneer in the renaissance of Turkish wine. Memduh Erdoğan, Mehmet's grandson, now runs the company, focusing on classic Anatolian varieties, especially the local white emir, which typically is planted as low-growing bush vines, even in such places as the nearby Zelve Valley, a UNESCO World Heritage site with fairy chimney rock formations and old cave dwellings and churches. Rustic and rich yet fine, Kocabağ's wines represent not only good value but are increasingly more stylish.

> Favorite wines: 2009 Emir, Yesilyurt/Cappadocia (12%); 2009 Kalecik Karasi, Kapadokya (14.5%)

Kavaklidere Wines, Akyurt, Ankara Province (www.kavaklidere.com)

Kavaklidere is Turkey's largest producer of wine (more than 900,000 cases a year) and the oldest private winery, founded in 1929 by the And family in Ankara and now owned by the Başman family and directed by Ali Başman. Kavaklidere owns more than 1,300 acres (560 ha) of vineyards in virtually all of Turkey's finest wine-growing regions. Based in Anatolia, the Başmans especially work their original vineyards in the Ankara area, which are planted almost exclusively with the native variety kalecik karasi.

For some in the Turkish wine industry Kavaklidere is the 800-pound gorilla in the room: too big, too powerful, too interested in churning out huge quantities of average commercial wines. We beg to differ; better analogies would be to the Jackson Family Estates in California or the Antinori family in Tuscany. Like their wineries, Kavaklidere is still family owned, enlarging its holdings while pioneering innovative styles and high quality at all prices. Kavaklidere steadfastly promotes indigenous wines, contributing knowledge to local growers and spreading Turkish wine culture abroad; it exports 20 percent of its production.

Some of the most impressive vineyards are at the starkly beautiful Côte d'Avanos estate in the heart of Cappodocia, near the Red River Valley and the town of Gülşehir. Like much of Cappadocia, the climate is continental, with desert-like rainfall of 12 to 16 inches (300 to 400 mm), cold snowy winters, and a lot of wind; it is located nearly 3,300 feet (1,000 m) above sea level and has decomposed calcareous loam-clay soils over volcanic rock that are quite poor and free draining. As a result the yield, even with tightly spaced vines, is low. The heart of Kavaklidere's production is 475 acres (190 ha) planted in native varieties like kalicek kalesi, narince, emir, and öküzgözü. Other vineyards are located in Ankara, Elaziğ, and Güney.

Expert guidance from the respected Bordeaux winemaker Stéphane Derenoncourt augments the experience and astute leadership of Kavaklidere's staff, which produces more than 40 wines of remarkably good quality across the board. The tighter spacing in newer vineyards has reduced yields per plant, thus yielding finer grapes. At Côte d'Avanos, for example, the average yield, even for cabernet sauvignon, is about half that permitted by appellation regulations in the top districts of Bordeaux, about 1.6 tons per acre (26 hl/ha).

Kavaklidere's wines are generous in fruit and forward in taste, yet the best are quite capable of aging for as long as a decade. Kavaklidere is one of the few Turkish producers making unique fortified wines from the classic indigenous Anatolian grapes, narince and öküzgözü.

Favorite wines: 2010 Kavaklidere Prestige Narince, Kapadokya (13.5%)

This beautifully crafted and strongly flavored yet elegant narince was produced from 18-year-old (first planting) vines at Côte d'Avanos and with 20% aged and fermented in French oak barrels. Bright orange blossom aromas lead to inviting lime-zest, chalky-mineral flavors with good acidity to balance the dry and slight quinine astringency on the finish, which in this case adds more depth, inviting one to drink it with something grilled, especially fish.

2009 Kavaklidere Prestige Kalecik Karasi, Kalecik/Ankara (13.6%)

Turasan Cappadocian Wines, Ürgüp, Cappodocia (www.turasan.com.tr)

Founded in 1943 by Hasan Turasan, Turasan is a legacy winery that produced a mere seven hundred cases of its first vintage. Today, under the direction of Turasan's grandson, also named Hasan, the firm has evolved into one of the largest, most respected wine producers in Turkey. More than 1,200 acres (500 ha) of vineyards are divided between two parcels, one near Ürgüp, the other near Mount Erciyes. The young French winemaker Eduard Guerin has greatly improved Turasan's quality, crafting more elegant wines by cutting yields, using better oak barrels, and shortening the time in oak to preserve the fruit.

Ruins at Magnesia, a few miles inland from Ephesus south of Izmir, highlight the large Temple of Artemis. Magnesia was a major wine-producing center during the late Hellenic to Roman period.

Baalbek was the largest Roman temple complex in the Empire, and the Temple of Dionysus/ Bacchus is one of the largest, finest, and well-preserved of its type.

The Touma family, who owns Clos St Thomas in Lebanon's Beka'a Valley, converted a limestone grotto cut from the rock at their winery into a small chapel. Each year, just before harvest starts, they celebrate with a mass.

Gaston Hochar, winemaker and co-owner of Chateau Musar with his father, Serge, decants the 1977 Chateau Musar in the winery's cellar for the authors.

Making wine at the fringe—harvesting syrah at the Zumot family's St Thomas vineyard at Sama, near the Syrian border. Local Muslim townspeople and migrant Syrians pick the fruit.

Galil Mountain vineyard in winter near the border with Lebanon visible in background, in northern Galilee.

Eli Ben-Zaken has guided his Domaine du Castel, located high in the Judean Hills west of Jerusalem, to the highest ranks of Israeli wine lists, and this hillside vineyard's fruit near Tzuba is a key part of his success.

Gaia Estate's vineyard in Nemea grows superior agiorgitiko grapes under proprietor Yiannis Paraskevopoulos' meticulous care.

Famous for millennia, Samos fine old Muscat vines produce various styles of deliciously rich and fine sweet wines under the guidance of the Cooperative of Samos, the sole producer of this ancient wine.

Domaine Porto Carras began the renaissance of Greek wine nearly 40 years ago, and agronomist Leon Zikas carries on this legacy today at the domaine's beautiful vineyards overlooking the Aegean sea.

Mount Athos' Saint Panteleimon Monastery is the home of Tsantali Winery's Mount Athos vineyard located at the tip of the easternmost finger of the Halkidiki Peninsula.

The sandy volcanic soils of Santorini allow assyrtiko vines to grow very old, with tap roots often extending several meters deep and laterally.

Pebbly, sandy volcanic soils, desert-like climate and no phylloxera all contribute to the extraordinary longevity of Santorini's vines. This 150+-year-old vine, trained in the traditional basket style providing sun shade to the clusters, may live another two centuries.

The harshly beautiful landscape of Santorini provides a stunning setting for vineyards such as these near Pyrgos, overlooking the great caldera formed by the volcanic eruption of 1600 BCE.

The vineyard at Ürgüp, primarily calcareous, is planted strictly in French grapes. The vineyards near Erciyes are planted in friable gray-blue rock that resembles schist; these vineyards are at a lower altitude, about 3,000 feet (900 m), and are planted primarily with classic Anatolian varieties and syrah. Turasan now produces more than 100,000 cases a year. It is a winery on the move and, with quality improving, a lovely and popular destination for wine lovers who are visiting Ürgüp's many worthwhile tourist sites.

Favorite wines: 2011 Turasan Rosé (13%); 2009 Turasan Seneler Öküzgözü-Boğazkere, Elaziğ-Denizli (14%), a blend of 75% öküzgözü and 25% boğazkere

Kayra Wines, Elaziğ, eastern Anatolia (www.kayrawines.com)

Although Turkey was neutral during World War II, it felt compelled to control vital industries, including alcohol production. This winery remained under state control until 2005, when it was sold to private interests and christened Kayra. One of the largest producers of wine in Turkey today, Kayra, led by the American winemaker Dan O'Donnell, has expanded into quality production, increased its lineup of wines, and actively educates people about wine. O'Donnell, a big burly man, loves working in one of the more "frontier-like places I could have chosen, given my previous work in California, but it is often frustrating."

Elaziğ is somewhat remote, in the middle of southeastern Anatolia, and to settle here and make wine was a challenge. The surrounding landscape is reminiscent of La Mancha in Spain or eastern Washington State: dry, desertlike, and windy with an extreme climate. People have been growing grapes here for millennia, O'Donnell says, beginning with the Hittites. "When I came here, the original estate vineyard was planted to cabernet and merlot," he said. "We budded it over to the local varieties, öküzgözü and boğazkere. Working with a number of truly individual, special, indigenous varieties in a faraway land was also appealing to me."

One of O'Donnell's biggest problems is finding good fruit and knowing what kind it is. "Vines here have different names for the same variety, like öküzgözü, and getting fruit ripe in this climate, with soils containing high limestone content and shale, is a challenge." He says the problem in buying grapes is that it often requires talking to whole villages because land is still held in common. "The idea of private ownership and development simply hasn't caught on here," he says. "People are suspicious of anyone looking at the grapes. On occasion during harvest I have been shot at by suspicious locals, who think that I am trying to organize the theft of their grapes."

The winery has its own small vineyard in Elazığ and more in Şarköy that contribute strongly to top-tier wines, and the dry weather means Kayra can farm organically.

When asked about viticultural practices in southeastern Anatolia, O'Donnell laughed and said, "What viticulture? With a few exceptions there is no incentive to reduce crop level, or change to trellising from the ground-hugging bush vines to gain better quality. Like I said, it's the Wild West."

Remarkably, Kayra makes very good wine at moderate prices. At the high end, Kayra Reserve, Kayra Imperial, and the revived Buzbağ brand show quite excellent character with wine from various regions.

Favorite wines: 2008 Kayra Vintage Öküzgözü, Single Vineyard (Şükrü Baran), Elazığ (14.5%)

> *Kayra's vineyard near Lake Keban offers a superior example of just how rich and deep a wine the big-berried öküzgözü grape can produce. This wine is a deep, opaque black ruby, with a bouquet that combines classic öküzgözü black cherry and raspberry liqueur aromas with light dill and vanilla from the American oak barrels in which it was aged. Full-bodied, dense flavors are backed by firm but not harsh tannins, finishing with dark plum and cherry flavors, ferrous overtones, and a firm structure. Keep until 2016 or so, and serve slightly cool to decrease the initial warmth of the alcohol.*

2006 Kayra Imperial Öküzgözü, Elazığ and elsewhere (14%)

Shiluh-Süryani Sarabi Vineyard, Midyat, Mardin Province (www.suryanisarabi.com)

Approximately 25 miles (40 km) north of the Syrian border, in what is considered northern Mesopotamia, an area heavily populated by Kurds, one of the most fascinating wineries on our journey is reviving a 1,500-year-old wine tradition. Yuhanna Aktaş's new vineyards, cave, and winery are outside the ancient town of Midyat, east of the more ancient city of Mardin. Nearby are the ruins of the ancient Roman trading city of Dara, which is still being excavated and home to the first Mesopotamian dams and irrigation canals.

Syriac Christians began to settle in this area around the fourth century CE, made wine, practiced their form of Orthodox Christianity, and spoke Aramaic, the language of Jesus. The area is now heavily populated by ethnic Kurds, Syrians, and Turkish Muslims, but the small community of Syriac Christians, which counts Aktaş as a member, still holds to some of its age-old customs.

Aktaş's family has owned vineyards here for many years, producing home-made wine and table grapes. In 2003 the family set up its company, Ninve, named for the ancient Assyrian capital, Nineveh. Two years ago Aktaş and his friend and partner, Jacob, decided to revive the Syriac Christian wine tradition and named the new winery Shiluh, which means peace in Aramaic/Syriac. For this well-known silversmith in Midyat, creating a winery and planting new vineyards is challenging and nerve-wracking, given the political and religious issues in Kurdish southeastern Turkey. The landscape is not a desert, as one imagines Mesopotamia to be, but hilly farmland at a high altitude (2,925–3,575 feet/900–1100 m) and a mix of sand and limestone terra rossa, which is ideal for vines. Grapes have been here for millennia; the lack of water is the main issue. The local variety of grape is boğazkere. Two other white varieties, mezruna and kerkuşh, are grown nowhere else. Some vines are a hundred to two hundred years old, Aktaş said, adding, "We do have some phylloxera here, but enough of the old vines have survived, and most of the vines are bush-trained to conserve water and shade the fruit."

Suryani (Syriac) wine is an old concept, Aktaş notes, "but in Midyat, we are the first winery. Only Suryani people speak Aramaic. We are the descendants of the Sumerians and Assyrians, and took on Christianity quite early. Most of our people abandoned their lands and homes in this area due to the troubles beginning a half-century ago." Only about eighteen thousand Syriac Christians are living in Turkey today; fifteen thousand in Istanbul, the rest in Mardin and surrounding villages.

What is Suryani wine, and what makes it different? Aktaş notes that "wine is clearly a very important aspect of Christianity, and important to this region for six thousand years. Monasteries of our faith were established in and around Mardin beginning sixteen hundred years or so ago, and they [the monks] made wine, farmed vineyards, [which] were highly prized." During subsequent centuries the Muslim population in the area cut the Suryani off from what was happening elsewhere. Consequently their traditional style of production has not changed much.

"Firstly, the vineyards are still farmed as of old, organically," Aktaş explained. "We don't have much disease pressure here due to the low humidity, cold nights, and dry summer days. At harvest we crush the grapes, white or red, and ferment them in large clay jars buried in the ground for 45 to 60 days. The wines are then kept for many months in tanks before bottling without filtration or fining. That's it." The method, we noted, is similar to Columella's description of wine making in Italy in the first century CE, as well as to Georgia's *qvevri* tradition (see chapter 12).

Shiluh Suryani wines are truly biblical wines because the winery uses ancient production methods and because it connects directly to a wine-making tradition straight out of the Bible. It was common practice that once the grapes were trodden in stone lagars (the Portuguese name for what in Hebrew is called a *gat* or treading basin), the juice flowed through a channel down into the stone cistern or large clay jars below to finish fermentation and age, before being decanted off into amphoras or wineskins. Because of the ritual connection to the Eucharist, the wine had to be unadulterated by any modifications such as filtration in harmony with the spirit of the biblical text and rituals of the Syriac Church. The Aktaş family's wines, while made with a modern press for example, are certainly true to the family's convictions, their terroir, and to a long-forgotten tradition.

Favorite wines: 2010 Şiluh Kustan, Mezruna and Kerkuşh (13%)

> *Kustan is the nearby village that is the source of these grapes, blending 80% mezruna with kerkuşh, all from older vines. It has a lightly nutty bouquet with hints of dried peach or apricot skins and is certainly not as fruity as modern white wines often smell. It offers full-bodied flavors of vanilla, citrus skin, and dried fruit, and its viscosity suggests a light sweetness that contributes to a lingering finish freshened by good acidity. This wine is deliciously interesting and definitely traditional.*

2010 Şhiluh "Manastir," Boğazkere Midyat (13.5%)

Turkey is the home of key viticultural areas where the Apostle Paul traveled, through such cities as Pergamum, Ephesus, and Antioch, where followers of Jesus first called themselves Christians. Şhiluh Suryani emulates biblical wines even for Eucharistic purposes, attempting to revive a forgotten tradition of fine wine in a region once famous for its wines. The other new Turkish wine-makers we met along our journey have great enthusiasm for their country's historical wine legacy. Based upon our tastings across the vast landscape of modern Turkey, that enthusiasm is now often matched by the results in the bottle. Moreover, the wealth of characterful, indigenous varieties that Turkey grows provide a brilliant palette upon which to draw forth even more inter-esting wines as producers further understand their potential and how best to optimize it.

Eight

LEBANON

His shoots shall spread out; his beauty shall be like the olive tree, and his fragrance like that of Lebanon. They shall again live beneath my shadow, they shall flourish as a garden; they shall blossom like the vine, their fragrance shall be like the wine of Lebanon.

—Hosea 14:5–7

THE MODERN ERA

The history of wine in Lebanon is nearly as old as wine itself. The spread of the domesticated vine and production of wine into "the Lebanon" from the north began as early as the sixth millennium BCE. Modern Lebanon's wine industry was nearly ruined by the civil war of the 1970s and 1980s. Despite more recent political problems and the 2006 war with Israel, Lebanon's wine sector has continued to grow in size and reputation. What is it about this remarkable country of four million people that allows an ancient wine culture to thrive and grow under daunting conditions?

For centuries individuals in the mountains, the Beka'a Valley and the hills north of Beirut made wine and arak, the national anise-flavored distillate, for their own consumption. Monasteries also needed wine; most made their own, but quality overall was uneven, and the grapes used were often of dubious quality and character. Lebanon produced superior wines in ancient times and in Roman times was a hotbed of Dionysian religious/cult practices. The Great

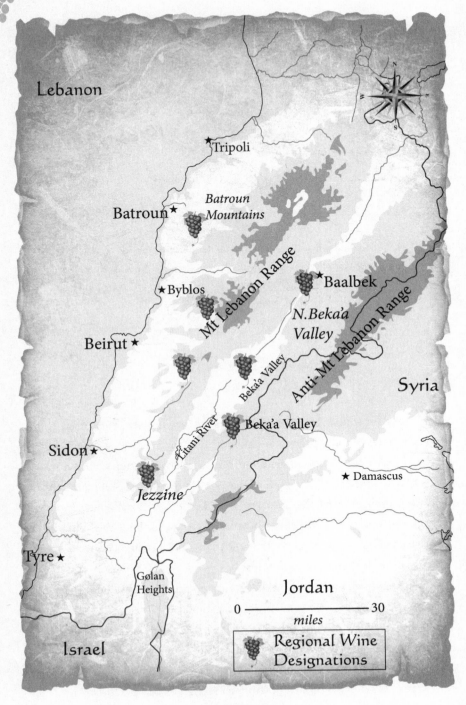

Lebanon

★ Tripoli

Batroun Mountains

Batroun ★

★ Byblos

Mt Lebanon Range

★ Baalbek

N.Beka'a Valley

Anti-Mt Lebanon Range

Beirut ★

Beka'a Valley

Syria

Litani River

Beka'a Valley

Sidon ★

★ Damascus

Jezzine

Tyre ★

Gølan Heights

Jordan

0 ———— 30

miles

Regional Wine Designations

Israel

Temple of Dionysus at Baalbek in the northern Beka'a Valley is a testament to that history.

Lebanese experts realized a half-century ago that sophisticated wines could not be made from the few indigenous varieties remaining, like Merweh. The loss of high-quality indigenous varieties in Lebanon likely is the result of centuries of Muslim rule and replacing wine grapes with table grapes while losing good genetic stock.

In his excellent book *Wines of Lebanon,* Michael Karam asserts that the country's oldest winery is the Armenian Catholic Bzummar Monastery, which has made wine continuously since its founding in 1749. The largest dedicated winery in Lebanon today, Chateau Ksara, began in 1857 when Jesuit monks in the Beka'a Valley inherited a 62-acre (25 ha) vineyard and decided to make wine.

Under the Treaty of Versailles (1919), Lebanon became a French mandate, or temporary colony, which exposed the country to French culture. During World War II, Beirut became the "Paris of the Middle East," a key banking and financial center and a place to enjoy life, including good wine.

By the 1920s and 1930s certain wealthy families had started or expanded wineries: Gaston Hochar at Chateau Musar in Ghazir, the Brun family at Domaine des Tourelles (founded in the 1880s), along with the Nakad family in the Beka'a. Wine growing in Lebanon expanded when several family wine producers whose fortunes were tied to arak production established vineyards in the 1930s and 1940s and satisfied the burgeoning urban population's demand for wine and brandy.

The breakthrough came in the late 1950s and early 1960s, when Hochar persuaded a few French buyers to try his Chateau Musar wines. The distinctive personality of the wines, and Hochar's daring to put Lebanese wines up against top French and other international wines, opened the world's eyes, and Lebanese wines developed an international reputation.

At the Bristol Wine Fair of 1979, Michael Broadbent, MW, the United Kingdom's then most distinguished wine critic, tasted several of Hochar's wines. Broadbent was impressed by their quality and was surprised that the best wine in the group was a 1959 vintage red. When wine journalists traveled to Lebanon, they found that excellence was not confined to Hochar's winery but could also be found at producers like Chateau Ksara and Chateau Kefraya.

The civil war, followed by the Israel-Lebanon conflict that began in 1982 with Israeli occupation of the Beka'a and southern Lebanon and lasted until 1995, almost completely shut down Lebanon's burgeoning wine export market. Only after the Lebanese Civil War ended did the economic and political situation change. Muslims and Christians alike began investing in wine as good business. The high profile of some new investors, such as Carlos Ghosn of Renault in IXSIR, also contributed to some easing of government sanctions against alcohol and made it easier to promote Lebanon's unique and long wine history worldwide.

Today several top Lebanese brands are available throughout Europe and the United States. The help of foreign wine makers, coupled with a talented younger generation that has studied in France and Italy, has sent Lebanese wine quality to a level not seen since the Roman period, when wines from Beirut, Tyre, and Sidon were classified at the second-highest level, just below top Roman *crus*. We visited most of the top wineries of Lebanon and strongly believe that Lebanese wines should again be accorded the respect they held two thousand years ago.

CLIMATE, GEOGRAPHY, AND WINE REGIONS

Lebanon had the same warm climate during Phoenician times that it does today, but human depredation of forests and less efficient irrigation has done damage to its ecosystem. Centuries of warfare led to the loss of the famous cedars of Lebanon (used to build Israel's temple, palace, and ships) in the Mt. Lebanon range behind Beirut. Erosion and forest loss allowed vineyards, once grown on the poor steep slopes, to creep closer to the sea.

Lebanon's mountains get solid rainfall; their limestone geology is mostly porous, making for extensive aquifers that store rain and snowmelt, rendering drought less a problem than erosion damage. The contemporary lack of trees to hold the soil on slopes leads to severe erosion, unlike when trees were present two to three thousand years ago.

Coastal Lebanon, like Israel, has a Mediterranean maritime climate, with moist sea winds and rainfall mostly in the winter and spring. It is generally warm, slightly humid, and without strong temperature changes day to night. Mountains rise steeply to more than 4,900 feet (1,000 to 1,500 m) east of the coast; the summit of Mount Lebanon is 10,020 feet (3,083 m) above sea level. Most coastland is inhabited, so room for vineyards is sparse, mostly on the slopes behind the coastal littoral above 1,148 to 1,312 feet (350 to 400 m), where they are visible near Ghazir or farther north in the Batroun Mountains (both north of Beirut).

The arid Beka'a Valley, across the central mountains from the coast, grows 90 percent of Lebanon's grapes. They are nurtured by a deep aquifer beneath the limestone, clay, and terra rossa. All the vineyards are dry-farmed; only young plants are irrigated. Yet the Lebanon Mountains and the Anti-Lebanon range have the strongest effect on the climate, similar to how the Cascade Mountains affect Washington's climate.

The mountains hold most of the moisture. In the winter they receive snow and rain, more than 39 inches, while the coast receives rain, but the Beka'a receives little. The valley floor is about 2,600 feet (800 m) above sea level, and the vineyards on the highest slopes are planted at an altitude of about 4,600 feet (1,400 m), where it can be cold. The Beka'a is dry and semiarid, much like Washington State's Columbia Valley, but growers have access to water from mountain aquifers and the Litani River.

Some vineyards are planted at altitudes as high as 5,500 feet (1,700 m), though this practice was more common centuries ago. Many mountain vineyards and towns were inhabited by Maronite Christians and Druze for centuries. Recent decades of war, and the contemporary pressure to make more land available for housing, have significantly decreased mountain wine production.

In the Beka'a Valley the geology supports viticulture nicely. Lebanon literally is composed of limestone from the Jurassic and Cretaceous periods when dinosaurs roamed. The pale white limestone, often streaked by iron oxides (terra rossa), is quite friable, cracked by water for eons and buckled by earthquakes. Lebanon's name comes from the Proto-Semitic word for white because of its limestone and snow.

Joe "Assaad" Touma (Thomas in Arabic), owner-winemaker at Clos St. Thomas Vineyards in the village of Qab Elias in the Beka'a, noted that "one of the key reasons for focusing on merlot was precisely due to the similarity of soils we have with Bordeaux, which could be a contributor to the structure of the tannins and the bigger style of our merlot."

For the northwest, not far from the coast, the climate is more moderate than in the Beka'a, with smaller day-night temperature differences and more humidity. Lebanon in general can produce fine wines, primarily because of its well-drained limestone soils, high altitude of most vine-growing areas, and how the Lebanon Mountains block and trap cool marine air. We begin our exploration of Lebanon's fine wine in the ancient area of the Batroun Mountains, working our way south and east to the Beka'a Valley.

BATROUN MOUNTAINS REGION

Coteaux de Botrys Winery, Eddé-Batroun (www.coteauxdebotrys.com)

The oldest winery in north Lebanon, Coteaux de Botrys Winery (Slopes of Batroun), was created in 1998 by Joseph Bitar, whose daughter Neila is now in charge. Located in the town of Eddé, the estate vineyard overlooks the Mediterranean. Botrys is the ancient Phoenician name for the city and port now called Batroun, meaning grapes in Greek. During the Roman Empire the mountains behind Botrys/Batroun were well known as the "cellar of the Roman Empire," Neila Bitar said. Phoenicians undoubtedly had high regard for the quality of the region's wines, as did the Greeks, who also regularly traded here, shipping wine to their colonies as far west as Sicily.

Most of their vineyards are about 50 acres (17 ha) and are scattered on low slopes (650 to 1,300 feet/200 to 400 m) overlooking the sea. The production of Coteaux de Botrys focuses primarily on Mediterranean varieties like Rolle, Marsanne, syrah, and mourvèdre; the landscape strongly resembles Provence. The Bitar family's superb enologist, Yvan Jobard, nephew of the legendary François Jobard of Meursault in Burgundy, has reduced yields in the vineyard, producing polished yet minerally wines that show potential for the region. Seven other wineries now in the region speak to its revival after thousands of years of being Lebanon's fine wine-growing area outside the Beka'a.

Favorite wines: 2009 Coteaux de Botrys Cuvée de L'Ange (13.5%); 2010 Coteaux de Botrys Prince Blanc (14%)

Batroun Mountain Vineyards, Batroun (www.batrounmountains.com)

Assaad Hark, the gregarious owner of Batroun Mountain Vineyards, likes to say he is a "man of two countries, one vineyard." Hark was born in Lebanon,

lives in Batroun, and also lived in Minnesota for several years, where he studied engineering and still maintains a residence and import business. Bitten
by the wine bug, he did the short course on viticulture and enology at the
University of California, Davis, before coming home to Batroun and planting
vineyards in 2004. He has 30 acres (12 ha) in six villages and farms organically,
with high-density planting (5,500–9,500 vines/ha), which is different from the
practice of other Lebanese growers. The wines are generous, fresh, and well
structured.

> *Favorite wines: 2010 Batroun Mountains Goutte d'Or (13%); 2009
> Batroun Mountains Prestige Rouge (13.5%)*

IXSIR, Basbina (www.ixsir.com.lb)

Perhaps the most controversial and exciting new wine project in Lebanon,
IXSIR (Arabic for elixir) is a dream come true for three friends who started the
winery in 2007. IXSIR is the most glamorous Lebanese newcomer, with state-
of-the-art cellars built completely underground, beneath the seventeenth-
century Seigneurial House, which has been carefully renovated to house
tasting rooms and a restaurant.

IXSIR's owners are dedicated to producing expressive wines from six top
terroirs in Lebanon and have spent a fortune acquiring the land for planting
new vineyards at elevations of 1,300 to 5,500 feet (400 to 1,700 m) throughout
the country. They also work with established traditional farms whose owners
agree to meet IXSIR's specifications. The scale of the investment and the ultra-
modern approach being taken in an inherently conservative area have created
a certain "envy" of IXSIR among other more established producers. The es-
teemed winemakers Gabriel Rivero of Spain and Hubert de Boüard (Chateau
Angelus, Bordeaux) contribute to IXSIR's success.

IXSIR's owners intend to create not just a local regional winery but a
showcase for the country's vinous possibilities. Based on the first few wines
they have made, using strict grape selection, gentle extraction methods, and
the best oak barrels, their cosmopolitan approach appears promising.

> *Favorite wines: 2009 Altitudes IXSIR Rouge (13.5%); 2010 Altitudes IXSIR
> Rosé (12.5%).*

CENTRAL MOUNTAINS AND MT. LEBANON

Chateau Musar, Ghazir (www.chateaumusar.com)

Perhaps the most famous Lebanese wine producer, and the third largest, is Chateau Musar. Its grand winery and cellars loom over the lovely hill town of Ghazir and the Mediterranean. A fortress stands next to the winery. Indeed the Mzar Castle cellars, built in the seventeenth century, now contain Chateau Musar wines. Ghazir is the family seat of Serge and Ronald Hochar, whose family arrived in Lebanon as French Crusaders during the twelfth century and never left. Serge and Ronald's father, Gaston, had studied in Bordeaux, where he befriended Ronald Barton, the owner of Chateau Leoville Barton, and then returned to Lebanon. With Barton's help Gaston Hochar slowly built up his winery. In the period between World War II and Lebanon's civil war (1976–90), wine was still a luxury, even among Christians, though the Hochars and others prospered as Lebanon's economy developed and Lebanese began to drink better wine.

Political unrest has not dampened the Hochars' faith in their country. The civil war often meant harvesting grapes behind the front lines in the Beka'a. In 1984, a famously difficult year, harvest was delayed forty days because of the fighting. Somehow Gaston Hochar managed to make a wine under extreme duress. "We made only eighteen thousand bottles of Musar, picked in late October, a month late. It took us five days, almost, to get the fruit to the winery, by which time it was already fermenting. It's not wine … it's my Madeira," Serge told us. The wine is a tribute to the Hochars' fortitude; it is unique and flavorful, in a madeirized, earthy-aggressive way. Moreover, Hochar's fortitude is a tribute to his perseverance and an argument against mixing war with wine!

Today's wines at Chateau Musar reflect 70-year-old traditions, including organic viticulture with bush-vine plantation and a high vine age. The reds are 40 to 80 years old, while the ungrafted merweh and Obaideh white grapes, planted in a vineyard behind the village of Ghazir at 4,300 feet (1300 m), are 80 to 130 years old. Chateau Musar uses only concrete fermenters; Serge Hochar and his son Gaston, also a winemaker, don't like stainless steel. They age wine almost exclusively in older wooden casks.

Chateau Musar's wines are controversially praised and denigrated by consumers and critics for their noncontemporary nature. They have a decided funkiness, an earthy character or slight oxidation because of their significant levels of volatile acidity (VA). Wine color is less deep and sometimes can reveal rustic, acetic, or gamy scents that mask the more pure flavors and real potential of the wine. One cannot argue with Serge Hochar's comment that the VA lifts the aromas of the wine, necessitates longer aging to appreciate them, and that Chateau Musar's red is not a wine for everyone. Decanting the red in advance helps to clean the wine of sediments and aeration helps it release its volatile aromas.

Recognizing, however, that most consumers today cannot wait many years to enjoy their wines and prefer more clearly fruit-driven fresh flavors, the Hochars decided in 1995 to start bottling with lower levels of VA and slightly increase the levels of sulfur dioxide to maintain freshness longer. This is especially notable in Musar Cuvées. Nevertheless Musar's are atypical of Lebanese wines, but everyone should try them, as they are genuine expressions of a place and the personalities of their creators.

Favorite wines: 1977 Chateau Musar Red (14%)

> *The Musar Red reminds us that sometimes patience is a virtue. This red is a blend of cabernet, cinsaut, and carignan from vineyards in the Beka'a. Like younger Musar reds, it was not too dark in color on its release in 1983. We remember first tasting this 1977 vintage in the early 1980s; now it is much richer, with more obvious sweet cinnamon, pepper, and black cherry flavors, and it is mildly tannic. When we first tasted it, it had already revealed the lifted earth aromas and slightly sharp acidity of oxidation that are not good signs for aging. We liked it 30 years ago for its vitality but questioned the faulty aspects, which generally do not improve with time, making for a wine that would decline quickly. Today this wine, which seemed too fragile for aging, is still going strong, with a personality not unlike its maker: resilient. Today it has a light brick-garnet color and a haunting, delicate cherry bouquet, with floral-spicy scents underneath. Pretty and minerally, with dried cherry flavors, good tannin, and fine integration, it seems much cleaner and fresher than it did when young. The delicate graphite and violet aromas and warmth of flavor that evolve with aeration make this a wonderful and delicious old wine today. Serge Hochar said, "The problem is . . . this wine talks to us." Indeed it does, to this day and at least for another decade.*

2003 Chateau Musar White (13.5%)

Chateau Fakra, Kfardebian Valley, Kesrouan District (www.fakra.com)

Carlos Adem, a professor of biochemistry, was born in Argentina, educated in England, and now is a wine grower in Argentina, France, and Lebanon. He started the wine business in 2000 and created the Chateau Fakra brand by working with grapes purchased from the Beka'a. Fakra is named for a village at 5,200 feet (1,600 m) in the Mount Lebanon massif, where an ancient temple complex dating to Roman times sits. The temple was dedicated to Adonis and Zeus, and Dionysian rites were also practiced at Fakra; certainly this part of Lebanon was as a key center of Dionysian worship. Most of Adem's fine vineyards are scattered throughout the Beka'a and make robust wines.

> *Favorite wine: 2007 Chateau Fakra Collection Privée Cabernet-Syrah, Beka'a Valley (13%)*

Chateau Belle-Vue, Bhamdoun (www.chateaubelle-vue.com)

Bhamdoun is where Naji Boutros grew up, where his grandfather owned the Hotel Belle-Vue at 3,600 feet (1,100 m) in the mountains east of Beirut, a famous grape-growing region. More than five hundred people from the town were killed during the Israel-Lebanon conflict in the early 1980s, which decimated the population.

Boutros remembers getting up early to work in the fields. He also remembers the Israeli tanks that occupied Bhamdoun and the Syrian and Lebanese artillery that shelled the town. Much of the town was destroyed, including the old landmark hotel. He left at seventeen, went to the United States for college, and earned degrees from Notre Dame and Stanford in engineering and management. There he met his American wife, Jill, and then embarked on an international career with Merrill Lynch while living in New York and London, where the Boutroses raised four children and were comfortable.

Dismayed by the sadness of the town during a visit while he was living in London in 1996, Naji Boutros realized he had to return to preserve the wonderful local culture and restore a sense of community to Bhamdoun. The family moved to Bhamdoun three years later. Bhamdoun is halfway between Beirut and the Beka'a Valley. On the advice of a Lebanese winemaker who had worked in California, Naji Boutros planted cabernet where his grandfather's hotel had stood.

When Joseph Khairallah, a Bhamdoun native, heard that this crazy young man had returned home from abroad to replant vineyards, Khairallah proclaimed, "No one will plant those vines but me—it's my valley." He offered his services and knowledge about farming to Boutros, and Khairallah has been with Belle-Vue ever since and now is the vineyard manager. Boutros has more than 60 acres (about 24 ha) in production, an expensive proposition because Bhamdoun's proximity to Beirut makes real estate pricey.

The first harvest was in 2003. What makes Bhamdoun special for wine? Boutros considers the differences between the mountains and the more famous Beka'a far below. The Beka'a Valley is more fertile, he says, and it's quite easy to dig down a few feet and find water. The Beka'a also is about four degrees warmer during the year than Bhamdoun. The soils here are extremely porous; higher up they are more calcareous. Lower down, it's terra rossa over the limestone, so they planted syrah and merlot there, and cabernet at higher elevations.

All their vineyards are organic, with high iron content, not unlike parts of Pomerol and Saint Émilion in Bordeaux. Low yields, less than half a ton per acre, also mean higher costs as the intensive farming work requires employing more local people, which actually is part of the idea. Boutros and his family believe they have a duty to help Bhamdoun as well as make fine wines. They donate US$1.00 per bottle sold to fund scholarships for children at the local school. As the Boutroses write on their website, "What began as the lonely efforts of a handful of individuals has blossomed into village-wide support and excitement as we better appreciate the wisdom of the Arabic proverb, 'One hand alone cannot clap.'" The wines are made under the guiding hand of the consulting enologist Diana Salamé, who studied in Dijon and is one of only two women winemakers in Lebanon.

Favorite wines: 2006 Chateau Belle-Vue la Renaissance Vin Rouge (14%)

Boutros's premier merlot-cabernet blend, which in 2006 was 55% merlot, 45% cabernet, is a nearly opaque black ruby. Aged in 90% new French oak barrels ("the fruit just gobbled up the new oak," Salamé notes), the bouquet has vanilla aromas, intense scented cassis, and black cherry pastille scents. Full bodied, the fruit is lithe and elegant; the tannins are fine and so integrated with the oak that the fruity finish is seamless. This wine is like a Bordeaux in focus and style and will keep well until 2018.

2010 Chateau Belle-Vue Petite Geste, Mont Liban (13.5%)

BEKA'A VALLEY

The Beka'a, as locals call it, has for thousands of years been the key viticultural area in Lebanon. The Romans built the largest temple complex in the Near East in Baalbek; the two key temples are dedicated to Jupiter (Zeus) and Dionysus, grafting divinity and worship of the two Roman gods to the more ancient Phoenician gods—which no doubt included older incarnations of Dionysus. The Temple of Bacchus (Dionysus), one of the best preserved ancient temples in the world, reflects the importance of the Beka'a for wine two millennia ago. Today the ruins here are a must-see for any wine lover.

Byblos and Tyre were the main ports from which wine was shipped, but the Beka'a is probably where most of it was made. Legend has it that the Egyptian god Osiris washed ashore in a coffin in Bibylos (his treacherous brother Seth had lured Osiris into the coffin). For the Egyptians, Osiris was like Dionysus, god of vine and wine. The Greeks believed that Phoenicia (Lebanon) was one of the birthplaces of Dionysus, at Nysa.

No matter the mythology, the Beka'a has all the conditions needed to grow grapes. Also, its location allowed direct trade routes between mountain ranges (west to east) and up through the desert as far north as Turkey. The valley is sunny most of the year, with warm summers and cold, wet winters; the altitude is high enough to mitigate the worst heat and pests. Run-off from Mount Lebanon and underground aquifers provide sufficient water for grapes.

Clos St. Thomas, Qab Elias (*www.closstthomas.com*)

"Our family started in the arak business here in the Beka'a in 1888, and we started making wine for arak in 1952," Joe "Assaad" Touma related while driving through his vineyards. "But it wasn't until after the civil war was over in 1990 [that] my dad [Said Touma], with my older sister Nathalie, really [began] wine production as a major enterprise for us. They found this rocky site up on the hill out of town, and dug cellars in the limestone 30 meters [more than 98 feet] down. We had found a natural cave during the process, and they dedicated it as 'Chapelle de St. Thomas,' our family's namesake."

Today the family controls 153 acres (62 ha) throughout the Beka'a at altitudes of 3,000 to 3,600 feet (900 to 1,100 m). The Touma family, like most winemakers in the Beka'a, is Christian. Parts of the Beka'a, particularly to the north around Baalbek, are under Hezbollah rule and strongly Muslim, but most of the mid-Beka'a down to Kefraya is fairly tolerant and has mixed populations. Consequently, at harvest Touma relies on Bedouin families who arrive regularly each year, and other local Muslims. Most of the local Muslim farmers in the Beka'a now grow wine grapes, since they get better prices from the needy wineries than they do for table grapes, which is surely a paradox. The Touma family also hosts an annual harvest party—everyone parties at night, and then picks the first grapes the next morning.

Aging takes place in French and American oak barrels; only the top-level wines see new oak. For aging Lebanese *cèpages* (such as cinsault and carignan), Touma prefers American oak but French for cabernet or merlot. Clos St. Thomas is one of the only producers of pinot noir in Lebanon, an unusual grape for the Mediterranean climate. Touma buys fruit from a young vineyard that has an altitude of about 3,600 feet (1,100 m), and by fermenting it cool turns out vintages like the 2008 and the upcoming 2011 that are remarkably elegant, aromatic, and surprisingly well textured. "The soils are not unlike Burgundy with limestone and red clay, and the slope is fairly steep," Touma notes. After tasting a range of wines in the cellar, and of course his father's marvelous arak and new cognac-type brandy, we can say that Clos St. Thomas certainly is a leading light in the Beka'a Valley.

Favorite wines: 2006 Chateau St. Thomas Red (14%)

"The war with Israel began in July and ended towards the last week or so of August, and our town was not immune to shelling," Joe Touma recalled. "Our harvest began the first week in September, so there were no Bedouin to harvest as they were afraid to return. So, we had to call our friends—everyone picked, even my dad, who is not so young anymore. But it turned out a fine vintage, as we had about 200 mm [about 12 inches] more rain than average during the winter, and it wasn't too hot. We were very lucky and blessed to have so many friends help us."

The flagship wine of Clos St. Thomas is a blend of 40% cabernet, 40% merlot, and 20% syrah. This wine is a lovely mature, medium ruby-garnet color, and its bouquet is redolent of deep plum, cassis, and a touch of garrigue, that combination of dried herbs, brush, and earthy spices like black pepper so often seen in Mediterranean French wines. Full bodied, with excellent fruit intensity balanced by still youthful chewy tannins, this lovely wine reminds us of a cross

between a fine Washington wine and a Right Bank Saint Émilion Bordeaux. It should age well and reflects the Beka'a character accurately.

2007 Clos St. Thomas les Emirs (14%)

Domaine des Tourelles, Chtaura (www.domainedestourelles.com)

The most historic winery in Lebanon, Domaine des Tourelles, owes its existence to an enterprising young Frenchman, François Eugène Brun, who while a young man was hired by an Ottoman company to help engineer the new Beirut-Damascus road. When he got to the key junction town of Chtaura in the Beka'a in 1868, he immediately fell in love with the area (and a young woman) and decided to make wine, arak, and other spirits. He became the first commercial producer in Lebanon. Seventy years later his sixteen-year-old grandson, Pierre Brun, took over the winery when his father, Louis, died of Asiatic flu. Pierre Brun studied formally at Montpellier, taking further lessons about how to make liqueurs and fine arak and learning from locals that the finest anise seeds came from around Damascus. He was one of the first producers to stock his own seeds, which he bought directly from farmers in Syria. Domaine des Tourelles's arak is still considered one of the finest in Lebanon.

When Pierre Brun died in 2000, he left no will and had no descendants. Subsequently two local family friends, Elie Issa and Nayla Khoury, bought the property and vowed to preserve Brun's legacy, his office, and the old winery cellars. They upgraded the technology and returned to making fine wines. Today Issa's daughter, Christianne Issa, is the manager; she works with her brother Fawzi, the winemaker, to produce several thousand cases every year. Fawzi Issa studied in France, then worked for a time at Chateau Margaux and René Rostaing in Côte Rôtie, experience that taught him how to make syrah.

Today Domaine des Tourelles has 50 acres (20 ha) all around Chtaura and Kefraya, high up in the Anti-Lebanon range near the Syrian border. "The soils here are terra rossa and limestone," Christianne Issa notes, "but more clayish where Jean Michel Fernandez, our winemaker, planted the tempranillo, our grand experiment."

Domaine des Tourelles retains its glow by still using old concrete fermenters. Visiting old cellars transports one back to a simpler age. The wines reveal a depth of flavor and modern fresh intensity that are compelling. Domaine des Tourelles is a legacy winery in excellent hands today, making modern wines that reflect the new Lebanon.

Favorite wines: 2007 Domaine des Tourelles Marquis de Beys (14%); 2010 Domaine des Tourelles Blanc (13%)

Cave Koroum, Kefraya (www.cavekouroum.com)

A winery that produces nearly 85,000 cases a year and is owned by Muslims? In Lebanon? Indeed. Cave Koroum's owners, Bassim Rahal and Sami Rahal, and their family have been in the wine and grape business for more than 50 years. Their village of Kefraya is predominantly Muslim, and its main product is grapes. While growing grapes is not against Islamic beliefs, making wine is often considered to be.

The family sold its wine grapes to producers for decades. In 1997–1998 a crisis in the industry resulted in a precipitous decline in the demand for wine grapes, so the Rahals and the village began to make their own wine rather than lose more than 300 tons of fruit. Today Kouroum is one of the most modern wineries in Lebanon, with a beautiful view from the entrance terrace across the vineyard hills to Mount Lebanon's massif.

Bassim Rahal says they have never looked back. Sami Rahal told the author Michael Karam, "It [wine] is a part of life and a part of living. Neither the Bible nor the Qur'an says don't work. Two thousand people rely on grapes, so what I do is between me and my God and no one else. People say you are the first Muslims to make wine. I say so what? What is wrong with that?"

For the Rahals and Kefraya Village, the quality of the wines affirms they made a good, smart choice.

The vineyards, particularly the older cinsault grapes for which the Kefraya area is renowned, are located on rolling slopes at altitudes higher than 3,250 feet (1,000 m), with the terra rossa limestone and rocky soils typical of the higher Beka'a. And what was once unfashionable is being made fashionable again, as other producers have also reexamined the quality older heritage varieties, either in blends or by themselves. These wines truly represent the taste of Lebanon. Here at Kouroum wines are flavorful, well priced, and characteristic of their village's terroirs.

Favorite wine: 2003 Cave Kouroum 7 Cépages, Kefraya (14.5%)

This wine is an exotic, powerful yet finely balanced blend of seven varieties: 25% each of syrah and cinsault, 10% each of grenache and carignan, 15% cabernet, and 15% pinot noir and merlot. The wine is medium ruby in color, and its nearly mature bouquet highlights cassis, licorice, cracked pepper, and some tar and rose notes, with nicely balanced tannins and ripe berry, leathery-meaty flavors. 7 Cépages reflects a fascinating mix of the old and new Lebanon in a bottle.

Chateau Kefraya, Kefraya (www.chateaukefraya.com)

Across the road from Caves Kouroum, Chateau Kefraya, the showplace winery created by Michel de Bustros in the village of Kefraya, represents another triumph of one family's determination in the face of civil war. The original chateau, built on an artificial hill made by the Romans, was constructed in 1946. In 1951 de Bustros planted a few vineyards in recognition of the Beka'a Valley's long association with vineyards. He did this with a particular eye for the specific "terroir" of Kefraya village, with its variety of soils from limestone-chalk to limestone-terra rossa and rocky clays.

Fast-forward two decades. While the local predominantly Muslim town (70 percent Druze) may have thought de Bustros crazy to plant wine grapes, he soon had the top older wineries (Musar and Ksara) clamoring for grapes. He subsequently expanded his holdings to more than 700 acres (300 ha). In 1976, as Israeli tanks crossed into southern Lebanon and war raged, he decided it would be better to make his own wine, so in 1978 he formed a partnership with a French company and built an estate winery. The first wartime vintage, 1979, was great.

Shortly after that initial success, the increasing ferocity of the war plunged the Beka'a Valley and Kefraya into a long, difficult period. De Bustros never left the property due to concern for problems that could arise without him there to solve them, and he was always fearful of what could happen to his family and his property.

He found a new and more adventurous French winemaker, Yves Morard, who was willing to work at Kefraya in trying times. Morard stayed through 1996, crafting wines while the fighting raged. In 1984 the Israeli army captured Morard and took him to Israel; he was suspected of being a member of the Palestine Liberation Organization. Morard explained he was a winemaker. The

Israelis questioned him relentlessly, but with some assistance from the French Embassy in Israel, he was released to France. He flew right back to Lebanon.

Even during the war business was good, and de Bustros realized he needed to expand, and more investors to make that possible, so the current Druze leader, Walid Jumblatt, and others came on board in 1987. Jumblatt is now the majority owner. With the end of the civil war, Chateau Kefraya was poised for growth and planted cabernet, syrah, mourvèdre, and other varieties, and hired a new winemaker, Jean Michel Fernandez from Spain.

Beginning in 1996 he created a revolutionary new blend that illustrated just how great Lebanese wines could be. Mostly cabernet, with 40% syrah and mourvèdre, the 1996 Comte de M debut vintage was aged in new French oak for one year and then in bottle for three years. It stunned the world. Comte de M showcased the Kefraya terroir in a style that was recognizable to international wine critics yet distinctly Lebanese. Today Fabrice Guiberteau continues to craft impressive lineups from the chateau's vineyards at elevations of 2,900 to 3,600 feet (900 to 1,100 m). Guiberteau studied and trained in Bordeaux for many years and has brought to Chateau Kefraya a more rigorous approach, cutting yields and using as much older vine fruit as possible. Kefraya is the second-largest winery in Lebanon, with perhaps the most consistent lineup. Even better, Le Relais Dionysos, its restaurant, is one of the few places to drink good wine with fine food in the whole Beka'a.

Favorite wines: 2007 Chateau Kefraya Comte de M, Kefraya (14%)

> *The star in the Kefraya firmament, and one of the best wines in Lebanon, if not the whole Levant, the 2007 blend of 40% cabernet, 40% syrah, 10% carignan, and 10% mourvèdre has a nearly opaque black ruby-purple color. It was aged in new French oak barrels and has some smoky-vanilla aromas, but more evident are deep black berry, roasted meat, and herbal-mineral and tar-like scents, likely contributed by the mourvèdre. This wine is densely textured, all its flavors are integrated, and they echo the bouquet, which is rich in tannins. Here is a fresh, inviting, and deeply focused wine that can age beautifully until 2020.*

2008 Chateau Kefraya Les Bretèches, Kefraya (14%)

Chateau Ksara, Zahle (www.ksara.com.lb)

Chateau Ksara has multiple distinctions: it is the oldest winery in modern Lebanon (begun in 1857 by Jesuit monks); the largest winery in the country today (it produces about 210,000 cases a year); and the only winery with 1.25 miles (2 km) of Roman caves under the chateau. The caves, which were excavated around 1899, were discovered by local children who were following a fox that was stealing chickens. Finally, the Jesuits decided in 1902 that they just had to have the first observatory in the Middle East, primarily to measure seismic activity and rainfall. Today the five Beka'a vineyards encompass 840 acres (340 ha) planted at altitudes of 3,100 to 3,600 feet (950 to 1,100 m) on typical Beka'a soils.

In the 1860s a Father Kirn and his brethren discovered an adequate water table and clay-chalk/limestone–terra rossa soils. Even while Lebanon was under Ottoman rule, the Jesuits could make wine for religious purposes. After World War I, Chateau Ksara became a commercial venture for the monastery, entering into an age of growing sales, better vineyards, and well-regarded wines.

In 1972, however, the Vatican urged all monasteries to divest themselves of commercial ventures, ending a century of monastic wine making in Lebanon and forcing the sale of this chateau to a local businessman, Jean-Pierre Sara. Civil war struck a couple of years later. Ultimately wartime forced an ownership change in 1991 to Charles Ghostine. Improvements have continued, especially regarding lower yields and more selectivity. Chateau Ksara's production ranges from commercial wines for easy drinking to highly reputable wines made with great care.

Favorite wine: 2007 Chateau Ksara, Cuvée de Troisième Millénaire (13.5%)

Massaya, Tanail/Chtaura (www.massaya.com)

Massaya means twilight in Arabic, a reference to the rosy color of the Anti-Lebanon Mountains at dusk. The Massaya winery is located on the Beka'a Valley floor in Tanail, the owners' hometown. From its founding in 1997, Massaya has been a bellwether of Lebanon's wine renaissance since the civil war. The brothers Ramzi and Sami Ghosn were forced to flee Tanail in the mid-1970s as troops entered the area where their parents' country property and vineyards were located. Both attended school and worked in the United States and France. Two decades later their father pleaded for them to return home, with Sami the first to return in the early 1990s. But Sami hated living in Beirut and decided to revive the family farm.

help and her consultant, friend, and neighbor is Domaine Wardy's winemaker, Diana Salamé. The wines will no doubt continue to evolve, even in the absence of Coteaux du Liban's guiding light.

> *Favorite wine: 2010 Coteaux du Liban Blanc du Clos, Vallée de la Beka'a (13%)*

Heritage Winery, Qab Elias (www.vinheritage.com)

Heritage Winery has a great heritage indeed. Dargham and Wissam Touma, the owners, are cousins of Joe Assaad Touma of the nearby Clos St. Thomas. Heritage has had its own winery only since 1995, when Dargham Touma, a hobbyist winemaker with a doctoral degree in food sciences, decided to get serious about making Beka'a Valley wine. Wissam Touma observed that they own just 15 percent of the vineyards that produce their grapes. "In the Beka'a it wasn't common until recently for wine producers of our age and medium size to own most of the vineyards we use," he notes. Because so many winemakers of their generation are well educated and are running local wineries, the over-all consistency and quality of the wine is much higher now. The key, however, is maintaining the style of Beka'a wines while making them fresher. Heritage's new blend, Le Fleuron, emphasizes forward fruit and round flavors yet still has that hint of sauvage, or wildness, that is the Beka'a, and this wine is affordable. The Lebanese wine writer Michael Karam has called it "Lebanon in a bottle."

> *Favorite wines: 2006 Heritage Plaisir du Vin, Beka'a Valley (13%); 2007 Heritage Grand Vin Bourgeois, Beka'a Valley (14%)*

Chateau Ka, Chtaura (www.chateauka.com)

The Kassatly family business started selling bulk wine in 1919. In 1968 Akram Kassatly returned from France and with his brothers decided to build a new winery in their hometown of Chtaura. The civil war, which began in 1975, forced them to abandon the project, and all the wine was destroyed. When the war finally ended about 15 years later, they decided to reinvest in the building and converted it to make syrups and other nonalcoholic beverages, a safer investment. But in 2005 Adam Kassatly, Akram's son, decided to make wine again under the Chateau Ka name. (In the ancient Egyptian religion, *ka* was the embodiment of a person's essence, breathed in at birth, and it was what made the person alive.)

Chateau Ka relies on Bedouin harvesters, who were naturally reluctant to be in the area during the Hezbollah-Israel War in 2006. But the *ka* of Chateau Ka showed great strength, and a fine vintage was harvested under stressful conditions. Today Jean Tannoury is in charge of an expanded domain, including vineyards around Baalbek. Ownership is critical there, since this area of the Beka'a is controlled by the local Hezbollah government. Hezbollah's strict interpretations of Islam make it difficult for independent growers, who are mostly Muslim, to sell grapes for wine to a Christian producer. Kassatly's reward for enduring the vicissitudes and struggles of the previous three decades is that the family now makes about 25,000 cases of flavorful and affordable wine each year.

Favorite wines: 2010 Chateau Ka Source Blanche, a blend of muscat, sauvignon blanc, semillon (14%); 2006 Chateau Ka Fleur de Ka, a blend of cabernet, syrah, and merlot (14.5%)

Chateau Khoury, Zahle (www.chateaukhoury.com)

Brigitte and Raymond Khoury began planting their vineyard, located on slopes 3,900 to 4,300 feet (1,200 to 1,300 m) above Zahle, in 1995 and now have about 39 acres (13 ha) with fine views across the Beka'a, especially on snowy winter days. Their family, originally from Alsace, decided to plant grapes atypical of Lebanon: Riesling, Gewürztraminer, and pinot noir. Their first vintage was 2004; in 2005 their son, Jean Paul Khoury, took over production, which remains small and family oriented.

The vineyards face multiple directions and are often 3 or 4 degrees Celsius cooler than on the valley floor, which is particularly favorable for the late ripening Riesling and Gewürztraminer. Yields are low on the Khourys' organic farm. The wines are refreshing and different overall from those of most other Lebanese producers, given the Alsatian origins of the family.

Favorite wines: 2010 Chateau Khoury La Rêve Blanc, Zahle, a blend of Riesling, Gewürztraminer, and chardonnay (13%); 2007 Chateau Khoury Cuvée Ste. Thèrése, Zahle, a blend of 80% Caladoc and 20% pinot noir (13%)

Chateau Nakad, Jdita (www.winenakad.com)

Chateau Nakad, founded in Jdita by Joseph Nakad in 1923, is one of Lebanon's most historic wineries, literally founded on the site of an old Bronze Age winery; an ancient stone winepress welcomes visitors to the modest winery. Nakad originally was an arak producer and started to make wine after World War I to sell to the French. The arak business declined after World War II, and the sons decided to focus on wine in 1956.

Nakad's son Selim noted that the civil war hit them hard, especially after Israel invaded Lebanon in 1982 and cut off travel between Beirut and the Beka'a, forcing the brothers to stop making wine.

Yet Selim and Bassam, the two brothers most engaged in the winery, persevered throughout the 1990s and today still make traditional, meaty wines that are affordable and true to Beka'a tradition.

Favorite wine: 2004 Nakad Chateau des Coteaux (14%)

Domaine Wardy, Zahle (www.domaine-wardy.com)

Domaine Wardy has been producing wine under its own name since 1998, but the company traces its history to a great uncle who started making arak and home wine in 1893 under the name Ghantous-Abu Raad. Aziz Wardy, the current manager, is a member of the family that continued to make arak through war and disasters but by the early 1990s had decided that fine wine was the future. In 1996 the vineyards were producing a reasonable crop, and Salim Wardy, Aziz's father, started making varietal wines. This was a departure from the tradition of blends that had arisen because vineyards were planted in a mixed way. In 1998 Salim Wardy released his first three varietals, cabernet sauvignon, chardonnay, and sauvignon blanc, as well as blends.

Domaine Wardy was the first in Lebanon to employ a female winemaker, Diana Salamé, who helped create the flagship Wardy Private Selection blend and also consults for others. Domaine Wardy, meanwhile, has become one of the most important Lebanese brands globally, with wines that have innovative packaging, fair prices, and, most important, excellent quality.

Favorite wines: 2010 Domaine Wardy Sauvignon Blanc, Beka'a (13%);
2005 Domaine Wardy Private Selection Red, Beka'a (13.5%)

SOUTHERN LEBANON

Karam Winery, Jezzine (www.karamwinery.com)

Habib Karam is one of the smallest wine growers in Lebanon; his winery, begun in 2003, makes only six thousand cases a year. He is a senior captain for

Middle East Airlines and sells a lot of wine in the United States, where he and his brother have an import company. Karam is the only winery in southern Lebanon. It is in the mountains of Jezzine, only a two-hour journey by car from Beirut, assuming Lebanese Army patrols let you through, fearful that potentially hostile Hezbollah forces may later "interrupt" your journey. Vineyards existed in these mountains before the Romans, according to Habib, and, given the altitude (3,600 to 4,300 feet/1,100 to 1,300 m), most are on old terraces. Farming is traditional, with bush vines on terraces and wider planting because of the lack of water. These frontier wines are worth looking for, and we hope others will join Karam in southern Lebanon to revive the ancient terraces, as the area is the country's "Wild West" for wine.

Favorite wines: 2006 Karam St. John, a blend of syrah, cabernet, and merlot (13.8%); 2008 Karam Corpus Christi, a Bordeaux-syrah blend (13.7%)

Lebanon's wines are as fragrant today as they were three thousand years ago. Wineries in Lebanon today connect us directly and simultaneously to the ancient and modern Bible wine trail.

Nine

JORDAN AND NOTES ON EGYPT

More than for Jazer I weep for you, O vine of Sibmah!
Your branches crossed over the sea, reached as far as Jazer; upon your
summer fruits and your vintage the destroyer has fallen
And Gladness and joy have been taken away from the fruitful land of Moab;
I have stopped the wine from the wine presses; no one treads them with shouts of joy;
the shouting is not the shout of joy.

—Jeremiah 48:32–33

RECENT HISTORY

People in Jordan probably began to grow wine grapes earlier than the third millennium BCE. Certainly the Jordan valley and Jericho had vineyards by the fifth millennium BCE. Ammonite wine (from Amman), famed from the early biblical period, was accepted for Temple offerings in Jerusalem. By Christ's time Moab in southern Jordan, where Petra is today, had a fine reputation; the number of Nabatean winepresses cut into the rock there reflects concerted vinicultural (grape growing and wine-making) activity. Nabateans, an early Semitic tribe who spoke an early form of Aramaic and lived in various places, including Moab, actively maintained the great Silk Road, used to transport wine from southern Arabia into the eastern Mediterranean and back through their kingdom. The Nabateans, masters of desert hydrology and irrigation systems, later held drinking bouts in great style, according to the Greek historian Strabo, and worshiped Dushara, their precursor to Dionysus.

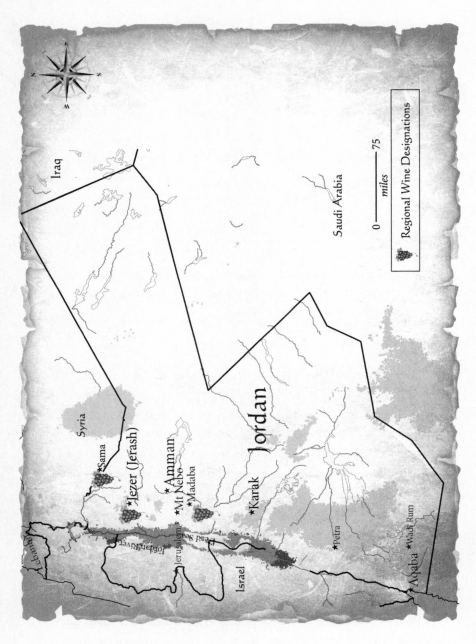

Jordan today, the area east of the Dead Sea, was at various times part of the Assyrian Empire, Palestine, and Syria, among others. The terrain, altitude, and climate, particularly in the ancient northern kingdoms of Gilead and Ammon (where Amman is located), are quite similar to those of the Beka'a Valley of Lebanon, Galilee, and the Jerusalem Hills in Israel. Wine and olives were the logical crops grown, and the area became famous as a result. The epigraph makes clear how important wine was in Jordan: Sibmah (north of Mount Nebo, known today as Mount Pisgah), for example, was famous for luxuriant vines and summer fruits (Isa. 16:8; Jer. 48:32). Modern Simia has extensive ancient ruins including large sarcophagi, with winepresses cut into the rock nearby.

The Jeremiah passage that opens this chapter goes on to say, "I will bewail with the weeping of Jazer the vine of Sibmah." Jezer is today's Gerasa-Jerash, then a Canaanite town and an important Roman city; now it has spectacular ruins and continues to be home to fine vineyards in the hills above the city. According to the Polish archaeologist Tomasz Waliszewski, who has worked in Jordan and Israel for many years, Jordanian wine was highly reputable even after the Roman era, and it was so important to the local economy that its cultivation continued despite the rise of Islam.

Much of eastern and southern Jordan is desert, but the slopes of the Pisgah range, which fronts the Dead Sea all the way north to Lake Tiberias, have the right conditions for making good wine. On the east-facing sloped plateau, the little moisture that falls allows for forests and crops to grow. The altitude of Mount Pisgah, where Moses looked down upon the Promised Land (Deut. 34:1), is 2,240 feet (690 m); the Dead Sea, the lowest point on Earth, is 1,312 feet (400 m) *below* sea level.

Wine pitchers from the middle Bronze Age (eighteenth century BCE) have been found in excavations around Mount Pisgah. During the late Roman imperial period and into Byzantine rule, monks and merchants created many vineyards around the city of Madaba, famous for its mosaic map of the Holy land region from the sixth century CE, and nearby Mount Nebo/Pisgah, where Moses is said to have been buried. A Byzantine mosaic depicting a wine pitcher with grape clusters attached was unearthed at the nearby monastery of el-Kaniseh and attests to the importance of wine grapes in this area.

This is where modern Jordan's wine trade began.

After Syrian troops helped him reclaim his land and remove the squat-
ters, Sami Ghosn revived the vineyards and started making raki and selling it
in a stylish new package, while Ramzi remained working in France, though he
too, came home in the mid-1990s to partner with his brother in the growing
business. This provided the capital to begin making wine, but the Ghosns still
needed outside partners. In 1998 they formally joined forces with Dominique
Hebrard, former owner of Cheval Blanc; Hubert de Boüard de Laforest of
Chateau Angelus; and Daniel Brunier of Vieux Telegraphe in Chateauneuf du
Pape to begin Massaya.

Today, under Ramzi Ghosn's tutelage, Massaya produces 25,000 cases a
year, including an innovative top-level Bordeaux-based wine introduced in
1998: cabernet blended with ourvèdre and syrah, something their French
partners never considered. They named it Gold Reserve. Most of Massaya's
red grapes grow near Baalbek with organic farming. From the beginning the
Ghosn brothers have intended to shake up the Lebanese wine scene. Consider
it youthful enthusiasm and perhaps rebellion, but their quality wines and
sincerity about removing the tarnish from Lebanon's war-torn image are
undeniable.

> Favorite wines: *2009 Massaya Gold Reserve Red (14.5%)*
>
> *This is a unique blend of half cabernet, 40% mourvèdre, and the balance of
> Syrah, aged two years in French oak barrels, 30% of which are new. Deep black
> color entices you to inhale the rich concentrated bouquet of cassis, black plum,
> and graphite-mineral. The flavors are equally compelling, showcasing rich fruit
> intensity enrobed with firm tannins, balanced acidity, and long finish. Here's a
> wine to keep for another decade.*
>
> *2011 Massaya Rosé, Tanail Estate, Beka'a (13.5%)*

Coteaux du Liban Winery, Zahle (www.libancave.com)

Started in Zahle in 2000 by the Burgundy-trained Nicolas Abou Khater,
Coteaux du Liban aimed to produce traditional wines and use innovative means to achieve more "vital and spirited" wines, as his widow, Roula
Ghantous-Abou Khater, told us. All the grapes come from nearby vineyards,
including the Coteaux's, at 3,600 feet (1,100 m), and the wines have received
solid marks from the beginning. Just as the winery's fortunes were entering a
new, prosperous level, Nicolas died. Roula decided to carry on with her family's

Zumot Winery and Vineyards, Amman (www.zumot-wines.com)

Modern Jordan's wine industry, as small as it is, began in 1954 when Bulos Zumot, an Amman businessman and the father of the current owner, Omar Zumot, decided to make and sell his own wines. Jordan had a few small wineries, including some affiliated with local monasteries. But, as in neighboring Lebanon, many growers were Muslim and concentrated on table grapes. Bulos Zumot dreamed of putting Jordanian wine back on the map, of reviving the quality and renown the country had earned two millennia before.

The Zumots found their inspiration in the wonderful mosaics and atmosphere of Madaba's Byzantine monuments and churches. After much exploration they found a perfect vineyard plot not far from the Church of Saint George, giving the new winery's wines their brand name. The Zumot Winery and Vineyard was set up in 1996, and the first wines arrived in 1999. From the beginning Omar Zumot wanted a noninterventionist policy in the vineyard—the Zumot vineyards would be farmed organically, and that practice continues today.

Omar Zumot says, "There was no one really to learn from, since no one had wine grapes." He had studied abroad, drunk widely of French wines, and toured vineyards in many countries. He began importing wines, opened a wine store in Amman, and hosted tastings for visiting scholars, diplomats, and business people. He became friendly with like-minded young new producers in Lebanon, Israel, and France; knew what good wine should be; and was aware of the challenges of making fine wine in Jordan. Omar Zumot learned from everyone and in time the Saint George wines got better, while sales grew along with demand.

Soon after the turn of the twenty-first century Zumot Winery bought land in two radically different northern Jordan sites, one on the forested slopes above the ancient Roman city of Jerash and the other on the Syrian border at Sama.

The vineyard above Jerash is at 3,200 feet (1,000 m) and sits on terra rossa limestone and some clay. The altitude, with its cooler temperature and southeast-facing slopes, gave Omar Zumot the idea to plant pinot noir here; the results were remarkable, he notes. Maybe it's not Burgundy, but the site has proved quite suitable for that finicky variety, as well as for chardonnay. Harvest in Jordan, Zumot observes, is all done by hand and usually starts in early August. Canopy management to protect the clusters from sunburn is critical to success, he adds.

The Sama vineyard is on fairly flat ground composed of clay, basalt, and limestone at an elevation of 2,000 feet (600 m) and requires irrigation from aquifers. "We bought the property in 2003–2004," Omar Zumot notes, "when it was originally a military base. There was the house here, for officers, which we have updated and use for events and guests. When you look north towards Syria, you see a small guardhouse up on the rise there—that's the Syrian border and a Jordanian border patrol guardhouse. Our harvesters are from the local Bedouin village, as well as Syrians who come over to help in the fields—at least they did before the current crises of the past year [2011] in Syria." As part of his organic farming Zumot planted thousands of wild herbs to encourage predator habitat for beneficial insects. He uses cover crop to fix the nitrogen in the soil, a vital issue in the depleted aridity of the region, where soils often have low organic compound levels.

Organic farming and irrigation have greatly aided him in achieving his goals. The result: many Zumot Saint George wines have won medals and positive recommendations at major international wine judgings and from key wine critics worldwide.

"Unfortunately, the mind-set that everybody had was that Jordanian wine was mediocre wine," he told CNN interviewer Arwa Damon of *Inside the Middle East* in 2010, "but Jordan is like its wine. You come to Jordan, and you are always pleasantly surprised. The country is welcoming, just like its wines." Zumot uses the best equipment and barrels for his wines, and in a few years he has created an estate with more than 540 acres (220 ha) dedicated to most of the classic varieties, as well as experiments with sangiovese, carmènere, and even chenin blanc grapes.

Favorite wines: 2010 Zumot Saint George Viognier Winemaker's Selection (14%)

> *Zumot's Viognier reveals typically opulent, overt floral, juicy peach, and ripe apricot aromas. Flavorwise it is fleshy, with deep near-tropical flavors that are balanced by solid acidity, minimal oak character, and good length. The intense character is in the same league as similar wines from the better producers in Lebanon and California.*

2008 Saint George Reserve Cabernet Sauvignon (14%)

Quite youthful in appearance, aroma, and taste, this blend is primarily from Sama. Its deep ruby-purple color conveys intensity, which is evident in the elegant yet strong floral-cassis aromas that signal fruit from a cool climate. The palate is thickly textured and dense, probably from Sama's warmer climate. Deep licorice, blackberry, and distinctive red bell or chipotle pepper flavors emerge on the finish, along with notable graphite-mineral accents and excellent persistence. It is a fleshy cabernet that could use until 2016 to soften, yet it is excellent now, indicative of Jordan's potential.

NOTES ON EGYPT

In researching this book we had hoped to visit modern Egypt to compare what we might find relative to the wealth and importance of ancient Egyptian wines. Alas, the political situation did not permit this. Our previous experience with modern Egyptian wine is highly limited, as virtually none is exported. When Islam conquered Egypt in the seventh century CE, the great heritage of ancient wine was effectively lost until archaeological excavations brought to light the magnificent tomb paintings depicting wine's high position in Egyptian society.

The only wine not destroyed by Islam was Coptic monastic wine, made under the duress of potential Muslim interference, and often secretly, behind monastery walls. Our only experience with an Egyptian wine, a chenin blanc consumed about eight years ago, was not a fortuitous one; the wine was flat, with little to recommend it.

As in antiquity most Egyptian vineyards are in the Nile delta region near the Mediterranean, which has a relatively milder climate than farther south and mostly silty soils. Today Egypt has new wineries, Sahara Vineyards near Luxor and Shahrazade Winery on the Red Sea coast across from Sharm el-Sheikh. Their fruit, including the native variety *bannati* from near Luxor, comes partly from the Nile delta. Little has changed in five thousand years: growing grapes in the desert is a challenge. While the irrigation technology is now available, taking advantage of it requires tremendous diligence (and financial means) to produce high-quality grapes.

The largest Egyptian wine producer today, Gianaclis, was started by a Greek immigrant in 1882. The company today makes wine from three vineyards, one near Luxor (Sahara Vineyard), and the others in the Nile delta. The most commonly found wines in Egypt are its dry red called Omar Khayyam; its dry white, Cru des Ptolémées; and a rosé called Rubis d'Egypt.

In 2005 our colleague Alder Yarrow tasted a large variety of Egyptian wines in-country and found most of them oxidized, flat, and/or simply dull. He wrote: "I'm sad to report that while Egyptian wine may have been revered throughout the ancient world, either standards have changed or much has been lost through the ages. Some . . . charitably describe Egyptian wine as an acquired taste, but mostly, it is just bad. . . . In other countries with bigger markets such production would be driven out of business by the competition, but sadly, the market in Egypt is mostly tourists who show up for a few days, buy a bottle with dinner, and then go away, albeit with a bad taste in their mouths." The two most prominent varietals cultivated in modern Egypt are pinot blanc and cabernet sauvignon, with vineyards located around Lake Maryut.

Recently, however, with a liberalizing of the economy that started before the ouster of Mubarak, and access to better technology and the guidance of enthusiastic foreign winemakers, Egyptian wines have registered modest improvement. Unfortunately, few small producers have the wherewithal to produce wine of higher quality.

Gianaclis, whose wines are better than most but still modest, caters to a captive market, much as producers of Provencal rosé do; Gianaclis has a huge tourist influx and no incentive to produce wine of higher quality. The market simply isn't there. We think it likely that, given the current political climate, Egypt will not soon rediscover the rich wine tradition that once made it famous and was so much a part of its ancient culture.

Perhaps the Egyptian wine industry, once a major protégé of the Canaanites' and an innovator in labeling, imports/exports, and making age-worthy wines, is gone forever. We can only hope that the vine brought out of Egypt (Ps. 80) may be replanted there—allowing Egyptians to experience their rich heritage once more.

Ten

ISRAEL

Also I will restore the captivity of My people Israel,
And they will rebuild the ruined cities and live in them,
They will also plant vineyards and drink their wine,
And make gardens and eat their fruit.

—Amos 9:14

MODERN HISTORY

Israel became a modern, independent country on May 14, 1948. For the first time in approximately 2,600 years, since Sargon II of Assyria defeated the Kingdom of Israel in 721 BCE and Judah fell to Babylon in 597 BCE, a Jewish state existed. Yet Israel always had wine, even under nearly a thousand years of Muslim rule. In the mid- to late nineteenth century, when the Ottoman Empire allowed Jews and other foreigners to return to Palestine (the ancient name), among the earliest to heed the call were several who wanted to rebuild the Promised Land of wine.

Certainly Christian monasteries had made wine in Palestine for centuries—Latroun Monastery still makes wines—but there was little else. Sir Moses Montefiore of England, the Jewish financier and philanthropist, visited Palestine in the mid-nineteenth century and encouraged local Jews to plant vineyards and work the land. Wineries existed prior to his first visit, as early as 1848. By the 1870s other pioneers had imported French grape vines, including Rhône varieties like carignan. The biggest boost to a renewal of wine

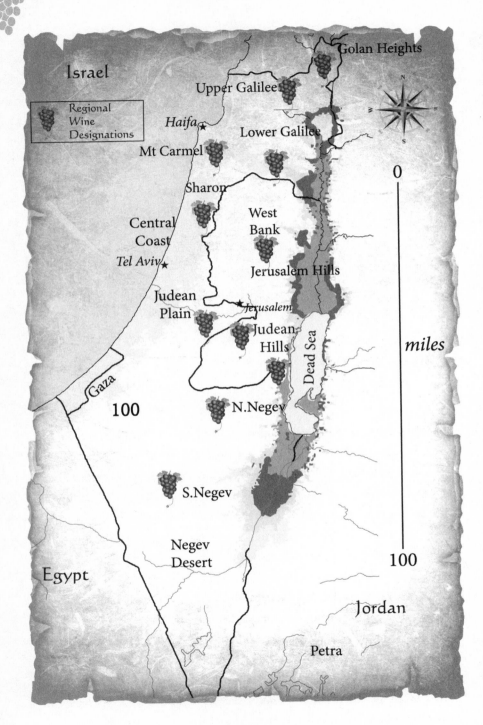

Israel

Regional
Wine
Designations

Golan Heights

Upper Galilee

Haifa

Lower Galilee

Mt Carmel

Sharon

West
Bank

Central
Coast

Jerusalem Hills

Tel Aviv

Judean
Plain

Jerusalem

Judean
Hills

Dead Sea

Gaza

100

N.Negev

S.Negev

Negev
Desert

Egypt

0

miles

100

Jordan

Petra

production came in the 1880s, when Baron Edmund de Rothschild of Chateau Lafite Rothschild decided to start making wine in the Shomron (Samaria) area south of Haifa in an effort to help struggling colonists in Israel. He wanted to make good Bordeaux-style wines, of course, and "brought in his guys from Lafite, built two big stone wineries with all of the state-of-the-art equipment of the era, one at Zichron Ya'acov in 1892 and Rishon Le Zion in 1890, planting malbec, cabernet franc and sauvignon and the rest," Adam Montefiore of Carmel Winery told us (he is the great-great-grandnephew of Sir Moses). Carmel became the name of Rothschild's property, after nearby Mount Carmel. *Carmel* derives from the Hebrew Kerem-El, God's vineyard.

"The first plantings failed for three reasons: growers were paid on yields, and these French varieties were low yielding; the vines became infected with phylloxera, which arrived in the early 1890s." So cuttings then had to come from a nursery in Kashmir, India. Lastly "people didn't want more expensive wine. They wanted cheap wine, so the experiment failed," Montefiore told us.

Rothschild stuck with it, as did early settlers whom he helped by setting up a cooperative system to supply his wineries; it remained important to the wine industry for nearly another century. Rothschild also brought in American rootstocks. Before the phylloxera took its toll in 1890–1891, Israel had about 6,900 acres (2,800 ha) of vineyards; by 1914 it had only 2,200 acres (880 ha), the result of Rothschild's decision to restrict vineyard plantings because he feared overproduction would lead to market collapse. By 1963, however, Israel had 110,000 acres (4,450 ha) of vineyards and produced 21,000 tons of wine grapes annually.

Israeli wine production continued to improve despite these initial setbacks, until three events occurred that brought growth to a grinding halt: the Russian Revolution, Prohibition in the United States, and Egypt's decision to ban importation of wine. Most of the production and markets that survived were devoted to sacramental wines—the strong, sweet wines Jews worldwide were conditioned to use in saying kiddush on the Sabbath. The planting of cheap productive wine grapes like Carignan, Alicante, Ugni Blanc, and Clairette was advanced in the 1950s, followed by Petite Sirah, Colombard, and Emerald Riesling in the 1970s. While new wineries such as Segal (now part of Barkan) and Eliaz (now Binyamina) did start post–World War II, wine consumption in Israel remained low, less than 4 liters per person.

Independence in 1948, however, brought an influx of settlers obeying the call of aliyah (ascent), immigration to Israel, and many went into farming. Between 1948 and 1979, for example, 1.4 million Jews made that journey. Viticulture expanded to supply grapes for the sacramental wine that Israelis required but also overseas Jewish communities that were growing and eager to support the new Israel. Buying Israeli wines was one way to do so.

In 1972 Dr. Cornelius Ough of the University of California, Davis, visited Israel. His report electrified the industry. After he visited the Golan Heights in northern Israel on the border with Syria and Jordan, Ough concluded that it had ideal soils and climate for wine grapes. Until then most vineyards had been established in the coastal areas south of Haifa and southeast of Tel Aviv. The first vines were planted in the Golan in 1976, and in 1983 Golan Heights Winery was founded. The 1980s were a difficult time for Israel economically and socially; the invasion of Lebanon in 1982 and the Intifada in 1987 created tension and disruption throughout Israeli society. Golan Heights Winery's first wines were revelatory and eventually blossomed into a garden-scape of new wineries. Older wineries modernized and rejuvenated their lines, and Israeli wine growers who studied enology and marketing at UC Davis or in Australia came home. Today Israel has more than 240 wineries that produce about 3 million cases from 12,000 acres (5,500 ha) of wine grapes. Planting vineyards and making wine is indeed modern Israel's future.

CLIMATE AND GEOLOGY

Put simply, Israel's climate ranges from hot Mediterranean-maritime in southern Israel to warm maritime-Mediterranean along the coastal areas north to Haifa. In the Negev and around the Dead Sea, a desert climate prevails—hot, dry days and cold nights. In the uplands and areas like the Jerusalem Hills, the altitude of 2,300 to 3,300 feet (700 to 1,000 m), cools things off considerably, creating a semi-continental climate; snow in winter is not uncommon.

The landscape along the drive north into the mountains of Galilee and the Golan Heights toward Mount Hermon looks like northern Italy or France in winter. It can be quite cold but sunny and the climate continental. Most rainfall is in winter and ranges from a paltry 8 to 12 inches (200 to 300 mm) in the desert areas to more than 40 inches (1,000 mm) farther north along the coast. Compared to the earliest period of grape-growing in Israel five to seven thousand years ago, the climate is drier and warmer.

Geologically speaking, most of the country's vineyards, except those in the Golan Heights and parts of Upper Galilee, are located on sedimentary or metamorphic sites. Millions of years ago the area was seabed, pre-Cambrian deep metamorphic rock formed by tremendous pressure. Then, as the super-continent separated, along with other phenomena, the deeper layers under the sea or continental landmass lifted. Most coastal areas are essentially limestone and sandstone seabed. As one moves eastward and into higher altitudes away from the coast, into the Judean Hills or the mountains of Galilee for example, limestone dominates, but there are also basalts from volcanic activity. Millions of years of water erosion created the iron-rich terra rossa typical of these up-land mountain areas.

Northeast of the Sea of Galilee, the Golan Heights rose from massive vol-canic eruptions and lava flows; several cinder cones are still visible. Rocky ba-salts with little soil are common. In the southern desert areas like the Negev and the Dead Sea basin, a combination of Jurassic limestone and sandstones, eroded and faulted over the eons, forms the basic geological structure.

GRAPES, APPELLATIONS, AND THE
WINE ECONOMY IN ISRAEL

Israel really doesn't have any indigenous varieties of merit, or at least any that are known. Experiments are being conducted on a plot of old vines found near Ashkelon, most of which are believed to be old varieties favored by the Muslim population for eating. But only DNA analyses and tests will determine whether any of these heirlooms have promise for wine. Meanwhile, Israeli producers have planted almost every important French variety and several Italian ones, such as barbera and sangiovese. Chardonnay, sauvignon blanc, cabernet, and merlot dominate.

As for appellation, Israel has no real official system like France or Greece, with definitive rules about what grapes can be used, or how much wine can be legally produced. Rather, the country is generally divided into five growing regions: Galilee, Shomron, Samson, Judean Hills , and the Negev. Each is sub-divided into smaller ones. For example, Galilee has four subregions: Upper

Galilee, Lower Galilee, Golan Heights, and Tabor. Where possible, we will give the appellation for the *winery's* location. An advantage of this system is that wineries can buy fruit outside their own region that may be better or quite different. One should bear in mind that in Israel, as in the United States, there are no strong rules with regard to appellation, except geographical location.

The concept of terroir increasingly drives more producers, for example, to explore the Jerusalem hills area, even though producers in Shomrom have traditionally made wine from coastal vineyards. Israel's principal wine regions are virtually the same as they were 2,500 years ago.

Today's Israeli wines provide consistently good quality, ripe forward flavors, and rich fruit. The industry still struggles with somewhat higher prices than its competitors in the international marketplace for two reasons: almost everything—equipment, bottles, corks, and the like—must be imported, and the Israeli shekel (IS) has appreciated in recent years; and making wine according to kosher laws is expensive (see chapter 5). Most Israeli wineries produce kosher wines for economic reasons: if you want to sell wine in grocery stores, it has to be kosher, because that's all they will stock. Also, even most secular Jews in Israel still hold to some old traditions. The wines themselves are no different, except they are more expensive because of the extra labor required.

Let's begin our Israeli wine tour alphabetically by producer within each region, from north to south.

GOLAN HEIGHTS

The Golan Heights is Israel's newest old area for modern wine production. While the remains of Canaanite period "gats" are found at sites throughout the Heights, modern winemaking here only was revived after the 1967 war with Syria, which controlled it until then.

Assaf Winery, Kidmat Zvi, Golan Heights (www.assafwinery.com)

Assaf Kedem made wine in South Africa and at another winery in the Golan before starting his own winery in 2004, with his vineyard first planted in 1990. He now has 40 acres (16 ha) at altitudes of 1,600 to 2,600 feet (500 to 800 m).

Kedem is well respected in Israel where he serves as consultant to others, and he was one of the first people to plant pinotage, South Africa's signature variety, in Israel. His son Orem assists with wine making at their estate vineyard. Like many small family wineries in Israel, the Kedems' is not kosher. Their wines are richly flavored and extroverted in style.

Favorite wines: 2011 Assaf Pink Zinfandel, Golan Heights (12%); 2009 Assaf Cabernet Sauvignon Reserve, Golan Heights (11% cabernet franc) (14.5%)

Chateau Golan, Moshav Eliad (www.chateaugolan.com)

Uri Hetz, Chateau Golan's winemaker since its founding in 1999, studied his avocation in Oregon and California. Chateau Golan uses only estate-grown fruit from the lower southern Golan plateau, an elevation of about 1,300 feet (400 m). This area is less rocky than the northern Golan, with more clay, deeper soils, and better water retention. Hetz makes about six thousand cases each year from 50 acres (20 ha). He is unapologetic about not making kosher wine: "I couldn't stand it to not be able to touch my barrels or taste my wines when I need to."

Favorite wine: 2009 Chateau Golan Reserve Syrah, Golan Heights (14.5%)

Golan Heights Winery, Katzrin (www.golanwines.co.il)

It's safe to say that this winery, begun in 1983 by a group of local kibbutzim and moshavim (members of an agricultural cooperative) and overseen by an American winemaker, has been as instrumental in creating modern Israeli wines as Rothschild's Carmel Winery was in the revival of Israeli wine a century ago. Golan Heights began planting vineyards in 1976, at altitudes ranging from 1,300 to 3,900 feet (400 to 1,200 m) in the shadow of Mount Hermon, the highest peak in the Levant (9,232 feet/2,814 m). From 6,000 cases in 1984 the winery's production has expanded to nearly 600,000 cases today, all consistently good, some superb.

The Golan's climate is semicontinental, and its high altitude with basaltic, free-draining soils provides a unique environment that head winemaker Victor Schoenfeld points out, "duplicates the conditions of wine-growing as if we were 800 km farther north, closer to north-central Anatolia; not far from Mount Ararat, actually." It probably is the coolest region in Israel.

The winery makes wines under three principal brands: Golan, Yarden, and Gamla, the latter two for premium wines that can age. Because the winery has 1,500 acres (600 ha), its vines spread across the Golan Heights, Schoenfeld uses sophisticated tools to monitor quality in both the vineyards and winery, including a new tracking system that allows the team to perform cellar operations simply by clicking on a giant computer screen on the wall. Moreover, Golan Heights is at the forefront of bringing into Israel new vine cuttings, including official French government-approved ENTAV selections, and propagating clean cuttings through its nursery operation.

The devotion to viticulture drives Schoenfeld and his team; the northern Golan vineyards, which are at the higher altitudes, have stony soils of low pH and high basalt content; they provide many of the best white wines, like sauvignon blanc and chardonnay. The southern Golan vineyards, planted at lower altitudes, are slightly warmer, have soils with higher pH and often with more loess and silty sand, and provide better conditions for the best red wines, such as syrah and cabernet. The winery's moderate crop levels average 4 tons per acre for reds, though single vineyard selections often yield much less. Golan Heights Winery produces many excellent wines here, and many are available abroad—the winery exports nearly 35 percent of its total production. And these wines are kosher, too.

Favorite wines: 2008 Yarden Cabernet Sauvignon El Rom, Golan Heights (14.5%)

> *The El Rom Vineyard of Golan Heights Winery is at one of the highest altitudes, 3,600 feet (1,100 m), in the northern Golan, near the Syrian frontier; its vines were planted between 1983 and 2004. The opaque black-ruby color of the Yarden Cabernet Sauvignon El Rom alerts you to what is coming—deep blackberry, cassis, violet, and delicate oak scents confirm the rich intensity of the fruit. Powerful yet polished tannins are enveloped by high-extract, graphite-laced fruit with a lovely, elegant filigreed texture. This wine is completely different from the Bordeaux-style Israeli cabernets like Castel but equally well balanced.*

2011 Yarden Sauvignon Blanc, Golan Heights (13.5%)

Pelter Winery, Kibbutz Marom Hagolan (www.pelterwinery.co.il)

Tal Pelter's winery isn't much to look at—a modern warehouse. His background is impressive—he studied at Hebrew University, took a degree in wine science from the University of Perth, Australia, and spent several vintages working at Australian wineries, where he gained valuable experience. You know something special is going on when you enter the winery and are given a glass of an excellent *méthode champenoise* sparkling wine. Pelter is one of only two producers of such wines in Israel (Golan Heights is the other); the wine is refreshing, lively, dry, and delicious. Pelter searches out different terroirs for his various wines, including Golan Heights, the Judean Hills, and the Upper Galilee. His is not a kosher winery—he takes a hands-on approach, working with growers and managing his own vineyard. High altitude is key, he notes. Pelter's wines overall are expressive and rich, though not inexpensive, befitting someone who is fanatical about getting everything right and desirous of staying small.

> *Favorite wines: 2011 Pelter Gewürztraminer, Galilee (13.2%); 2008 Pelter T Selection Cabernet Sauvignon, Golan Heights (14.4%)*

GALILEE

Galilee means many things to many people, especially Christians, yet it is more than just the area around Lake Kinneret (Tiberias), the Wedding at Cana or the hilltown of Safad, famous for its orthodox Jewish learning centers. The mountains and valleys that spread across this large area of northern Israel to the Lebanese border has been prime wine-growing country for millennia, and currently producing wines that are at the top of every critic's best of Israel lists.

Galil Mountain Winery, Kibbutz Yiron (www.galilmountain.co.il)

Founded in 2000 as a joint venture between Kibbutz Yiron and Golan Heights Winery, Galil Mountain Winery is a spectacular new winery. This estate vineyard is located at 2,200 feet (675 m), not far from the Lebanese border, and most of the vineyards are found here as well. This area of the Upper Galilee, winemaker Micah Vaadia points out, "is quite different from the Golan. There the volcanic basalt soils are only 2 million years old, very young soils. Here at Galil Mountain ours are 120 million-year-old terra rossa limestone soils formed when the mountains uplifted from the ocean floor." Elevations range from 1,400 to 2,600 feet (420 to 780 m) with moderate temperatures, presenting wines with excellent structure and acidity in most vintages.

Vaadia received his master's in enology from UC Davis and feels fortunate to make wine here because the vineyards allow him to craft a wide variety of wines, yet he also "feels part of an ancient tradition of winemaking in this area extending back 3,000 years. Archaeologists have found many old gats in the area, including one near our vineyard at Malkiyya by the border. And the lintel above the entrance to the fourth-century CE Baram Synagogue—2 kilometers away—has grape clusters carved into it."

Galil Mountain makes about eighty-five thousand cases each year from five sites, totaling 222 acres (90 ha). The highly efficient kosher winery is set up for gravity flow, and wines are robust, flavorful, and rich.

Favorite wine: 2010 Galil Mountain Barbera, Upper Galilee (14.5%)

Ramot Naftaly Winery, Moshav Ramot Naftali
Upper Galilee (www.ramotnaftaly.com)

Yitzhak Cohen, Ramot Naftaly's founder-winemaker, began growing grapes in the Kedesh Valley below the moshav in the mid-1990s. Tel Kedesh, a Canaanite citadel, had been famous in ancient times for its wines; archaeologists have unearthed from the site old coins that show grapes on them. The Kedesh Valley, Cohen explains, is "quite cool, as it is in a bowl surrounded by the hills, so cold air stays trapped until about 10 a.m. It is one of the coolest sites in northern Galilee, a great area for red wines, though only moderately high altitude [1,300 feet/400 m]." To age his red wines Cohen usually uses only Italian-style 20 hl *botti*—big oval casks. "My grapes have a lot of structure and tannin, and don't need small oak barrels," he notes. His kosher wines are amiable, with strong personalities, just like their creator.

Favorite wines: 2007 Ramot Naftaly Barbera, Upper Galilee (13%); 2008
Ramot Naftaly Cabernet Sauvignon Reserve, Upper Galilee (13.5%)

Shvo Vineyards, Jish/Gush Halav Upper Galilee (www.shvo.co.il)

Brand new, with small production but a grand vision, Gaby Sadan's Shvo Vineyards and winery in Upper Galilee reflect his great international wine experience and his many years at Golan Heights Winery. The Shvo winery, in a dilapidated old apple-processing shed in Jish, an ancient Maronite Christian and Muslim town, uses solar panels for energy. Sadan has spent his money on the vineyards and began planting 25 acres (10 ha) at 2,600 to 3,000 feet (800 to

900 m) on the slopes of Mount Merom in 2006. He planted *en gobelet* (as bush vines) 6 acres (2.5 ha) of grenache as he had seen the success of that variety in Australia. Sadan hopes to produce five thousand cases; now he makes half that amount every year.

Sadan planted syrah in a location with limestone, gravel, and flint soils along with a unique quartz concretion called brainstone. The steep site is exposed to direct breezes from the sea, which is only 12 miles (20 km) west, and its annual rainfall of 32 inches (800 mm) is high enough to allow dry-farming. He focuses on Rhône blends, sauvignon blanc, and barbera. The future looks bright, judging by the early wines we tasted.

Favorite wines: 2009 Shvo Vineyards Red Blend, Upper Galilee (14%)

> *This is a deliciously floral, southern Rhône-like blend, despite the inclusion of 20% Barbera. It is based on syrah (45%) and further includes grenache and mourvèdre. Deeply colored, it has strong aromas of dark berries along with spicy licorice and hints of roasted meat. The nicely tannic flavors unfold with lovely fruit purity and mineral-graphite top notes. It finishes strong and well balanced, and it deserves aging until 2019.*

2010 Shvo Vineyards Barbera Rosé, Upper Galilee (13%)

SHOMRON (SAMARIA)

Shomron is where ancient Israelites drank fine wines from lavish bowls and conducted drinking festivals (Amos 6:1). It was known for its fecund vineyards, treading of grapes, wine making, and fine wines (Judg. 9:27). Samaria's coastal areas were among the first to be planted millennia ago, and again in the modern era, beginning with Baron Rothschild. Yet Shomron also extends into the mountainous area north of Jerusalem, incorporating such famous wine areas as Shiloh.

Binyamina Winery, Binyamina (www.binyaminawines.com)

Founded in 1948 as Eliaz Winery (after the owner's son, who was killed in the War of Independence) and renamed Binyamina Winery, this winery now is owned by a local group of Israeli business people. Previously a producer of staid wines, Binyamina now is one of Israel's better producers of fine kosher wines and its fourth largest. The reason for its success lies in its direct control of excellent vineyards across the land, from the deep Negev to the Golan Heights, and investment in new technology. The fines wines are crafted by Sasson Ben Aharon, the chief winemaker, and his second-in-command, Asaf Paz (see also the Vitkin Family Vineyard).

While we were visiting Binyamina, Ben Aharon explained why being a kosher winery frustrates some Israeli winemakers and how the new owners of Binyamina helped resolve a difficult issue. "In a kosher winery there is a major problem of not being able to work the wines during the High Holidays and Shabbat. We cannot, as winemakers, touch the wines except to have one of the observant Jewish workers do what we need, which is both frustrating and time consuming, especially when they are not around at all on the holidays. So the owners bought expensive new equipment, especially a computer-controlled temperature and pumping system, after we explained the economic and quality-control aspects to them. Now we can be gone three or four days even and still have complete control by programming before the holiday begins."

Binyamina also has a separate brand, The Cave, which is a super-premium production of cabernet-based wines from its best vineyard, made in small amounts and aged in the sixteenth-century man-made cave near Zich'ron Ya'acov that was used in the 1890s by Baron Edmund de Rothschild.

Located south of Mount Carmel's lower slopes, Binyamina has revived early modern Israeli varieties like old vine carignan and grenache and excellent mature vine zinfandel, and also produces modern classics from cabernet and syrah. Overall the wines are generous, supple, and ripe, as well as good value.

Favorite wines: 2008 The Chosen Diamond (13.5%)

> *The Chosen, the winery's high-end label, is a reflection of the winemaker's creativity, named for the Hoshen stones (the biblical term for the carefully chosen precious stones set in the breastplate of the high priest). For the Diamond the cabernet (50%) is from Kidmat Zvi in the Golan and Kerem Ben Zimra in the Upper Galilee, while the syrah (40%) and petit verdot (10%) come from vineyards at lower elevations in central Israel. With restrained oaky character though aged in 90% new French oak barrels, there is no dominant oaky aroma. Rather, this has wonderfully polished, rich, and stylish vanilla and blackberry flavors integrated with hints of graphite, herbs, and balanced tannins. Diamond should age well through 2018.*

2008 The Cave, Upper Galilee (13.5%)

> A wine to reckon with from its first vintage in 2000, the Cave comes from a spe-
> cial, low-yielding vineyard in Upper Galilee and is aged for 24 months in French
> oak. This vintage is 67% cabernet sauvignon and the rest merlot, with 2% petit
> verdot. Although it is unlike Bordeaux in character, it is equally polished and
> elegant, the bouquet discretely complex, with herbs, light tobacco, oak spice, and
> black currant. This medium full-bodied wine has flavors that are bright, inte-
> grated with fine tannins, and a finish that has a hint of roasted cherry. It should
> mature well through 2018.

2009 Binyamina Carignan, Lower Galilee Reserve (13%)

Carmel Winery, Zichron Ya'acov (*www.carmelwines.co.il*)

Telling the story of Israel's largest and oldest active winery would take far
more space than we have, but here are a few highlights to fan your curiosity.
Three Israeli prime ministers worked here: David Ben-Gurion, Levi Eshkol,
and Ehud Olmert. "Carmel was a successful Zionist business," noted Adam
Montefiore, Carmel's wine development director, who also writes on wine for
the *Jerusalem Post*. "Zionism means 'working on the land to make it your own,'
and Labor Zionism is what settled the country, through the efforts of people
like Ben-Gurion and Chaim Weizmann, the first president." Carmel made the
first oak-aged wine in Israel in 1976, too.

Carmel today makes one million cases of wine each year and controls
3,470 acres (1,400 ha), all under the guidance of Lior Lacser, the chief winemaker, who studied in Burgundy. Since the late 1990s he has worked hard to
modernize the old wineries, planted new, higher-quality vineyards in Galilee,
pioneered planting in the Negev, and regraded all the vineyards so he pays for
grapes according to quality, not quantity.

"The changes brought by the new management allowed us to stop producing anything except wine, brandy, and juice," Montefiore explained. "Ten years
ago all Carmel wines were mevushal—now none are. We now separate wines
into four different tiers with Carmel Fine Wines, including prestige blends
and single vineyard wines at the top, Appellation and Private Collection in the
middle, and Selected for easy drinking, inexpensive wines. Selected is now the
largest-selling brand in Israel." To us the turnaround is remarkable. We tasted
our way through two dozen wines, and the top wines are consistently expressive,
while the more commercial wines are true to type and offer solid refreshment.

Favorite wines: 2008 Carmel Mediterranean Blend (13.5%)

> The blend is a tribute to Baron Rothschild's legacy and Lacser's modern vision, an effort to reinvent a "taste of Israel." Crafted with wine from vineyards all over Israel, its composition is 35% old vine carignan, 22% syrah, 20% petit verdot, 18% petite syrah, and 2% each of malbec and viognier. Enticingly aromatic, with scents of smoky bacon, garrigue herbs, violet, and black pepper, the flavors are well balanced and solid. This lovely medium full-bodied blend finishes with notes of graphite and black cherry; it's quite elegant yet full without being coarse. It's delicious now and will be even better in 2015.

2010 Carmel Single Vineyard Riesling, Kayoumi Vineyard Upper Galilee (13%)

Margalit Winery, Caesarea (www.margalit-winery.com)

Professor Yair Margalit started his now legendary vineyard and winery in 1991. At the time he was teaching at Technion University and writing two influential textbooks on wine chemistry. Today he is researching a new book and still making fine wine, assisted by his winemaker son Assaf. Margalit Winery has 25 acres (10 ha) of vineyards producing just 1,800 cases a year; 70 percent comes from the original vineyard at Kadita in Upper Galilee, the rest from near Binyamina, all with Bordeaux varieties plus a little petite syrah. The early vintages were quite full and perhaps a bit rustic. Since 2001 Assaf Margalit has been "trying to make a more elegant style, between New and Old World wines, more expressive of our terroir." Margalit's wines are not kosher.

Favorite wine: 2009 Enigma, Galilee and Shomron (14%)

Recanati Winery, Emek Hefer Industrial Zone
Hadera (www.recanati-winery.com)

Recanati Winery, a medium-sized winery (eighty-five thousand cases) located in an industrial park not far from Caesarea, makes some of the most consistently flavorful wines in the country. It has one of Israel's finest winemakers, Gil Shatzberg, who took over in 2008 from an equally respected man, the American Lewis Pasco.

Lenny Recanati, the owner, is truly passionate about wine and has allowed Shatzberg the opportunity to make wines according to what the vineyard potential offers. The company controls 275 acres (110 ha), many in top Upper Galilee sites or in the Judean Hills.

Shatzberg worked at Trefethen Winery in Napa Valley in 1991 and sees his challenge today as "making wines with less massive character and more fruit finesse and lower alcohols, though 2010 presented a challenge in that area." He limits the amount of new oak, matching precisely a particular cooper's barrels with the wine best suited to it. A student of Israel's recent wine history, Shatzberg produces one of the best old-vine carignans from the only head-trained vineyard in the country, in the Judean Hills. Equally refreshing is Recanati's reasonable pricing, even for Reserve wines. The wines are kosher.

Favorite wine: 2011 Recanati Rosé, Upper Galilee (12%)

Saslove Winery, Kibbutz Eyal (www.saslove.com)

Owner-founder Barry Saslove, an engineer, came to Israel to fight in the Six-Day War in 1967 and stayed on to become one of Israel's finest wine educators. Then he decided to put his money where his mouth was and started the winery in 1998. Since 2002 his enthusiastic daughter Roni Saslove has made the wines with her father's guidance, although she has a master's degree in enology from Brock University, Ontario. The family owns a vineyard at Kadita in the Upper Galilee and also buys fruit from nearby vineyards at high altitudes to make seven thousand cases of nonkosher wines a year. Most vineyards are farmed organically. Roni Saslove's pet project, begun in 2004, is her Kadita Dessert Wine, a multivintage, cabernet-based port-style wine with 17 percent alcohol; it is quite elegant and not as heavy as most ports.

Favorite wine: 2008 Saslove Adom Cabernet Sauvignon, Upper Galilee (14%)

Smadar Winery, Zichron Ya'acov (www.smadar.com)

Named after founder-owner Moti Shapira's daughter, Smadar is a lovely old legacy from the last century, now part of Zichron Ya'acov's wine renaissance. Shapira is the great-great-grandson of Ze'ev and Esther Shapira, among the original Rumanian Jewish immigrants who settled in Zichron Ya'acov in 1882 and helped develop the original Carmel vineyards. Shapira launched his brand in 1998, creating his small winery and wine bar at his guesthouse in the center of town. The wines originate from 7.5 acres (3 ha) of vineyards at nearby Ein Toot and a 40-year-old carignan vineyard. A small family *garagiste* project,

Smadar is definitely worth searching out for the forthright intensity and generosity of its wines, much like their producer.

Favorite wine: 2007 Smadar Old Vine Carignan, Shomron (13.5%)

Vitkin Family Winery, Kfar Vitkin (www.vitkin-winery.co.il)

Vitkin is truly a family affair—Sharona and Doron Belogolovsky, along with Sharona's brother Asaf Paz, started Vitkin Family Winery next to their house on the moshav founded decades ago by Doron Belogolovky's grandparents. Paz, who studied in California and Bordeaux, convinced his brother-in-law, a stonemason by profession, that they should make wine. That was in 2001. Sharona Belogolovsky, the architect in the family, figured out how to turn the barn into a winery. By 2002 the family had decided to focus on Mediterranean varieties, as well old Israeli standards like French columbard, and, given Paz's travels, pinot noir and Riesling, too. Fruit is sourced from the whole country, "our Israeli journey," as Paz wryly calls it, primarily from cooler locations in the Judean Hills and Upper Galilee. The exception is the superior old vine carignane source from Zichron Ya'acov south of Haifa. The family now makes five thousand cases of kosher wine per year. Paz's wide experience has expanded their thinking. Vitkin now uses only 350-liter puncheons (casks) for the Mediterranean varieties; new barriques (225 liter) being too strong for them, and Vitkin now makes consistently interesting, deeply flavorful, wines.

Favorite wines: 2008 Vitkin Carignan Old Vines, Shomron (14%)

> *The grapes for this wine come from the same old head-trained vineyard as Smadar's; it has low yields and produces wine of a dark black-ruby color. Strong, gamy black plum and strong cedar-smoke aromas combined with graphite provide an auspicious introduction to the flavors; these come from the vineyard, not the barrel. Ripe wild blackberry and roasted cherry flavors envelop the firm tannins. This wine is slightly rustic in a positive way, and it's one to hold on to until 2015 or so.*

2011 Vitkin Dry Riesling, Judean Hills (11.8%)

JUDEAN HILLS

The promise of the Judean Hills begins with the blessing of Jacob in Genesis 27:28 that anticipates many vineyards and dewfall that causes them to grow fecundly. This is where the god Eshcol lived and where spies found huge grape clusters that required two people to carry them on poles (Num. 13). The same attributes make them prosperous today, as the often steep slopes, terra rossa soils, and semi-continental climate provide ideal conditions to grow intensely flavorful grapes, often in the same locale as wines famous three thousand years ago.

Clos de Gat, Kibbutz Har'el, Ayalon Valley (www.closdegat.com)

Considered one of Israel's top wineries since its first vintage in 2001, Clos de Gat is still Israel's only estate vineyard, located near where Joshua defeated the five kings. More recently its tasting room was Yitzhak Rabin's headquarters during the 1948 War of Independence. Named after the three-thousand-year-old *gat*, or winepress, found while clearing the land for vineyards in 1998, Clos de Gat has 47 acres (19 ha) planted. The winemaker-owner Eyal Rotem studied in Australia, though it was his partnership with Kibbutz Har'el that led to Clos de Gat's beginnings. Today it produces eight thousand cases of nonkosher wine annually.

The vineyard is in a low-lying bowl between hills at an elevation of 820 feet (250 m). Daytime temperatures are not extreme, and nights are cool. The soils are comprised of limestone and clay with chalk rendzina (humus-rich soil formed from the weathering of rocks, especially limestone and gypsum). The presence of the *gat* is evidence that wine has been produced here for a long time, but Rotem chose the site because "no one in this area was making wine, and the soils showed excellent potential." He uses ambient yeasts and French oak barrels, with all reds "punched down" by hand during fermentation to mix the skins and solids with the juice for good extraction. Yields are quite low, about two tons per acre. Clos de Gat's wines show flair, elegance, and richness, along with definitive structure more akin to France than Australia.

Favorite wine: 2007 Clos de Gat Ayalon Valley, Judean Hills (14%)

> *Rotem's superbly crafted flagship Bordeaux blend is dominated by cabernet sauvignon, with merlot and petit verdot. Its dark ruby color leads to pleasing aromas of black cherry, tea, cassis, and fine oak spice. The wine was aged for 18 months in new French oak casks. Between Bordeaux and Washington in character, this wine has plenty of rich cassis-berry fruit, integrated oak-vanilla, creamy yet firm tannins, and a long finish that suggests a fine future—as long as 2020 or so.*

Domaine du Castel, Moshav Ramat Raziel (www.castel.co.il)

Eli Ben-Zaken's property lies in the hills a few miles west of Jerusalem. Ben-Zaken gave up his previous career as a Jerusalem restaurateur, planted vines on his property's terra rossa limestone-clay soils in 1988, and made his first wine in 1991. Another vineyard overlooking a steep wadi, a dry canyon-like wash, was planted soon after in nearby Tzuba. He took as his motto words from Winston Churchill's speech during the London Blitz, when he felt as though he "were walking with Destiny, and that all my past life had been but a preparation for this hour and for this trial. . . . I was sure I should not fail." Chutzpah? Well, no. Domaine du Castel is considered one of Israel's finest wineries. Today it has several parcels totaling about 40 acres (16 ha) of vines. Ben-Zaken, who is fond of Bordeaux wines, emulated that area's philosophy, planting densely—11,000 to 16,500 vines per acre (4,400 to 6,700 vines/ha; the average in Israel is 5,400 vines per acre, or 2,200 vines/ha, according to Ben-Zaken). He makes about 8,500 cases of kosher wine each year, and he has gained worldwide renown for the restrained, nuanced, yet deeply flavorful wines he makes.

> *Favorite wine: 2008 Domaine du Castel Grand Vin, Jerusalem–Haute Judée (14%)*
>
> > *Ben-Zaken's top wine displays elegant claret-like finesse and structure, with fine tannins, graphite, and black fruit flavors and cassis-cedar aromas mixed with dried herbs. It's not a big wine, more a pretty, stylish Saint Julien Bordeaux type that should age gracefully through 2020.*

Tzora Winery, Kibbutz Tzora (www.tzoravineyards.com)

Tzora is the beloved bequest to terroir of its late creator, Ronnie James, called the "doctor of terroir" by his friends and colleagues. James spent years in agriculture, scoping out the various landscapes of the Judean Hills, locating unique sites for grapes, some dating to biblical times. Tzora's vineyards, first planted in 2001, cover two key sites, Neve Ilan at 2,000 feet (600 m) above the Ayalon Valley near Clos de Gat, and the home vineyard at Shoresh (2,600 feet/800 m), high on northwest-facing hillside terra rossa limestone soils. The young winemaker is Eran Pick, who studied at UC Davis and worked in Bordeaux, where he initially met Tzora's famed consultant, Jean-Claude Berrouet, for decades the technical director of the renowned Chateau Pétrus. Tzora's plan is to further develop James's vision of producing distinguished wines without being overwhelmed with technological wizardry. Only four wines are made, all kosher.

Favorite wine: 2010 Tzora Neve Ilan Chardonnay, Judean Hills (14%)

JERUSALEM HILLS

Ella Valley Vineyards (www.ellavalley.com)

Located in the beautiful and historic Ella Valley, where David fought Goliath and where vineyards have been planted for millennia, Ella Valley Vineyards began in 1998. Owner Danny Valero desired to create a premium winery that would attract agritourists headed to Kibbutz Netiv HaLamed-Heh. The first wines were made in 2002, and today the lovely winery has two vineyards, Aderet at 1,500 feet (450 m), a warm site on limestone and not far from the ancient town of Itry, which includes a fine rock *gat*; and at Nes Harim at 2,500 feet (750 m), a cooler site on terra rossa.

Udi Kaplan manages the winery, overseeing the vineyards, while Lin Gold, who studied in Australia, is the vivacious winemaker; she joined Ella Valley in 2011. For both the goal is producing terroir-driven high-quality kosher wines at different price points. Although Ella Valley is known for well-crafted wines, Gold is concentrating on producing more refined, less powerful wines.

Favorite wine: 2010 Ella Valley Vineyards Chardonnay, Judean Hills (13.5%)

Gvaot Winery, Givat Harel, Shiloh (www.gvaot-winery.com)

This beautiful vineyard site near ancient Shiloh in the West Bank hills north of Jerusalem is where Joshua "divided the land to the sons of Israel according to their divisions" (Josh. 18:10). Shivi Drori, the winemaker, is an agronomist by training and a wine lover by culture. His recent research: analyzing the DNA of Israeli grape varieties that survived the Muslim takeover centuries ago. "About 35 varieties survived," he notes, "mostly big berried, fleshy table grapes with low sugar accumulation. We have 26 being examined via DNA extraction with known names. The trick is to see if they are related to better varieties, or if these can be propagated in a better way to make good wine."

Drori decided in 2000 to plant a vineyard on the escarpment 2,600 feet (800 m) above the deep Shiloh Wadi in an area historically given over to vineyards on the ancient terraces of terra rossa limestone and rendzinas. The site of the ancient temple at Shiloh lies across from the vineyard, and the area clearly has aptitude for wine-growing. Drori made his first wines in 2005 and remains a small producer, turning out just two thousand cases a year. His wines, which are kosher, reveal fine intensity, and visitors get a bonus, the chance to see several ancient Samarian winepresses.

Favorite wine: 2010 Gvaot Pinot Noir, Harel Vineyard (13.5%)

> *Drori is convinced Shiloh is an excellent area for pinot noir, and this first vintage speaks the truth. It is light ruby-violet in color, with true pinot aromas of black cherry and slight oak-vanilla that lead to similar fruit flavors, medium tannins, and a firm but cool finish indicative of the refreshing climate, especially at night.*

Sea Horse Winery, Moshav Bar Giora (www.seahorsewines.com)

One of Israel's most eccentric, smallest, and most distinctive wineries, Seahorse started with *Lying Down in a Cool Dark Place*, a documentary-fantasy about Israel's wine industry by Ze'ev Dunie, a Jerusalem indie filmmaker. His curiosity aroused, he spent time working with the late Ronnie James at his nearby Tzora Winery, learning how to make wine. Dunie started Seahorse in 2000, with wines named variously for film directors (Fellini), artists (Munch), or writers (Camus). Dunie loves quirky wines, so his are devoted to Rhône grapes, chenin blanc, and even zinfandel. The elfin Dunie's philosophy is simple: "I don't have a vision of the wine when I start making it. I try to go along and figure out what's the best approach to these grapes. I let the young wines lead the way, not try to control them." Dunie's wines are just as remarkable as their creator; they are not kosher.

Favorite wines: 2009 Seahorse James Chenin Blanc, Shomron (13.5%);
2009 Seahorse Munch Petite Sirah, Jerusalem Hills (ca. 14%)

Tzuba Estate Winery, Kibbutz Palmach Tzuba (www.tzubawinery.co.il)

As soon as we met Eitan Green, Tzuba's manager, he showed us a wonderful limestone-carved winepress from the First Temple period that was found "when we started cleaning up the area on the grounds. We then found the remains of a guard tower built from the stones taken out of the old vineyards, most likely twenty-six hundred years ago." Green, who grew up in Westchester, New York, has lived at the kibbutz, home of the winery since 1948, for 40 years and works with Paul Dubb, the winemaker, who is a native of South Africa. The original vineyard was created 15 years ago by Eli Ben-Zaken of nearby Domaine du Castel but planted by Dubb. At 125 acres (50 ha), Tzuba's is the largest vineyard in the Jerusalem hills. The firm was begun in 2005, according to Green, to develop wines "distinctive to the Jerusalem hills."

Stephen Sherman, the winery's agronomist, later showed us what has been excavated during the last half-century across the road from the winery: a large compound of winepresses dating from the ninth century BCE through the first century CE.

The estate controls all its vineyards, and the wines are kosher. Green points out, and we noted this too, that a recent trend in Israel for smaller wineries is to move away from varietal wines to blends. Tzuba produces consistent, elegant wines that reflect its high elevation (2,900 feet/895 m) and cool sites.

Favorite wine: 2008 Tzuba Metzuda Dry Reserve (14%)

NEGEV

The Negev, where Abraham sojourned, experienced a much cooler climate and more water during the early Bronze Age than it does now. That is why ancient winepresses have been found there. During a period when the Israelites had learned about irrigation, biblical writers make reference to a forest (Ezek. 20:47) and watercourses in the Negev (Ps. 126:4). Just as wines were produced then, they are produced today, often in the same places, such as Arad.

Yatir Winery, Tel Arad (www.yatir.net)

Yatir Winery is located just a five-minute drive from the great archaeological site of Tel Arad's Canaanite ruins in the northeastern Negev at 1,625 feet (500 m). The winery was founded as a joint venture of Carmel Winery and local growers in Ramat Arad in 2000. The vineyard is just 15 minutes from the scenic Yatir Forest, Israel's largest, at an elevation of 2,900 feet (900 m). The climate is significantly cooler where wine has been made for three thousand years, evidenced by the large number of stone winepresses found. The forest is at the southeastern edge of the Judean Hills and thus the reason for the Lion of Judah on its label. Ya'acov Ben-Dor, Yatir's manager and an amateur archae-ologist, told us that the Romans took a lot of wine "from this area as taxes. We also think this is where Lot and his daughters took refuge in the caves where wine was stored—it is not far from Hebron. King David bought wine from here as well. Today we have to use electric fences, as we still have problems like the ancients with jackals and gazelles, even hyenas, who come and eat the grapes."

Yatir Forest's wines are made by the gregarious and widely traveled Eran Goldwasser, who has a degree in enology and worked in Australia, then at Carmel, before being promoted to run Yatir Winery. Goldwasser insists that the vineyard makes these wines; yields are naturally low (about 3 tons per acre), so he never needs to use more than a total of 33 percent new oak casks for aging the red wines. These are rich, insistent, and strongly mineral-inflected wines, reflecting the thin soils and limestone clay–loess geology. The winery produces about 12,500 cases of kosher wine each year.

Favorite wines: 2008 Yatir Shiraz, Judean Hills (15%)

> *Given its ripeness, this is an amazingly well-balanced and delicious shiraz. Its color is nearly opaque, and it has meaty, blackberry-charcoal aromas: textbook shiraz/syrah. The flavors show harmonious oak, subtly infusing the ripe berry and roasted meat and fruit flavors with some nutty sweetness, while the finish is generous and balanced. It will be even better by 2015.*

2010 Yatir Viognier, Judean Hills (13.5%)

MORE WINERIES OF INTEREST IN ISRAEL

We visited and enjoyed the following wineries, all of which are worth searching out for their fine wines. We regret the lack of space to make detailed comments:

Amphorae, Shomron, www.amphoraewines.com

Bahat Winery, Ba'azalet Ha'Golan, Golan Heights, www.bazelet-hagolan.co.il

Barkan Wine Cellars, Samson, www.barkan-winery.co.il

Ben Zimra Winery, Upper Galilee, www.yekev-benzimra.com

Dalton Winery, Upper Galilee, www.dalton-winery.com

Flam Winery, Judean Hills, www.flamwinery.com

Miles Vineyards, Upper Galilee

Mony Vineyard, Judean Hills, www.walla.co.il

Odem Mountain Winery, Golan Heights

Na'aman Wines, Upper Galilee, www.naamanwine.co.il

Tanya Winery, Shomron West Bank, www.tanyawinery.co.il

Tishbi, Shomron Winery, www.tishbi.com

Israel's fine wineries should be part of any Holy Land tour people take to experience the archaeological revelations of ancient Israel. One should savor the great wines that Israel produces today while imagining just how amazing the wines were in the days of the patriarchs, prophets, sages, and Jesus. Israel's terroir, once the best of ages past, still flourishes today.

Eleven

GREECE

The peoples of the Mediterranean began to emerge from barbarism when they learned to cultivate the olive and the vine.

—Thucydides

Modern Greece has had its share of difficulties in recent years, including an imploding economy, but wine quality isn't one of them. Since the Classical Age (490–332 BCE), Greek wines have never been as good as they are today. The country's wine making has come a long way from even the early 1980s, when most visitors to the country still experienced horrible turpentine-flavored retsina (pine-resinated wine). It's no surprise that tourists wondered whether the praise for Greek cuisine and wines they had heard was a sick joke or if the only "glory that was Greece" lay among the ruins they scurried to visit.

A BRIEF HISTORY OF MODERN GREEK WINES

During the Byzantine period wine was still important to Greece. The Eastern Orthodox Church and nobility were the primary producers. Beginning in the twelfth century CE the empire gave preference to Venetian wine traders to the ruin of Greek producers, who saw their favorite styles copied by Italians and exported to Greece and Byzantium at preferential prices and poorer quality. When Byzantium fell to the Turks in 1453, Greece was allowed to continue wine production, but it was taxed and regulated so severely that effectively wine production ceased.

In a final blow the Turks destroyed Greece's vineyards during the 1821 revolution that led to independence from the hated Turks. Islands like Crete, which the Turks had not conquered, had continued to produce and export good wines, but by independence in 1830 these markets had collapsed.

The growing of wine grapes was revived in the nineteenth century and was based on small farm plots. Only the spread of phylloxera in western Europe in the 1870s led Greeks to plant more wine and table grapes, however. This brought new prosperity, as Greek grape producers exported wine and raisins to a wine-deprived West. After phylloxera finally invaded Greece in the early 1900s and vineyards died, the wine trade was not revived. Vineyard production in western Europe had returned to quantity levels last seen before phylloxera struck. These wineries no longer needed Greek wine to bolster their production.

As the Greeks' economy tanked, many emigrated between 1890 and 1925. A saving grace was the establishment of cooperatives that allowed farmers to sell their grapes at an agreed-upon price to a guaranteed buyer. But without quality incentives, this practice had highly negative consequences for Greek wine's reputation. Which isn't to say that all co-ops then created were poorly managed and made bad wines. One of Greece's best wineries today is the 80-year-old Agricultural Union of Samos, which makes one of the world's finest sweet wines. The two world wars further devastated the country, ruining agricultural land, decimating the population, inhibiting trade, and ultimately breeding a horrific civil war. Nonetheless a few families (Kourtakis, Boutari, Cambas, and others) managed to create substantial companies. By the late 1960s an improved economy allowed people to travel and study abroad, to experience the renowned wines and traditions of France and Italy, and see that retsina was not the only wine in the cellar.

Indeed the increased competition of the era propelled the large producers to start making wines that adhered to a new appellation of origin system. These Greek wines were produced from well-known French varieties (the first cabernet sauvignon planted in Greece arrived in 1950), along with important indigenous varieties.

New wineries like Domaine Carras used the services of famed French enologists like Emile Peynaud of Bordeaux to fine-tune and help craft their own terroir-based brands. The more ambitious producers established boutique wineries in the 1970s, and wealthy people who liked the cachet and had a true interest in wine began to invest in vineyards.

A NEW GOLDEN AGE

In 1985 the Athens Technical Educational Institute (TEI) established a formal degree program in enology. Soon it began to provide technically com-
petent professionals, while several now-famous producers, like Evangelos
Gervassiliou and Yannis Paraskevopoulos of Gaia Estate, took advanced degrees from Bordeaux, then returned to mentor this new group of young, mo-
tivated people. Aspiring winemakers realized they didn't need to go abroad to
get a good education because they could enroll in TEI's program.

Some would soon launch their own estates, others decided to create an
estate product and took over from parents who had sold to the co-ops. By the
1990s the once moribund Wine Institute's efforts to identify, develop, and improve Greece's important indigenous cultivars began to show results, providing better plant material for the new winemakers and their nascent vineyards.
This revived the growing of wine grapes in areas that had not been famous for
centuries, such as Santorini with its ancient assyrtiko and the resurgence of
Naoussa's xinomavro.

Today the biggest problem Greek winemakers face is not dissimilar to
what happened two thousand years ago, when the Romans conquered Greece.
Modern Greek wines of quality struggle in a similarly competitive marketplace and have a double hurdle to surmount: small quantities produced from
unfamiliar varieties and name-brand competition from elsewhere, without an
equivalent to the Roman aristocracy that considered Greek wines a mark of
sophistication and good "breeding" worth buying in large amounts. But new
programs and tourism do help to overcome these obstacles. Greece and its
modern yet tradition-laced wines are more exciting and delicious than ever. In
Greece one can try wines where Saint Paul or Caesar traveled and drink them
with local dishes, perhaps similar to those enjoyed by the ancients thousands
of years ago.

LAND

Greece is about the size of Wisconsin and nearly 75 percent mountainous. The
rest lies close to the sea, with many islands and miles of coastline. Greek vineyards hug mountain slopes, lie on relatively high plateau country, or overlook

the sea, sometimes all three. The geology of Greece is primarily sedimentary limestones and sandstones created by shifting tectonic plates that lifted the seabed and by millions of years of erosion and compression. Only the far northern areas, near Bulgaria or Albania, are primarily of volcanic or igneous matter. Several Aegean islands such as Santorini are purely volcanic. As elsewhere the individuality of a vineyard's soil composition defines much of its wine's style, factors that we will consider when we discuss individual producers. Equally important is weather.

CLIMATE

Greece lies between 34 and 42 degrees north, between Crete, which is not far from Africa, and Macedonia on the Albanian border. These latitudes provide classic Mediterranean climate traits—wet winters that are cool to cold; mild springs; warm, dry summers; and moderately warm autumns with rain returning in October. The temperature grows cooler the farther north one travels. The climate also changes as the altitude does. Although grapes were largely planted near the sea on easy slopes or terraced mountainsides in antiquity, modern Greek producers have also pursued more difficult and climatically challenging areas, often at elevations of 2,000 to 3,300 feet (600 to 1,000 m).

Inland and at higher elevations the climate becomes more continental, with much colder winters, including snowfall, and hot summers punctuated by thunderstorms. Islands with hot summers, like Santorini, plant vineyards so that they face north to avoid the worst heat. Many vineyards in Greece are farmed with no irrigation, so moving to cooler sites makes for smart farming and refined wines.

Winds blow frequently, especially in the islands and northern mountains, ventilating the vineyards and reducing mildew. Too much wind, however, whether it's hot or cold, can shut the vines down, preventing photosynthesis. This is one reason why some wines may have an alcohol content lower than expected; when photosynthesis shuts down, the vine accumulates sugar more slowly. This allows the time necessary for other metabolic processes that create phenolic compounds and flavors to mature and provide better balanced grapes.

APPELLATION

Greece's vineyards, both ancient and modern, are located within regions that are famous in literature and history. Greece's current wine law, enacted in 1971, uses these famous regions as the political and geographic foundation for categorizing wines, effectively dividing Greek wines into "quality wines" and "table wines."

The top-quality wines are designated Protected Designation of Origin (PDO); these include Greece's fine and endangered sweet wines, such as mavrodaphne from Patras and Cephalonia and the muscats Rio de Patras, Samos, Cephalonia, Limnos, and Rhodes. PDO-designated wines must be made only from Greek varieties and have strict production regulations. Not surprisingly they are some of Greece's most prized wines; some, like Santorini, Limnos, and Samos, certainly descended from styles that have been famous for two thousand years or longer. Among Greece's most famous dry wines, with their principal grape in parenthenses, are: Nemea (agiorgitiko), Mantinia (moschofilero), Naoussa (xinomavro) and Santorini (assyrtiko).

Many Greek wine labels are not translated or transliterated; the distinctive red or blue strip label affixed between the foil capsule and the top of the bottle provides an easy way to distinguish a PDO appellation wine. (Increasing numbers of PDO wines now include the anglicized name of the variety on the label.)

In these two highest categories use of the terms *reserve* or *grande reserve* is restricted to aged wines and governed by rules.

Recent legislation from the European Commission has created a new designation, Protected Geographical Indication, or PGI. Wines designated as such are closely linked to a specific geographic area. A third category established by the European Commission, Traditional Specialty Guaranteed (TSG), "highlights traditional character, either in the composition or means of production." In Greece retsina carries the TSG designation.

GRAPES

Following the wine trail in modern Greece is not unlike being in Italy; everywhere you turn a new wine made from a grape you never heard of is the local favorite. It may be Greek to you, but it makes the exploration even more worthwhile.

The main French varieties, however, are grown throughout the country and produce highly personable wines in the hands of pioneers like Hatzimichalis in Atalandi, a region in central Greece famous for its wines since the fourth century BCE.

Greece's current inventory of indigenous grapes is probably second only to Italy's in Europe. The most famous indigenous white grapes today are assyrtiko, malagousia, moschofilero, robola, roditis, and savatiano, though the last is not as capable of regularly producing fine wines, but it has been extensively planted for retsina. Most produce dry wines, although the assyrtiko is the backbone of Santorini's ancient and famous sweet *vinsanto* wine, made from sun-dried grapes and aged for several years in cask. Indeed the extraordinary aspect of Greece's wine scene is that it is a warm country, but its indigenous white wines often garner greater praise than the more logically acclimated reds. Various muscats also have been in Greece for thousands of years, but they probably originated farther east, in Asia Minor. Sweet muscats predominate, but excellent dry ones can also be found on Samos and Rhodes, for example.

Other indigenous white varieties to seriously consider are aidani, athiri, dafní, kidonitsa, lagorthi, monemvasia, thrapsathiri, and vilana. Of the foreign varieties in Greece, our favorite overall would be sauvignon blanc, with good chardonnays and semillon being made as well.

The top indigenous red grapes are the aforementioned agiorgitiko, mavrodaphne, and xinomavro. Many of these varieties are characterized by their ability to mature properly at relatively low alcohol levels. There are some, however, like xinomavro and mandalaria, that are strongly tannic and have firm acidity, too. While these wines can be quite tasty with typical Greek cuisine, solo they are a bit tough. Great progress has been made to adapt fermentation techniques and viticultural practices to yield more pliant wines.

Our favorite indigenous red varieties, in addition to those we have already mentioned, include mavrotragano, mandalaria, kotsifali, and liatiko (more for sweet than dry wines) in the Aegean, and limnio, limniona, mavroudi, negoska, refosco, stavroto, and vertzami in northern Greece. Of the foreign varieties, syrah enjoys particular success in Greece. Fine cabernets (sauvignon and franc) and merlot have been made in Greece for several decades, but syrah really entered the game only in the early 1990s at Chateau Carras in northern Greece.

Another happy surprise in Greece today is the quality and freshness of rosé wines made from indigenous and foreign varieties. Dry, sappy, crisp, and minerally, these are among the best anywhere in the world and among the top echelon with local dishes.

BACK TO THE FUTURE: NOTABLE GREEK PRODUCERS

Journeying through modern Greek vineyards is also a trip back in time through landscapes mentioned in Homer, Herodotus, and several classic Greek myths. Greece has hundreds of producers, and our intention is not to present an encyclopedic review or appraisal of all Greek producers; rather, we have selected those we think readers should know about and that we find especially interesting.

We begin our tour of Greek producers in northern Greece: Macedonia, Thrace, Epirus, and Thessaly. Unless noted otherwise, we use the anglicized names for places visited. Northern Greece is the general geographic area where Paul addressed his earliest letter to the Thessalonians, who basically quit their jobs and stopped working because they expected Jesus to return at any minute.

NORTHERN GREECE: THRACE, MACEDONIA, AND EPIRUS

Boutari Wineries, Naoussa, Macedonia (www.boutari.gr)

Historically among the most important family wine growers in Greece, the Boutaris family began producing wines here in 1879. Today their wineries produce wines in Santorini, Attica, Crete, Mantinea, and Goumenissa, with independent teams making estate-bottled wines under the watchful eye of Yannis Voyatzis, the long-time chief enologist. Despite what outside critics have said, "Xinomavro is not a harsh, tannic wine," Voyatzis maintains. "This issue arises because we [most producers/farmers] don't manage tannins well, and we are not getting full maturity. Low yields are important but [should] not [be] too low." Voyatzis recognizes that Naoussa is not an easy area. "We do a lot of microvinifications to understand vineyard blocks of our farmers better in order to help them," he notes. "Naoussa is a terroir region." Voyatzis takes account of xinomavro's difficult nature in the winery with new techniques like cold juice maceration, which has produced positive results. Boutari's Naoussa wines clearly express the potential for elegance with intensity that xinomavro can achieve. The Nemea wines from agiorgitiko vines show a similar degree of focus, intensity, and attention to growing the grapes properly, in order to do service to "the noblest Greek red grape variety," according to Voyatzis.

Favorite wines: 2004 Boutari Grande Reserve, Naoussa PDO (13%)

> *This wine is a lovely example of Naoussa's potential. Its light ruby-garnet color anticipates a detailed bouquet of dried tomatoes, black cherry, tobacco, and loamy earth. Slightly rustic flavors of sweet, dried sour cherry, balanced tannins, and good acidity contribute lovely finesse, subtlety, and brightness. A fine mature wine.*

2008 Boutari Agiorgitiko, Nemea PDO (13%)

Domaine Gerovassiliou, Epanomi, Thessaloniki (www.gerovassiliou.gr)

One of the most important domaines created in modern Greece, Domaine Gerovassiliou was founded in 1981 by Evangelos Gerovassiliou to produce Greek varieties in a modern manner. It is located south of Thessaloniki in an area that was famous for wine 1,500 years ago. In Epanomi the estate now comprises 138 acres (56 ha) of vineyards, the winery, and a fine wine museum that houses ancient amphoras and Greek pottery.

Gerovassiliou, formerly the enologist at Domaine Porto Carras, began research on one of Greece's best white grapes that had nearly disappeared, the malagousia. He began crafting modern versions of native varieties that were not typical of his area but were important to Greece's future—grapes like assyrtiko and malagousia, as well as the red grapes mavroudi, mavrotragano, and the ancient limnio, Aristotle's "limnios ampelos."

Gerovassiliou has been at the forefront of progress, especially as a mentor for younger producers in northern Greece. His wines are consistently intense and balanced, and they capture the essence of each variety.

Favorite wines: 2008 Gerovassiliou Avaton, Epanomi PGI (13%)

> *This is an astonishingly original blend of 40% limnio ("the oldest attested Greek grape variety," according to Gerovassiliou), 30% mavroudi, and 30%*

mavrotragano from Santorini. "Limnio needs color from the other varieties [both are quite dark]," he notes. Avaton is a ruby-violet color, and its aroma is full of ripe berries, violet with graphite overtones. This wine is medium full-bodied and richly textured, with flavors that combine dark berry fruit with a saline-medicinal character; it is unusual and deliciously refreshing. With fine tannins and some savory notes, Avaton is a complex wine that will be at its best between 2015 and 2018.

2010 Gerovassiliou Malagousia, Epanomi PGI (12.5%)

Kir-Yianni Estate, Yianakohori, Naoussa (www.kiryianni.gr)

Yiannis Boutaris, a scion of the great Boutari family, broke off from the family's business in the 1990s. But before he did so, he cleared forest in Naoussa between 1968 and 1976 to plant xinomavro at a higher elevation than usual and make a richer style. Eventually he struck out on his own, and his wines from that xinomavro vineyard have been acclaimed for 30 years. The original vinestocks came from Amyndeo and did not ripen well in the cooler climate. "The old vines don't get mature enough and have green tannins and high acid," Boutaris noted as we walked an older plantation. "We played around in 1998–99 with late harvesting, but it didn't work. About seven or eight years ago we started replanting with new clones that are much better. They ripen evenly, produce smaller clusters and berries, and we can harvest with full maturity at 13.5% alcohol, which is a wonderful benefit."

Xinomavro is a difficult grape, similar to Barolo's nebbiolo grape—both are relatively vigorous and have low color intensity, strong tannins, and high acidity—but Kir-Yianni's wines show the intelligent, detailed attention required to produce fine wine from a difficult grape in a challenging climate. The chance Yiannis Boutaris took by clearing forest for a new vineyard on an unproved site was well justified.

Favorite wine: 2008 Ramnista Reserve, Naoussa PDO (14%)

Tsantali Mount Athos Vineyards, Aghio Oro, Halkidiki (www.tsantali.gr)

Founded in 1890 by Evangelos Tsantalis, Tsantali is one of Greece's oldest, largest, and most consistently excellent wine producers, with the production decentralized in five wineries in different appellations. Among the most beautiful and important, with 247 acres (100 ha) of vineyards, is the Mount Athos estate, which surrounds the venerable Saint Panteleimon Monastery. In 1972 Tsantalis visited the ancient cliffside monasteries of Athos, a peninsula that juts into the Adriatic between the Singitic Gulf and the Gulf of Strimón. He was smitten by the monasteries' irreplaceable archives, holy spirit, and magical landscapes, including old terraces for vineyards, and decided to bring wine production back to the peninsula and "the monastic tradition of the Mount Athos wine to the outside world."

The Christian holy places of Mount Athos, which is at the tip of the peninsula, have existed for at least 1,700 years, with the first Eastern Orthodox monastery built during the eighth century CE. The monasteries are accessible only by boat and only to male visitors. "Probably there were no vineyards here in ancient times," Pannaiotis Kiriavides, the winemaker, notes, "but the monks likely started planting in the tenth century." The only woman allowed in the monasteries is the Virgin Mary, but anyone can visit the Tsantali winery and savor the wines.

Kiriavides explains that the vineyard lies on sandy-clay limestone soils filled with granitic material that contributes to drainage. The property is only 812 feet above sea level (250 m) at its highest point, but its slopes allow for fine luminosity. The vineyards had disappeared early in the twentieth century after they were wiped out by phylloxera; restoring them has taken decades, yet the climate is excellent with the surrounding forests and sea moderating the air temperature, while runoff from Mount Athos provides enough water to permit dry-farming.

Favorite wine: 2006 Tsantali Metoxi Chromitsa Red, Agioritikos PGI, (13.5%)

OTHER FINE PRODUCERS OF MERIT IN NORTHERN GREECE

Space does not allow us to fully discuss all the fine producers we visited and excellent wines we tasted in each region; there are simply too many. Here is a list of top producers worth seeking out in the marketplace and when visiting Greece.

Alpha Estate, Amyndeon, Florina (www.alpha-estate.com)

Favorite wine: 2008 Alpha Xinomavro Reserve Old Vines, Amyndeon PDO (14%)

Domaine Biblia Chora, Kokkinohori, Kavala,
Macedonia (www.bibliachora.gr)

> *Favorite wines: 2010 Biblia Chora Areti White (Assyrtiko), Pangeo PGI*
> *(14%); 2010 Biblia Chora White, Pangeo PGI (13%)*

Estate Porto Karras, Neos Marmaras, Halkidiki (www.portocarraswines.gr)

> *Favorite wine: 2010 Domaine Porto Carras Hellenic Portraits Assyrtiko,*
> *Sithonia PGI (13%)*

CENTRAL GREECE: EUBOEA, ATTICA, THESSALY

Avantis Estate, Mytika Lilantio, Evia (www.avantiswines.gr)

Apostolos Mountrichas made his first wine at Avantis winery in 1994, but his family's wine-growing history dates to 1830, when his great-grandfather started growing grapes on Euboea near Halkida. Avantis refers to the original settlers, the Avantes, of Euboea, an island off the east coast and separated by a narrow channel from the mainland. The Greeks call the island Evia, whereas it's Negroponte to the Italians.

The Avantes settled in Euboea in the early second millennium BCE and were known as warriors, important enough for Homer to mention in *the Iliad:* Book II: "The fierce Avantes held Euboea with its cities, . . . *rich in vines* . . . Elephenor of the race of Mars was in command of these; . . . chief over all the Avantes . . . fleet of foot and wearing their hair long behind, brave warriors, who would ever strive to tear open the corslets of their foes with their long ashen spears [emphasis added]."

Mountrichas's sustainably farmed vineyards are primarily composed of limestone loamy-clay around the winery, which his grandfather built in 1930. Mountrichas has also planted mavrokoudoura, an ancient, almost extinct, selection of the Aegean mandilaria grape localized to Euboea, with an extremely deep color. "I found this old guy with 60-year-old vines, and I took some cuttings," Mountrihas told us. "It's kind of like barbera." Avantis Estate has a range of consistently delicious wines with fine style at attractive prices.

> *Favorite wine: 2008 Avantis Estate "M" Mandilaria/Mavrokoudoura,*
> *Euboea PGI (14%)*

Katogi and Strofilia, Metsovo, Ioannina and Asprokambos, Nemea (www.katogi-strofilia.gr)

Two wineries and a shared vision united these two family-based wineries in 2001. Katogi Averoff was founded in 1959 by Evangelos Averoff in Metsovo, high up in the Pindus Mountains of Epirus. Averoff was one of Greece's greatest politicians, a strong believer in democracy, a national leader, and a leading intellectual. A wine lover, he found in the local monastery (now a museum) in Metsovo documents describing a strong local wine industry in the high mountains. This sparked the idea to create his own. Averoff went on to introduce the first cabernet sauvignon into Greece in 1969, based upon his pan-European viewpoint.

Averoff died in 1990, and his son-in-law, Sotiris Ioannou, carried on his work, developing new wines that combined French and native Greek varieties like agiorgitiko to acclaim. The winery has prospered and owns Giniets, the highest planted vineyard in Greece on the slopes of Mt. Pindus at 3,900 feet (1,200 m). Over time, however, Ioannou recognized that expanding or further improving the family's pioneering efforts to revive Greek viticulture would require new financing and more employees.

Similar visions, philosophies, and interests in encouraging more environmentally sound production methods eventually brought the Ioannous together with Strofilia winery to form Katogi and Strofilia SA in 2001. Combined, the company now has 272 acres (110 ha) of vineyards, more capital to invest, and a fine reputation for making some of the most interesting and complex wines in Greece. The wines are sold under two collections, or lines, Katogi-Averoff and Strofilia; across the board they are highly expressive, richly textured, and distinctive wines.

> *Favorite wines: 2007 Strofilia, Agiorgitiko Nemea PDO (13%); 2008 Katogi Averoff Rossiu di Munte Syrah-Traminer TO [table wine] Epirus (14%)*

OTHER PRODUCERS OF MERIT IN CENTRAL GREECE

Domaine Milonas, Kerotea, Attica

> *Favorite wine: 2010 Domaine Mylonas Asyrtiko Apopsi, TO Attica (13%)*

Papagiannakos Estate, Markopoulo, Attica
(www.papagiannakos-wines.com)

> *Favorite wines: 2010 Papagiannakos Retsina, Attica TSG [traditional Greek specialty style] (12%); 2010 Papagiannakos Kalogeri, Malagouzia PGI (12.4%)*

NORTH AEGEAN

Union of Vinicultural Cooperatives of Samos (EOSS),
Malagari, Samos (www.samoswine.gr)

Samos, just off the Turkish coast from Kuşadasi, and probably visible on a clear day from ancient Ephesus, has produced wine for millennia. We have evidence that the growing of wine grapes on Samos dates from around the twelfth century BCE, and the preferred style was dry and light, mostly red.

Muscat petits grains (muscat de frontignan) appears to have arrived on Samos in the mid-fifteenth century CE, after a resettlement of the island under Ottoman rule. This is the same muscat we know from Italy as moscato d'Asti, for example, or muscat de Beaume de Venise in France, which is considered the finest—most perfumed and elegant—of the muscat types.

Samos is quite a verdant island, with enough rainfall and a climate more moderate than Crete's; these conditions allow dry-farming. Samos has the highest peak in the Aegean Islands, Mt. Marathokampos at 4,700 feet (1,400 m), which blocks fierce winds or storms coming from the northwest. Most vineyards face north and are planted at elevations as high as 2,900 feet (900 m). Vineyards are mostly terraced, with bush vines of considerable age, and the soils are schistose, allowing fine drainage and limiting yields.

The Union of Vinicultural Cooperatives of Samos produces three levels of muscats (anthemis, nectar, grand cru), each with different production methods, residual sugar levels, and aging requirements. The delight of Samos muscat lies in the complex differences in taste, texture, and aroma that each method provides. All are consistently delicious.

> *Favorite wines: 2009 Samos Grand Cru VDN (Vin Doux Naturel) (15%)*
>> *The most prestigious of the co-op's wines is made by fortifying ripe muscat grape juice with brandy and stopping the fermentation with about 13 percent residual sugar. Produced from the highest and best exposed vineyards, this wine*

combines fresh grapey muscat flavors and the warm touch of alcohol, providing
weight and texture. The color is light topaz yellow. Delicately perfumed, it is
highlighted by spicy-floral cantaloupe and green-melon scents with pear. The
flavors are just medium sweet, showing refreshing acidity, no nutty aged charac-
ter, with pear, honey, and ripe orange on the finish. It's excellent served chilled.
2004 Samos "Anthemis" Vin Doux, Samos PDO (15%)

PELOPONNESE

Achaia Clauss Wines, Patras (www.achaiaclauss.gr)

The first private winery in Greece, Achaia Clauss Wines, was established in
1861, and today it is perhaps the most famous winery in modern Greece. The
German-born Gustav Clauss fell in love with Greece; after he visited the Patras
area with its beautiful mountains, he decided to stay and built a castle for a
home and a winery within it. He established vineyards in the area, using local
grapes, especially the "black grape of Dafne," mavrodaphne. He created the
sweet style of mavrodaphne known today. After World War I Greece seized the
German-owned winery as war reparations. In the interwar period quality suffered yet its original fame and German ownership probably saved it from being taken over by the Nazis during their occupation of Greece in World War II.

Great success came in the 1970s under the ownership of the Antinopoulos
family, when the winery created a refreshing dry white wine called Demestica
that was not a retsina. We can remember often drinking chilled bottles of it
while traveling in Greece in the early 1970s and enjoying its tangy, lemony
flavors with grilled octopus on Mykonos.

Today Achaia Clauss's fortunes seem strong again, with a new winery and
annual production in excess of two million cases. Fame rests on its excellent
fortified wines, as it did originally.

Favorite wine: Achaia Clauss Mavrodaphne of Patras Grand Reserve,
Mavrodaphne Patras PDO (15%)

Gaia Estate Winery, Koutsi, Nemea (www.gaia-wines.gr)

Yiannis Paraskevopoulos, a professor of enology in Athens, also teaches at
Bordeaux University's wine school, where he earned his doctoral degree. With
Leo Karatsalo, an agronomist, he created Gaia Estate in 1994 on Santorini,

then in 1996 purchased a small winery at Nemea, Peloponnese, perhaps the most prestigious red wine PDO in Greece. Their goal has always been to perfect the expression of Greece's native varieties, often pushing the envelope with new techniques.

"I have always been curious about our Greek wines," Paraskevopoulos remarked. "The original opinion of agiorgitiko [Saint Georges] was of a pleasant wine to drink immediately, but [it was] not special." To make a deep wine, however, has required immense efforts in the vineyards, lowering yields and improving clonal selection, which previously was lacking. A return to denser planting (14,800 vines per acre/6,000 vines per hectare) since 2002 has also provided richer flavors and more balance, he says. Paraskevopoulos's vineyards are planted at elevations of 1,800 to 2,500 feet (550 to 800 m) in limestone-marl soils, which hold moisture and allow for dry-farming.

To make a finer agiorgitiko Paraskevopoulos has adopted some techniques usually used for white wines. "I am now also doing batonnage [stirring particles at the bottom of the vat] in the barrel to increase the texture but not compromise the delicacy of the grape." But he has also returned to traditional larger oak vats for aging after initial fermentation in smaller French oak barrels.

Gaia Estate also makes one of the best, mostly gently resinated, retsinas in Greece (Nobilis Retinitis), just to prove that retsina can actually taste like a fine wine, by updating an ancient classic. As Paraskevopoulos once said, "Only retsina complements certain dishes in Greek cuisine—there is a need for it."

Favorite wine: 2010 Gaia Estate Notios Red, Peloponnese PGI (13%)

Domaine Skouras, Malandreni, Peloponnese (www.skouras.gr)

Since he founded Domaine Skouras in 1986, George Skouras has vaulted to the top level of Greek wineries, mostly based upon his commitment to developing the reputation of the Nemea appellation. His Mega Oenos (Great Wine) label was the first to blend agiorgitiko with cabernet sauvignon, and in 2001 he became the first in Greece to adopt screwcaps for his wines.

Skouras studied wine making in Dijon, and this certainly influenced his philosophy, as did working first at wineries in the Ionian Islands before establishing Skouras. Skouras's main production of reds is based on agiorgitiko, but he is enamored of the moschofilero (*moscho* = aromatic; *fileri* = variety), too. His results are dependably excellent; the wines have personalities as exuberant as their creator, along with flavor definition and complexity, making them among the best in Greece.

Favorite wines: *2008 Domaine Skouras Saint George, Nemea PDO (13.6%)*

> *Finesse, elegance, and depth all are in play with this wine, which is reminiscent of fine Barolo from La Morra. Indeed the aromas of agiorgitiko, especially when grown on clay soils and from mature vines, as this example is, are quite like barolo, with black cherry, licorice, roses, and some graphite. The wine, which is medium ruby-violet in color, was aged 12 months in second-use French oak barrels in order not to mask the fruit but soften tannins. This is what modern Nemea wine is all about.*

2010 Domaine Skouras Zoë Rosé, Peloponnese PGI (12.7%)

Domaine Spiropoulos, Mantinia (www.domainspiropoulos.com)

The largest and most important winery estate in the Mantinia area, Domaine Spiropoulos, actually started as a winery in 1860, but the current modern, highly ecoconscious estate and vineyards commenced in 1987. The owner, Apostolos Spiropoulos, studied enology at UC Davis in California and has continued to experiment with variations of the local moschofilero and to make wine in the Nemea PDO as well. His family winery and neighboring Domaine Tselepos are greatly responsible for the rebirth of the area for fine wine making and the renewed prestige of the moschofilero grape.

In 1987 he decided to start a family winery with financial aid from the European Union and planted mostly white grapes, because Greeks drank mainly white wine. The first wines were made at the new winery (located near the site of ancient Mantinea) in 1991. The vineyards are now certified organic, and the winery is ecofriendly and produces thirty thousand cases a year.

Spiropoulos notes that the main difference between the vineyards in Mantinia and Nemea is that the former are "mostly flat, while the latter [are] mostly on hillsides, though the elevation differences are similar." All the wines are consistently distinctive and true to their terroir.

Favorite wine: *2010 Domaine Spiropoulos, Mantinia Estate PDO (12%)*

Domaine Tselepos: Rizes, Arcadia (www.tselepos.gr)

Yiannis Tselepos can be considered one of the two godfathers of the modern Mantinia PDO along with Spiropoulos. When he initiated the Domaine

Tselepos vineyard and winery in that area in 1989, Mantinia was still relatively unknown and the wines rather rustic. Tselepos had studied enology at the University of Dijon, worked in Burgundy, and then came home to consult, finally building his own estate at Tegea after a few years. The vineyards, each with a different name, geology, and altitude, lie at elevations of 2,300 to 3,000 feet (700 to 900 m), perfect for crisp white wines. Here Tselepos crafts some of the more flamboyant, aromatic white wines from the indigenous, high-quality moschofilero variety. His several styles range from a champagne-method sparkling wine to a rich barrel-fermented version. In 2003 he entered into a partnership with Paris Sigalas of Santorini and his friend Alexandros Avantangelos to create the Driopi Estate in nearby Nemea PDO; Driopi specializes in the great local agiorgitiko grape.

The Tegea vineyard of 120 acres (50 ha) allows Tselepos to produce twenty-eight thousand cases annually. Tselepos, a big bear of a man, strongly believes in the advantage of old vines, some more than 70 years old. His experience and desire to get more flavor intensity into moschofilero led him to focus first on viticulture: "At our top vineyard, Saint Trichonas [the patron saint of winemakers, he says], we have excellent drainage on the terra rossa limestone soils, so we increased vine density to over 5,000 vines per hectare [12,350 per acre]. Now we crop at lower levels per vine to increase fruit flavor but still get reasonable yields to maintain viability."

Moschofilero, Tselepos maintains, benefits from some skin contact time to release its aromatics, often as long as eight hours. Creative innovations, such as producing a barrel-fermented version, are now allowed in the area. Tselepos notes that "in ancient Greece, our area was noted for its smoked wines [*kapneos* in Greek], so I thought that making a barrel-fermented moschofilero would be a closer imitation of the ancient wine." More likely, kapneos-style wine got its name from the grayish smoky color of the grape variety used, as Aristotle noted.

Yiannis Tselepos's wines are overtly intense yet clearly defined and sure of themselves; they walk the walk. In Tselepos's hands moschofilero can claim near-equal status with assyrtiko as Greece's finest white wine.

Favorite wine: 2010 Domaine Tselepos Moschofilero, Mantinia PDO (12%)
This classic, non-oaked version of the winery's flagship wine retains its aromas
as Tselepos ferments at low temperatures for nearly a month. The result exudes
floral-grapefruit skin aromas with hints of rose or gardenia aligned with quite

crisp lemony-saline flavors. Given that the grape has pinkish-gray skin when mature, there is even a touch of red currant or other red fruit flavors on the finish, adding to its engaging nature.

Monemvasia Winery, Monemvasia (www.malvasiawines.gr)

The name of this winery's website sums up its purpose: to revive and propagate the wonders of the native grape that first appears in historical documents from the twelfth century CE. It has now traveled the globe as malvasia, an emissary of Greece by way of the Venetians who controlled this part of the Peloponnese beginning in the fourteenth century. Monemvasia (only entrance) refers to the impregnable rock (it looks like a cross between a butte in Monument Valley, AZ, and Mont Saint Michel, minus the castle, and has been called the "Gibraltar of Greece") that is connected to the mainland by just a single narrow causeway. The local wine became the most famous export of the area, providing a fragrant soft wine more adaptable to warmer, humid sites than many others because of its fungal resistance; today it is important in Madeira, southern Italy, and even California.

George Tsimpidis set up his winery in 1997 and has done much research to isolate local selections and the best sites. Tsibidis wines show great personality and a deft approach to making this delicate aromatic variety.

Favorite wines: 2002 Monemvasia Winery Late Harvest, Monemvasia PGI (15%)

> *This wine represents a rare attempt to make a malvasia much like those of centuries ago. The amber-brown color highlights the long aging in old oak barrels, while the bouquet reveals ethereal tea smoke, olive, and Madeira-like scents. The flavor, medium sweet (16 percent residual sugar) and full bodied, has savory, nutty, dried fruit, and honey-caramel accents with great pungency and character. If this is what the medieval Venetians were sending all over the Mediterranean on their galleys, it's no wonder the wine became a legend.*

2010 Monemvasia Winery Asyrtiko, Monemvasia PGI (12.6%)

OTHER PRODUCERS OF MERIT IN PELOPONNESE

Antonopoulos Vineyards, Patras (www.antonopoulos-vineyards.com)

Favorite wine: 2009 Antonopoulos Malagousia, Achaia PGI (13%)

Cavino Winery and Distillery, Aigio (www.cavino.gr)

Favorite wines: Cavino Deus Mavrodaphne, Patras PDO (15%); Cavino Mavrodaphne Reserve, Patras PDO (15%)

Mercouri Estate, Korakochori, Ilias (www.mercouri.gr)

Favorite wine: 2006 Domaine Mercouri Cava Red, Letrini PGI (14%)

Oenoforos Estate, Selinous, Aigio (www.oenoforos.gr)

Favorite wines: 2010 Oenoforos Asprolithia, Roditis PGI (11.6%); 2008 Oenoforos Ianos Chardonnay, Aegion PGI (13.5%)

Parparoussis Winery, Achaia

Favorite wines: 2006 Parparoussis Muscat of Rio, Patras PDO (15%); 2003 Parparoussis Mavrodaphne Reserve, Patras PDO (15%)

Semeli Estate, Domaine Helios Winery, Koutsi, Nemea (www.semeliwines.gr)

Favorite wines: 2010 Semeli Mantinia Nasiakos, Mantinia PDO (11.5%); 2004 Semeli Domaine Helios Grande Reserve Nemea, PDO (13%)

Tetramythos Winery, Ano Diakpto, Aegialia (www.tetramythoswines.com)

Favorite wines: 2010 Tetramythos Roditis, Patras PDO (13%); 2010 Tetramythos Malagousia, Aigialia (13%)

Vatistas Winery, Laconia (+30 2734024132)

Favorite wines: 2010 Vatistas Kydonitsa, Lakonia PGI (13%); 2006 Vatistas Cabernet-Agiorgitiko, Lakonia PGI (14%)

CYCLADES ISLANDS

SANTORINI

Describing Santorini (Thera) requires many adjectives, but lush is not one of them. Aegean peoples have lived here for seven thousand years, as the ruins at Akrotiri attest. Located in the southern Aegean north of Crete, Santorini was known to the ancient Greeks as Kalliste, "the most beautiful"; it has a hot, dry, and windy climate—no soft, gentle breezes or tropical afternoon rains. The island represents the top of an enormous volcano that exploded catastrophically around 1600 BCE, causing a massive collapse of the crater and creating the stunning cliffs that overlook the huge sea-filled caldera. The eruption disrupted Mediterranean trade and destroyed Santorini's habitability for several centuries. Today it is home to an indigenous white grape variety, assyrtiko, and vines that may be the oldest in the world.

New settlers, Mycenaeans or Phoenicians, arrived around the thirteenth century BCE, bringing vines with them, evidenced by the large number of wine grape remains long buried under the protective ash at Akrotiri. This ash, pumice as light as a feather and heavier lava rocks that ejected from the volcano, provided a layered terrain for making assertive and unique ancient wines. Theran wine, with pulse sprinkled into it instead of barley meal, was common to the island after the eruption period.

Four hundred to five hundred years ago strong Venetian rule and influence led to the development of trade in Santorini's remarkable and unique white vinsanto (its name is a contraction of the Italian vino di Santorini). This is a rich and naturally sweet wine; several producers age their top wine for two decades or more in oak, and the results are truly heavenly.

The environment and strong mineral-laden volcanic soils provide unique circumstances for Santorini's flagship variety, assyrtiko. Santorini is isolated, and with virtually no rainfall for eight months, irrigation is not possible. But the lack of precipitation and the deep, sandy character of the soil with no clay make Santorini-grown grapes immune to phylloxera. Given that assyrtiko is still grown on original sedimentary limestone soils in the one part of Santorini that escaped the volcanic destruction, there is reason to believe the grape is an ancient native.

Harsh conditions dictate that the vines must be grown close to the ground for wind protection. The vines are grown in an ancient protective basket style known as ampeliá. Only one other place on Earth uses this technique, the windswept desert-like island of Pantelleria near Sicily. Not coincidentally, Pantelleria and Santorini were probably colonized by the seafaring, wine-loving Phoenicians, who adapted their viticulture to these windy, sea-salty dry places.

Ampeliá involves coiling and weaving the pruned branches coming out of the short trunk so that the leaves shade the fruit from harsh sunlight and conserve water evaporation while absorbing nightly dew, the only humidity the vine receives for months.

Also, the leaves prevent salt grains from pelting the delicate grape skins, ruining them.

When the vine reaches about 80 years old and becomes less productive, the grower cuts off the oldest and thickest branches and takes young shoots from the trunk, prolonging the life of the vine. Because the age of the vine is determined by its root system, this process can be repeated, we are told, four or five times, leading to vines that are three hundred to four hundred years old.

In addition to assyrtiko, Santorini produces several other Aegean varieties, such as the aidani and athiri white wines and the rare but exciting red, mavrotragano.

Estate Argyros Episkopi Gonia (www.estate-argyros.com)

Estate Argyros, which is more than one hundred years old, farms 86 acres (35 ha). The owner, Yiannis Argyros, who died tragically in December 2011, had taken over from his father, Matthew, in 1974, and for 30 years made what many Greeks considered the finest dry and sweet wines in Greece. His vinsanto Argyros, which we tasted with him, is aged for 20 years in 500-liter casks; these wines are without parallel for complexity, depth, and sheer deliciousness, though costly—and deservedly so. We tasted many vintages back to 1970, all awe inspiring. Mattheos Argyros, the son of Yiannis, is now in charge.

Most of the vineyards are on mountain slopes, and total production is moderate. The winery is simple and rustic, the wine making sophisticated enough. The vinsanto of Argyros is without peer, its dry white wines are intense, and its red mavrotragano excellent.

Favorite wines: 1988 Argyros Estate Vinsanto, Santorini PDO (14%)

> *This vinsanto was aged 17 years in older oak, then three years in newer barrels and blended with aidani and athiri. It begs comparison with the ancient nectar of the gods. The techniques used to make it are similar to those used to make wines in Israel two thousand years ago, except for being aged in oak*

*instead of amphoras. The color glows amber brown with a green rim. The
bouquet is extraordinary: honey and maple sugar, herbal tea, high floral tones,
and orange-muscat marmalade. Lusciously sweet, its liqueur-like flavors are
supported by fine acidity, a touch of oak tannin as backbone, and an incred-
ibly long finish—compelling us to believe this wine will be a wonderful treat
for another 50 years.*

2010 Argyros Estate Assyrtiko, Santorini PDO (13.2%)

Boutari Winery, Megalohori (www.boutari.gr)

Boutari invested in Santorini in the 1980s and rapidly gained immediate attention for the quality of its groundbreaking Kallisti Reserve assyrtiko, the first
barrel-fermented version of the classic wine of the island. The reputation of
Boutari's Santorini winery grew, and in 1988 the company built a stunning new
winery with lovely island-style architecture and tourist amenities. With vineyards at different altitudes Boutari makes about twenty-five thousand cases of
Santorini wines that represent good value and consistently high quality.

Favorite wine: 2007 Boutari Kallisti Reserve, Santorini PDO (14%)

Gaia Wines, Ekso Vrahies (www.gaia-wines.gr)

Ever curious, Yiannis "Johnny P" Paraskevopoulos came to Santorini in 1995
to try his hand with white wines on the island. His initial wine, Thalassitis
Assyrtiko, was crystalline in character and shocked early drinkers with its sub-
dued fruit character but high minerality and steely structure. Locals wouldn't
drink it, but Paraskevopoulos soon had a hit with a worldwide audience. In
2001 he turned an old tomato-canning factory into a winery. Today Gaia's
Santorini winery works about 150 acres (60 ha), producing about twenty-five
thousand cases a year.

Paraskevopoulos finds Santorini's extraordinary conditions provide nu-
merous surprises. "I didn't realize when I arrived," he remarks, "that the two
traditional [vine] training systems require about four times more labor than
typical trellising, nor that the minerality of the wines was so strongly linked
to vine age. If I had two centuries to find out if trellising would produce the
same degree of minerality, and as long-lived vines, I might try it, but I don't
think so."

Gaia's Santorini winery produces excellent wines that stretch the limits of assyrtiko. Paraskevopoulos is always trying new things, including drying his grapes for vinsanto in the shade, not sun, to retain more fruitiness.

Favorite wine: 2010 Assyrtiko of Gaias Wild Ferment, Santorini PDO (13%)

> *Fermented with indigenous yeasts, followed by partial oak aging, this wine has a bouquet that is more nutty than floral or mineral. The flavors are firm, slightly oaky yet balanced, and assertively marked by dried citrus and apricot skin flavors. With aeration the bouquet becomes more saline, the finish chewy, minerally, and nearly like that of a red wine. This is a wonderfully complex wine.*

Domaine Sigalas, Oia (www.sigalas-wine.com)

"Tourism was the engine for renovation of the wine business here on Santorini, beginning in the 1970s," Paris Sigalas related as we walked in one of his oldest vineyards. "I have a few vineyards on the hills below Oia but more on the plain below, where we are now at about 45 meters' elevation [148 feet]. This parcel has effectively existed for hundreds of years due to our ampeliá technique and layering of the canes."

Sigalas, a mathematician by training, started his winery as a hobby in 1991, but it is now considered one of the best producers on the island, responsible for bringing to prominence Santorini's finest unique red variety, the deeply colored and concentrated mavrotragano. His wines, now made with the assistance of the young enologist Charikleia Mavrommati, are refined and rich, with more body than some others. They have great fruit intensity and are extroverted, much like their producer.

Favorite wines: 2008 Sigalas Mavrotragano, Cyclades PGI (14%)

> *Sigalas rescued his mavrotragano grapes from near extinction when he first started working with them in 1998, planting 20 acres (8 ha) at high density from old vine cuttings; the yields typically are low, 1.5 tons per acre. This wine has an opaque black-ruby color, and its bouquet shows a lot of initial oaky-vanilla smokiness but also concentrated black fruit and fig aromas. The flavors maintain the bouquet's theme but add rich black licorice, velvety supple tannins, and powerful structure, followed by a long finish. Incredibly intense yet surprisingly refined, Sigalas mavrotragano is a special wine and can easily age until 2020.*

2009 Domaine Sigalas "Kavaliero," Santorini PDO (14%)

OTHER WINERIES OF INTEREST ON SANTORINI

Gavala Winery, Megalohori

Favorite wine: 2010 Gavala Assyrtiko (13%)

Santo Wines, Pyrgos (www.santowines.gr)

Favorite wines: 2007 Assyrtiko Santorini Grande Reserve, Santorini PDO (14.9%); 2003 Santorini Vinsanto Vin de Liqueur [fortified], Santorini PDO (15%)

Volcan Wines, Fira

Favorite wines: 2010 Assyrtiko-Mandilaria Rosé (13%); 2000 Kamaritis (vinsanto style) (11%)

Xatzidakis Winery, Pyrgos

Favorite wines: 2010 Assyrtiko Cuvée O (14%); 2003 Vinsanto (13%)

CRETE

PHYSICAL CHARACTERISTICS

Crete, the largest Mediterranean island, has a long history of civilization, even before the famous Minoan civilization (3000–1500 BCE), and of growing wine grapes. Minoans were definitely a wine-loving people, which is evident in many of their works of art.

Crete is mostly mountainous, with the ranges running in a central spine from the east to the west of the island, which divides the weather patterns. The south side is warmer than the north because of the hot African winds that blow into southern Crete from the Sahara. As one moves west, the climate become moderately cooler and more humid, definitely cooler than Santorini.

Crete has a relatively good water supply from snowmelt from its peaks, the highest of which are 8,000 feet (2,450 m) above sea level, and many streams. Crete's geology, unlike Santorini's, is primarily sedimentary clay-limestone from uplifted seabed.

GRAPES AND APPELLATIONS

Crete has four PDOs, three near Heraklion—Peza, Dafnes, and Archanes—and one at its eastern end, Sitia in Lasithi prefecture. It also has four regional PGIs: Kriti, Iraklion in the center, Lasithi to the east, and Kissamos near Chania in the west.

Crete has just a few local varieties, as well as transplants from the Cyclades Islands and Europe. The best white grapes are vilana and vidiano. Mandilaria, kotsifali, and liatiko are the most widely planted red wine grapes. In visiting many of the producers we found that where yields were well controlled, the wines were quite good, all else being equal. Most native grapes do not have high pigmentation, and the reds and whites are not especially aromatic. When Luke stopped in Crete during the first century CE en route to Rome, he probably drank wines from some of these varieties or their ancestors. And lest we forget, Ariadne, the wife of Dionysus, was the daughter of Crete's King Minos himself.

Domaine Economou, Ziros, Sitia (wineryeconomou.blogspot.com)

Eastern Crete has lovely cliffside towns, funky little seaports, and the beautiful ancient Minoan site of Gournia but relatively few vineyards. In Ziros, where old nongrafted vines can be found, Iannis and Natassa Economou make unique wines, some of the most thought provoking in the world, Cretan or otherwise. Iannis Economou studied wine making in Alba, Italy, worked awhile at Chateau Margaux in Bordeaux, speaks five languages, and makes wines that no one else would consider trying.

The Economous' winery is a warren of rooms in their seventeenth-century house in the village. Their 40 acres (16 ha) of vines provide just 900 to 1,800 cases a year, about 20 percent of what a vineyard of that size would on this island. What's going on? Iannis Economou works especially with a clone localized to Ziros of the old vine, nongrafted liatiko. The vineyard is farmed organically, and its sandy-schistose soils are exceptional, dry with no phylloxera. Iannis Economou creates wines that are unlike any other liatiko wines, often aged ten years in old barrels left outside before bottling for the sweet version.

"I like old school Italian and French wine making, where color is not so important, nor am I interested in making another powerful cabernet style of wine," he told us. Economou wines are extremely individual, from a unique place and a singular winemaker who makes wines much as people did centuries ago, except for the oak aging.

Favorite wines: 1998 Economou, Sitia V.Q.P.R.D. [PDO] (14%); 2000 Economou, Sitia V.Q.P.R.D. [PDO] (15.5%)

> *The sweet version is aged in the traditional style of the area: outside in half-full 300-liter old oak casks for ten years. Its full amber-brown color with a green rim resembles sherry. The bouquet, redolent of walnut and toffee, is similar to fine oloroso sherry, until one detects the wisp of wild herbs, as if a few drops of Chartreuse liqueur had been added. Its medium-sweet, full-bodied flavors are viscous and nutty, yet its firm acidity beautifully supports the lingering sweetness. As the Michelin Guide likes to say, "Worth a detour."*

Lyrarakis Estate, Alagni (*www.lyrarakis.gr*)

This family winery started selling its own wine in 1992, and 40 years of winemaking experience has allowed the Lyrarakis family to perfect the wines of its region. Bart Lyrarakis is the winemaker, and these days he is concentrating on vineyards in one of the higher elevations in Peza, 1,500 to 2,100 feet (450 to 650 m). Evidence of its ancient wine culture is everywhere in Crete; three Lyrarakis plots have remains of winepresses that were carved into the limestone rock in the mid-second millennium BCE.

He paid homage to his vineyards' heritage with his 2005 Lyrarakis Symbolo Grande Cuvée by placing on the red wine's label the symbol for wine, 𐂖, used by two ancient scripts, Linear B and Cretan hieroglyphics. Symbolo is a concentrated, powerful, and fragrant blend of syrah, cabernet, and kotsifali.

Lyrarakis is researching two rare and ancient varieties in particular, plyto and dafní, both nearly extinct. Lyrarakis has revived the two difficult white varieties; "Dafní means bay leaf in Greek, and is our last grape to be picked, and perhaps is an ancient variety. It's a bit sleeker, more salty or citric than plyto, which has more floral, fruity characteristics," Lyrarakis notes. All the Lyrarakis wines show high fruit intensity, sleek mineral flavors, and excellent character.

Favorite wines: 2010 Lyrarakis Dafní, Crete PGI (12%); 2008 Lyrarakis Syrah-Kotsifali, Crete PGI (13%)

Michalakis Estate, Metaxochori, Peza (*www.michalakis.gr*)

Emmanouel Michalakis got involved in the wine business in 1962, and since then Michalakis Estate has become an important domaine in Crete. Michalakis started out with inexpensive bulk wines and built the new winery in Metaxochori in 2003 to be near the estate's vineyards, which now have a more sophisticated range of grapes. The family owns 100 acres (40 ha) of estate vineyards, primarily in the Peza PDO, and also buys grapes. The winery, now run by son George Michalakis, produces about a hundred thousand cases a year.

The soils in Peza, says Dimitris Gouravas, the estate manager, have clay, some slate, and some limestone but are somewhat rocky. Michalakis has invested heavily in viticultural improvements, including planting at higher elevations (about 1,800 feet, or 550 m) and limiting production to a maximum of 3.6 tons per acre (58 hl/ha), depending on variety. Michalakis produces good to excellent wines that show fine regional character at the premium level.

Favorite wines: 2010 Michalakis Atarachos Rosé, Iraklion PGI (13.5%); 2008 Michalakis Estate Gold Cuvée Red, Iraklion PGI (13.8%)

OTHER PRODUCERS OF MERIT ON CRETE

Boutari Winery, Skalani (*www.boutari.gr*)

Favorite wine: 2009 Domaine Skalani Red, Iraklion PGI (14.5%)

Douloufakis Winery, Dafnes (*www.cretanwines.gr*)

Favorite wines: 2008 Douloufakis Syrah, Crete PGI (13.5%); 2010 Douloufakis Enotria (Red), Crete PGI (13.5%)

Winery Dourakis Andreas, Alikampos Chania (*www.dourakiswinery.gr*)

Favorite wine: NV [non-vintage] Dourakis Grenache Rouge (Rosé), Kissamos PGI (12%)

Mediterra Winery, Kounavi (*www.mediterrawines.gr*)

Favorite wines: 2010 Mediterra Xerolithia, Peza PDO (13%); 2008 Mediterra Mirambelo (Red), Peza PDO (13%)

DODECANESE ISLANDS

The Dodecanese Islands are grouped in the southeastern corner of the Aegean Sea, not far from the Turkish coast. Of the group, Rhodes and Kos have been famous wine centers for millennia—Rhodes created one of the most beautiful amphora shapes in the Hellenistic period 2,300 years ago. (See chapters 5 and 6 for more on the ancient wines and traditions of these islands.) Today Rhodes has the most wine grape vineyards in production, about 3,000 acres (1,200 ha), while Kos has much less.

CLIMATE, GEOLOGY, AND GRAPES

The Dodecanese climate is mild and maritime. The winds can be strong this far south, but generally they are tolerable, not like on Santorini. Summertime temperatures, while warm, are moderated by winds; we were surprised by the moderate alcohol levels of many wines, most less than 13 percent, which certainly is a result of the cooling sea winds.

Many vineyards are located at higher elevations, about 2,300 feet (700 m) on north-facing slopes. The geology runs to schistose rock and gravels on the slopes and more clay at flatter sites. Closer to the sea, on both Kos and Rhodes especially, the geology is ferrous limestone with clay uplifted from the sea.

On Rhodes the main white grape is athiri and the reds are mandilaria or amoriano, which are also the only ones permitted to obtain the Rhodes PDO appellation. The famous muscat of Rhodes also carries PDO status, along with muscat of Trani, a variation brought in by Italians from Puglia. On Kos, Oinampelos Winery has brought in malagousia, assyrtiko, and athiri for Greek white varieties but uses mostly French varieties for the reds, including syrah and cabernet, as well as tempranillo from Spain.

Enoteca Emery, Emponas, Rhodes (www.emery.gr)

Enoteca Emery has been in the Triantafillou family since 1923. It is located in Emponas, high in the mountains in the southwestern part of the island at an elevation of about 1,300 feet (400 m). The winery focuses on the classic local grapes, buying fruit from 175 acres (70 ha). Most vineyards are on hillsides as high as 2,460 feet (750 m) above the sea, with some on Mount Attavyros facing northwest. Stervos Chatzisavas, the winemaker, relates that the most expensive grapes on the island are the muscats. Overall the yields are low by anyone's standard, reflecting both the poverty of the soils and the climatic and geological constraints on the island.

Favorite wine: 2008/2009 Emery Efreni, Muscat of Rhodes PDO (14.5%)

KOS

Oinampelos Winery, Miniera Asfendiou (www.inambelos.gr)

One of two wineries currently producing wines on this small island, Oinampelos is owned by Mary Triantafyllopoulou; her son Christos makes the wine. Half their vineyards are by the winery and face northwest, not far from the sea or from the site where Saint Paul visited on his third missionary journey. Perhaps Paul had wine from the local vineyards? The main Oinampelos vineyard has 15 acres (6 ha) and is flat, with a heavier mix of red clay and sand compared to the winery's other vineyard, of 15 acres (6 ha), located on the other side of the island at higher altitude (1,000 feet/300 m) on Mount Díkaios. There the soil is a lighter, rockier schistose limestone and much less vigorous.

Reviving the wine industry in Kos has proved to be slow going but, according to Mary Triantafyllopoulou, fairly successful. "We have mainly brought in typical Greek white grapes from the island areas like Assyrtiko and Malagousia but also from France," she notes. "We are doing experiments with other native red varieties in hopes that they will eventually be allowed by the government. The Dodecanese Islands cannot plant anything now, not even for basic table wine." She is trying to get the legislation changed to permit grapes like aidani and mavrotragano. "The climate is warm but enough cool winds help to keep alcohol levels lower than one expects," Christos Triantafyllopoulos adds. The vineyards, first planted in 1996, now produce about 5,500 cases a year, an enjoyable lineup made by delightful people who are working to revive a lost culture on the island.

Favorite wine: 2010 Oinampelos Dikaios Athiri-Asyrtiko, VdT Dodecanese Islands (13%)

> *The grapes for this finely focused, elegant, and sprightly wine with excellent minerality and assertive flavors are grown on the slopes of Kardamaina near*

the sea. It contains equal amounts of athiri and assyrtiko, and the athiri was subjected to 30 hours of cold maceration to obtain more aromas and enhance the wine's structure. Flinty, green apple, citrus, and ripe peach skin aromas lead to medium-bodied flavors highlighted by dried apricot, refreshing acidity, and a fine finish.

RHODES WINERY OF INTEREST

CAIR, Rodos (www.cair.gr)

Favorite wines: 2010 CAIR Rodos 2400, Rhodes PDO (12%); CAIR Amandia Vin de Liqueur (Red), Rhodes PDO (15%)

Visitors to Greece should go to wineries and taste some of these marvelous Greek wines that enrich the Bible wine trail. In Peloponnese the wines of nearby Nemea hint at what the terroir produced in the time of Corinthian bacchanalian love feasts. The islands that Paul visited would have produced a different Eucharistic and table wine, and a sampling of those, now made in a modern style, will show some of the minerality and salinity of the wines that may have inspired Greeks to mix wine with seawater. The northern Macedonian wines feature some nuances that Christians in Thessalonica might have encountered as they waited for Jesus to return. Greece offers a rich heritage—almost every vineyard has an archaeological site, and many are located in places where Paul and other early Christians might have walked.

Twelve

SERIOUSLY, WHAT WINE WOULD JESUS DRINK?

(Or, Guess Who's Coming to Dinner?)

All sorts of images come to mind when we think about the Bible and wine and contemplate what wine would Jesus drink (WWWJD). How would a homeless peasant, Jesus of Nazareth, afford wine? The answer: through his charisma. He no doubt convinced people to supply his wine and his meals. People gave him money that was kept in a common money box (*glōssókomos*) overseen by Judas (John 12:6). Jesus's claim that he was homeless—"Foxes have holes, and birds of the air have nests; but the Son of Man has nowhere to lay his head" (Matt. 8:20)—indicates that people took him in and fed him.

Jesus loved "eating and drinking" and had a reputation of being a "glutton and a wino" (in Greek, *oinopotēs* means wine drinker, drunkard) (Matt 11:19; Luke 7:33–35). This revelation adds to the astonishment for those who cannot fathom a human Jesus. If he could produce *any* wine from water, what would he drink given modern choices? The question probably was not asked by any of his wealthier supporters when he stayed at their homes during his travels. Yet if Jesus were coming to our house for dinner, 'What wine could we serve?' would spark significant discussion and debate.

We attempted to answer that question by tasting a range of wines made in the ancient biblical manner. We reasoned that Jesus would drink wines that resembled those familiar to him. In several countries today a few enterprising wine producers have adapted practices not used for two millennia, partly as a reaction to modern industrial wine making and partly to satisfy their intellectual and artistic bents.

In chapters 5 and 6 we noted some ancient wine styles favored in the Levant, Greece, and Italy and those pronounced kosher in the Talmud. Today, Mas des Tourelles in the Rhone Valley (see box on p. 248) has re-created a Roman-style winery and has made authentic Gallo-Roman wines. History is on its side—the estate is located on the site of an old Roman villa and vineyard, with the remains to prove it.

What types of wine were available to Jesus that he would recognize today? Knowing this helps to identify which ones he might recognize. Some issues need to be considered first. No one in Israel today makes wines in the ancient manner. As a Jew, Jesus should only drink wines made by observant Jews and that have not been cut with water, yet he broke or allowed breaking the rabbinical rules of his day, such as picking grain on the Sabbath (Matt. 12:1), touching a near-dead body out of compassion (Luke 10:29–37), or healing on the Sabbath (John 5:15).

He may have enjoyed wines that were aromatized or had added flavorings like honey and pepper; the Talmud mentions wines like Inomillin, among others. First-century tastes leaned toward sweeter, though not necessarily stronger, wines than ours. Dry wines were also appreciated, although these were more difficult to do well, except by keeping amphoras buried in cool ground, as the amazing modern *qvevri* wines of Georgia have demonstrated through seven thousand years of continuous production.

Finally, Jesus traveled a great deal, and it's likely that circumstances, perhaps curiosity, and certainly thirst provided the opportunity to drink other types as well, even gentile wines in a gesture of friendship and goodwill. What Jesus would drink today ultimately depends on his sense of openness and community, a willingness to partake and share in the joy derived from good wine.

MAKING ANCIENT WINE THE RIGHT WAY

First, we should discuss in greater detail how wines were made in the first century CE. The archaeoagronomist Amos Hadas notes that "there is a great difference between the Roman smaller *dolia*-type winepresses and the larger, Levantine open basin *gat* [winepress in Hebrew] units." In both processes managing the heat generated during fermentation was the principal issue for ancient winemakers and required different approaches. One must follow different regimes fermenting the must to maintain the heat (smaller volume) in the dolia systems, compared to dissipating it in the open basin systems (larger volume). Therefore, "The vinification cycle is shorter for the basin systems (4 to 7 days) than for the dolia systems (10 to 15 days)."

Grape juice did not need to ferment on the skins for long in a small individual or family *gat,* one holding perhaps half a ton of grapes (500 kg) or less, before the juice flowed into the *yeqeb* (vat). Even during two weeks of fermentation, the grapes would not have generated enough heat or gas to ruin the resulting wine, as yeasts would not be starved of oxygen to metabolize sugar, thus allowing *Mycoderma* or *Acetobacter* to grow, feed off the sugars, and produce vinegar and terrible smells (a problem Columella nonetheless complains about at length). A small individual producer could pull from the basin to the large bowls—*pûr,* called in Hebrew *pûrâh*—a relatively clear, clean sweet wine.

In larger volumes this method would result in a spoiled wine, as an experiment in ancient wine-making techniques demonstrated in Israel in 1996–1997. Using the same grapes crushed and treaded in cleaned and restored small and larger-sized *gats* at the ancient Castra winepress site near Haifa, Yehoshua Gray, an expert in the restoration of ancient technology, showed that fermentation of treaded grapes in a larger *gat* (one that can hold at least 2,600 pounds, or 1,200 kg) must be allowed to proceed for several days to dissipate the heat, as well as the carbon dioxide generated while maintaining yeast viability, before decanting into the *yeqeb.*

It took about five days for enough heat and gas to dissipate before a wine was safe in the larger, open *gat* to finish the winemaking process, in order to prevent a stuck fermentation or worse yet. By draining the free-run fermented wine into the *yeqeb* after that time, the winemaker could press the pomace that remained in the *gat* and pour it into a separate *yeqeb,* then allow it to settle or filter it. This wine was healthy and smelled fit to drink. In the experiment wine made by drawing the juice out of the treading *gat* early and fermenting it in the *yeqeb* was, according to those who tasted it, "awful crap." The wine fermented in the treading *gat* for five days or more tasted pretty good, even a few years later.

WHICH WINES WOULD JESUS ENJOY OR RECOGNIZE?

Red wines made today according to ancient principles are not so different from contemporary wines, we learned. In the ancient world white wines were made the same way as in the experiment described by Dray and others, with skins, stalks, and pips all crushed and macerated together. Modern wines would be completely mysterious to Jesus—or any first-century Roman, for that matter. It doesn't mean that Jesus would not like them, but we think Jesus would not recognize them.

WHITE WINES

Ancient writers described fine wines produced in a wide range of styles using many unusual ingredients to add flavors. Thus Jesus might have known what Pliny tells us: "The resin of Judaea dries harder and has a stronger scent than even that from the terebinth tree, and Syrian resin has a resemblance to Attic honey. The resin of Cyprus excels all other kinds; it likewise is the color of honey, and has a fleshy consistency."

Retsina has been produced since at least the third millennium BCE (archaeologists have found wine jars from Crete from that period), but its production no doubt began in Anatolia, spread through the Levant, then to Cyprus and to Greece. Try Gaia Estate's Retinitis Nobilis, elegantly flavored with Aleppo pine resin, whose light resiny-herbal aromas and fresh and crisp fruit flavors are augmented by subtle camphor-pine flavors. A wonderful aperitif, this would be the perfect accompaniment for fresh fried fish from the Sea of Galilee or fried calamari from the Aegean.

Of more interest to most consumers would be pure non-resinated dry white wines. We are not sure what specific type Jesus would have drunk in Galilee, but white wines, aged and fresh, were highly appreciated throughout the Greco-Roman world. Today the most exciting, authentic descendants are Georgia's dry *qvevri* wines (fermented in the large sunken ceramic jars of that name), those made similarly in northern Italy, and the wines of Montilla-Moriles in Spain and Chateau-Chalon in France. The latter are derived from the *flor* yeast and made similarly to Jerez wines but without high-proof spirit fortification.

While not a country mentioned in the Bible, Georgia can be considered a principal stop on the Bible wine trail because of its seven-thousand-year history of making wine. Today Georgian winemakers using traditional techniques line their *qvevri* with beeswax before placing them in the ground. Grapes, white or red, are crushed or treaded first, and the whole lot is poured into the *qvevri* to ferment for weeks or months with no real controls. The wine is then removed, strained, and put into fresh smaller amphoras or bottled for aging or drinking. We visited Georgia in September 2011, observed *qvevri* wine production, and tasted many versions, primarily made from Georgia's top white indigenous varieties, rkatsiteli, mtsvane, and kisi. Truly the only concession to modernity of *qvevri* producers today compared to those of Jesus' time is the use of sulfur dioxide for preservation.

Josko Gravner, who uses similar methods in Friuli, Italy, on the Slovenian border, produced an especially good 2004 Ribolla Gialla (12.5%) that has a deep amber-orange color, anise seed and herb aromas, combined with dense, slightly tannic, flavors and a long nutty finish. No other wines are like them; a few are exported to North America and throughout Europe and are not expensive, though Gravner's is costly, due to very low production and high demand.

For Jesus's dinner we chose a 2009 Pheasant's Tears Rrkatsiteli from the Kakheti region of Georgia (12.5%) made by the American painter and winemaker Jon Wardeman at his Pheasant's Tears winery in Sighnaghi. His wine has a deep yellow-gold color and saline-mushroom, floral-herb, and olive scents. With aeration its medium-bodied, firm, and slightly tannic flavors reveal layer after layer, with notes of dried peach skin, almonds, and apricot balanced by solid acidity, and a chewy finish that is more like a red wine's.

Ancient writers like Pliny, Ovid, and Columella comment on white wines that are covered by a white flower yeast film and have potentially fine taste, provided they are not ruined by acetification (a different, dark *Mycoderma* film). This *flor* is a specific *Saccharomyces* yeast that grows under rare conditions, as in Montilla-Moriles (near Cordoba) and Jerez in Spain, and in eastern France's Jura appellation, Chateau-Chalon. Traditional producers of Montilla-Moriles wines made from the Pedro Ximenez grapes still age their wines in *tinajas,* large jars like *qvevri. Flor's* blanketing effect prevents oxidation/acetification of the wine beneath it. Fresh and nut-flavored wines like these were probably more common in the first century than today, since the ubiquitous method of maturation and storage in amphoras that were not always topped up allowed more oxygen to enter; necessary for *flor* development.

As the *flor* is a natural element, such wines would have been considered kosher and probably a style Jesus would have been familiar with. We thought to serve the Bodegas Toro Albalá Fino Electrico (15%) from Montilla-Moriles and the 2004 Berthet-Bondet Chateau-Chalon (14%). Both are fully dry wines, but they are much paler in color than the *qvevri* wines we have discussed. The bouquet of the fino shows the classic *flor* scent of salt air, lightly toasted almonds, and hint of apple blossom. The flavor is zesty yet deeply concentrated because of its extended barrel maturation. It is a more full-bodied wine than the Chateau Chalon, which shows the effect of the lower alcohol content from a cooler area and has the salty-briny flair of the Fino Electrico but fewer oxidative volatile aromas. Spiced apple, briny freshness, and lively acidity compliment the flavors, which are rich and well defined, capable of aging much longer. The ancients used certain spices and herbs, particularly fenugreek, along with seawater, to produce wines with nutty, oxidized, and aged flavors of unique complexity that mimic the effect of *flor*.

Coan wine was excellent medicinal wine, made by picking grapes a little early, drying them under the sun for three days, pressing them on the fourth, and then leaving them in casks to mature in the sun. The final step was to mix in a lot of seawater. This process, except for no longer aging the wine in casks left outside in the sun instead in a cool cellar) or mixing with seawater, is still the basis for Santorini's Vinsanto style. Pliny's description of Coan wine also calls to mind the ancient Jewish *ilyoston,* a sweet wine from grapes dried in the sun for three days and then gathered and trod in the midday sun. Surely Jesus would drink such a luscious wine.

A superb modern example of this sun-dried-grape (passito) style today is the 2004 Sigalas Vinsanto, Santorini PDO (9%) from Domaine Sigalas (see chapter 11). Vinsanto's assyrtiko and aidani grapes were picked and placed on straw mats to dry in the sun for ten days, then fermented in a tank, and subsequently aged for four years in old barrels. The mahogany-like color, rich caramel-raisin and sweet-tea bouquet, and lusciously sweet, viscous raisin-spice flavors leavened by a subtle saline finishing note, are extraordinarily delicious, completely in line with first-century palates. This will be our dessert wine.

RED WINES

Jesus no doubt would want to enjoy red wine as well as white. Wines made today using *qvevri* still put whole clusters in the vat to be broken up and crushed for fermentation, while some people have returned to treading the grapes as the most effective method, much as port wines have been made since 1700.

The best amphora-fermented wines we tasted paid attention to Columella's axiom that the wine should be checked after it has been fermenting for a month or less in the jars, and then racked off the heavy sediments into clean jars. We tasted two examples whose producers had not paid attention to this fundamental knowledge. Their wines were completely ruined by acetification, gaseousness, and the taste of spoilage.

Because Jesus would have appreciated a meal of roasted lamb, we chose a Georgian *qvevri* wine and a delightful Sicilian wine made in amphoras. From Sicily's east coast the 2010 COS Pithos, Sicilia IGT (12%) highlights two indigenous old Sicilian varieties; nero d'Avola (60%) and frappato. Wine has been made there since the eighth century BCE, when the Greeks colonized Sicily. COS makes this wine in small *dolia* with a capacity of 400 liters (106 gallons). The color has a lovely medium ruby-violet hue, definitely not a black wine. The aromas show earthy-floral, spice, game meat and pine notes, almost like a box of potpourri. These elegantly fresh cherry-violet and lightly mineral fruit flavors are balanced by delicate tannins, good acidity, and a round yet structured finish. Because it comes from a somewhat cooler area, this is probably a lighter wine than Jesus would have been accustomed to.

So we added two richer wines, a *qvevri* wine and a rich dried-grape Amarone wine, both of which offer flavors familiar to someone used to the powerful wines of the Levant. The 2008 Vino Terra Saperavi Selection from the Kakheti region (13%) truly shows the powerful yet nuanced character that Georgia's best red grape is capable of achieving. Dark black-violet color promises intensity and doesn't disappoint. The bouquet exudes dark ripe cherry and anise, with hints of graphite. The flavors are deep, velvety, and quite fleshy yet well structured, with no oakiness to hide the purity of the fruit and mineral extract.

"Some grapes will last all through the winter if the clusters are hung by a string from the ceiling . . . [and] before his time [early in the first century CE] priority at the table belonged to the Raetic grapes from the territory of Verona. Moreover, raisins are called *'passi'* from having endured the sun," Pliny reports. Raetic wines originated near the Alps and Verona, where Valtellina sforzato (the Alps) and Amarone di valpolicella (Verona) wines are made, the grapes dried using similar drying techniques from September to January, but maintained more hygienically in temperature controlled rooms today. According to Pliny, this area of northern Italy, as well as Gaul and Rhaetium (Switzerland), were where wooden barrels were first used for aging wine, beginning in the first century BCE.

Indeed drinking a mature Amarone such as the 1997 Mazzi Amarone della Valpolicella Classico Punta di Villa, made with red corvina (successor to Rhaeticum?) and other grapes dried for four months in an aerated attic (not under sunlight), then given a long fermentation in oak tanks and aged three years in old large casks, conjures Pliny's description for this style of wine. *Passum*-style wines were made throughout the Roman Empire, including Judea and Palestine. A jar fragment from Lachish (southwestern Israel) reads: "*Raisin wine;* wine made from black raisins." Mazzi's Amarone highlights mature ruby-garnet color and dark black cherry, raisin, and cooked plum aromas. These herald flavors that evoke a rich dark plum Christmas cake with brown sugar, spice, and prunes leading to a warm, raisin-like finish balanced by dry, slightly tannic, bitterness. In the time of Jesus this probably would have been a sweet wine. It is still made in that style around Verona today and is called recioto di valpolicella; terrific with chocolate!

THE ROMAN WINES OF MAS DES TOURELLES, FRANCE

The most exciting, unique wines we tasted are from this winery in the Rhone Valley east of Nimes, France. The southern Rhone Valley around Nimes was one of the first Romanized areas of Gaul, and the winery Mas des Tourelles (www.tourelles.com) was created in the 1980s on the site of a first-century CE Roman villa that is still being excavated. The Durand family owns the property and makes modern Rhone wines there, but its Gallo-Roman project is a true labor of passion. The Durands have actively planted a Roman-style vineyard and created a Roman-style winery, using re-created Roman equipment (press, treading floor, *dolia*) to make authentic ancient wines according to the precepts and recipes of ancient authors, especially Columella.

The first experimental wines using the ancient techniques were made in 1991 under the guidance of the archaeologists André Tchernia and Jean Pierre Brun, and the owner, a trained winemaker. Briefly, each wine was treaded in what Jesus would recognize as a *gat,* then pressed using a Roman lever press built from Cato the Elder's specifications. The wines were fermented and aged in *dolia* as large as 400 liters (106 gallons) and lined with pitch instead of beeswax, just as in Roman times. The differences in the three wines are great, but the quality of all is quite good. What some might denigrate as a gimmick was a true experiment here, given the amount of research and effort to ensure authenticity. Subsequently today, these are wines offered for commercial sale, unfortunately only in France.

The most unusual style is the 2007 Mas des Tourelles Turriculae (Vin de Gaule) (13%). Made according to a recipe from Columella in which seawater and *defrutum* (grape juice boiled down to a third of its original volume) are added, the wine is then aromatized with fenugreek, lemongrass, quince, and iris rhizome. In Roman times the *defrutum* was added two or three days after fermentation commenced naturally, and four days later they added concentrated seawater and powdered fenugreek. When fermentation was finished, a small amount of powdered gypsum was added to help settle out particulates as well as raise the acidity.

The result is wonderfully delicious. Dark yellow-amber in color, the wine has a bouquet that engages one immediately with hints of subtle orange, Asian herbs, *flor*-like nuttiness, dried apples, curry, and a hint of smoky-earthiness as well as sea air. The molecule responsible for the smell of nuttiness, as with *flor* wines, is found in fenugreek: small amounts lend nuttiness, but large amounts taste like curry. The flavors are fine, rich, dry, and full bodied, with refined fruit-nut, dried peach, and definite salty overtones. We mixed the wine with a little diluted saltwater to see how this would affect the taste, as this was a typical way to drink wine two thousand years ago. The flavors actually became rounder and more pleasant yet. No doubt Jesus would enjoy this wine, and certainly recognize the style.

The second wine, Mas des Tourelles Mulsum (13%), a widely recognized style in the Roman Empire, was served as an aperitif. It is made with red wine, according to Pliny. Here again, after the treading and decanting the grape juice into jars for fermentation, the winemaker adds an amount of honey equal to 5 percent of the volume of the juice and then mixed in about 50 herbs and spices. Jesus probably would recognize it as Inomillin, wine mixed with honey and pepper, among other things. The wine was lightly sulfured after fermentation was completed, and it was bottled a few months after that. The bouquet of this medium ruby–colored wine explodes with strong floral, cinnamon-clove spiciness. The flavors have a high-toned, slightly tannic, character, where the sweetness of

the honey lifts the front and middle tastes but fades to reveal a drier finish. Spicy cherry and floral flavors show remarkable ability to evolve in the glass as well, and we thought it would be a delicious wine with dark chocolate.

The last wine, a 2008 Mas des Tourelles Carenum (13.5%), was made from late-picked white grapes that had been treaded. After two days' fermentation the juice was spiked with spiced *defrutum* and crushed quince in a higher amount than for the Mulsum. Carenum has a velvety rich texture, with medium-sweet flavors balanced by a refreshing acidity matched to intense mineral-honey, herb, and quince flavors. The bouquet projects nuttiness, honey, and anise and lavender scents, with a hint of yellow raisin, even after being open nearly two weeks. It is delicately sweet yet has somewhat medicinal-herbal accents on the finish and is a complement to the farmhouse sheep and goat's milk cheeses we like to serve.

We are certain Jesus would enjoy these wines, as they directly speak to his times.

What wines would Jesus drink (WWWJD)? All of them. As the guest of honor, no doubt Jesus would be humble enough to try all these wines and would find them delicious and even familiar. While many are not easy to find, and in some cases are expensive, we chose wines to honor a special guest. One thing seems clear, now that we have concluded our journey: following the Bible wine trail can be done through reading, travel, and the glass. The writers of the Bible provided a wealth of beautiful language, descriptions, and (mostly) wise advice about how we as societies should live and relate spiritually to one of our most precious cultural legacies. "The fruit of the vine" has served throughout history as the primary mediator between heaven and earth, illuminating our humanity while often reminding us of our deeper connection with the divine. Whether at Jewish rites and holidays, the Christian Eucharist, consumption of meals, or enjoyment with friends, wine is a reminder that all of life is sacred and worth celebrating, wine glass in hand.

Notes

PREFACE

p. x   **I contend instead:** Patrick McGovern, *Uncorking the Past: The Quest for Wine, Beer, and Other Alcoholic Beverages* (Berkeley: University of California Press, 2009), 27.

CHAPTER 1: THE ORIGINS OF WINE

p. 6   **"Typical of the Thracian epiphany":** Edward Hyams, *Dionysus: A Social History of the Wine Vine* (London: Sidgwick and Jackson, 1965), 84.

p. 7   **Recent archaeological digs:** Patrick E. McGovern, *Uncorking the Past: The Quest for Wine, Beer, and Other Alcoholic Beverages* (Berkeley: University of California Press, 2009).

p. 7   **The first wine cultures emerged:** Ibid., 82.

p. 8   **As humans experimented:** Naomi F. Miller, "Sweeter Than Wine? The Use of the Grape in Early Western Asia," *Antiquity* 82 (2008): 944.

p. 9   **The Eurasian grape:** McGovern, *Uncorking the Past.*

p. 9   **Further, wild grapes have grown:** Michal Dayagi-Mendels, *Drink and Be Merry: Wine and Beer in Ancient Times* (Jerusalem: Israel Museum Press, 1999).

p. 10   **The drunken monkey hypothesis:** D. Stephens and R. Dudley, "The Drunken Monkey Hypothesis," *Natural History* 113, no. 10 (2004): 40–44.

p. 10   **Siduri functions as a wise female deity:** William Younger, *Gods, Men and Wine* (London: Wine and Food Society, 1966), 32.

p. 11   **"The wild beast Enkidu":** OB Pen II [CBS7771] col iii 96-101

p. 11   **In 3 Baruch and 4 Ezra:** Alexander Kulik, *3 Baruch: Greek-Slavonic Apocalypse of Baruch (Commentaries on Early Jewish Literature)* (Berlin: de Gruyter, 2010), 198–99.

p. 12   **Because the area around Mount Ararat:** Trevor Watkin, "New Light on Neolithic Revolution in Southwest Asia," *Antiquity* 84 (2010): 621–34.

p. 12   **Plausible evidence from recent research:** William Ryan and Walter Pitman, *Noah's Flood: The New Scientific Discoveries about the Event That Changed History* (New York: Simon & Schuster, 1998).

p. 13   **In 2000 Robert Ballard:** Ian Wilson, *Before the Flood: The Biblical Flood as a Real Event and How It Changed the Course of Civilization* (New York: St. Martin's Press, 2004).

p. 13   **According to Ryan and Pitman:** Ryan and Pitman, *Noah's Flood.*

p. 14   **The cradle of grape cultivation:** Patrick McGovern, Stuart Fleming, and Solomon Katz, eds., *The Origins and Ancient History of Wine* (Amsterdam: Gordon and Breach, 1995), 5.

p. 15   **About nineteen thousand years ago:** Arlene Miller Rosen, *Civilizing Climate: Social Responses to Climate Change in the Ancient Near East* (Lanham, MD: Altamira Press, 2007), 46–47.

p. 15   **The period included:** Ibid., 97–98. For a different view see Ryan and Pitman, *Noah's Flood.*

p. 15   **Paleoclimatologists note:** Catherine Kuzucuoğlu, "Climate and Environment in Times of Cultural Changes from the 4th to the 1st Millennium BC in the Near and Middle East," in *Scienze dell'Antichità: Storia Archeologia Antropologia* 15 (2009): 201. Università degli Studi di Roma "La Sapienza"; Edizioni Quasar di Severino Tognon srl 2010 (University for Studies, Rome, "La Sapienza"; published by Quasar Editions of Severino Tognon srl, 2010).

p. 15   **Evidence at archaeological sites:** Ibid., 204.

p. 16   **In the southern Levant:** Rosen, *Civilizing Climate,* 100.

p. 16   **Studies in the area:** Daniel Zohary and Maria Hopf, *The Domestication of Plants in the Old World,* 2nd ed. (Oxford, 1993).

p. 16   **Lighter loess (wind-blown deposits) soils:** M. Zohary, *Geobotanical Foundations of the Middle East* (Stuttgart: Gustav Fischer, 1973); Avinoam Danin, *Desert Vegetation of Israel and Sinai* (Jerusalem: Cana Pub. House, 1983).

p. 16   **For the descendants of Noah:** Rosen, *Civilizing Climate,* 129–30.

p. 16   **Botanical analyses showed:** Pam Belluck, "Cave Drops Hints to Earliest Glass of Red," *New York Times,* January 11, 2011.

p. 17   **Even earlier:** McGovern, *Uncorking the Past,* 180.

p. 17   **As trade increased:** José F. Vouillamoz et al., "Genetic Characterization and Relationships of Traditional Grape Cultivars from Transcaucasia and Anatolia," *Plant Genetic Resources* 4, no. 2 (2006): 144–58.

p. 17   **Grape pips unearthed:** McGovern, Fleming, and Katz, *Origins and Ancient History of Wine.*

p. 17   **From economic documents:** McGovern, *Uncorking the Past,* 97.

p. 18   **In fact viticultural knowledge:** Ibid., 176.

CHAPTER 2: FROM MESOPOTAMIA TO ISRAEL

p. 19   **A fine map:** Patrick E. McGovern, *Uncorking the Past: The Quest for Wine, Beer, and Other Alcoholic Beverages* (Berkeley: University of California Press, 2009), 132–33.

p. 20   **Besides, their alluvial soils:** Carey Ellen Walsh, *The Fruit of the Vine: Viticulture in Ancient Israel* (Harvard Semitic Museum Publications, Monographs, vol. 60.) (Winona Lake, IN: Eisenbrauns, 2000).

p. 20   **This was a Greek way:** William Younger, *Gods, Men and Wine* (London: Wine and Food Society/World Publishing Co., 1966), 55.

p. 20   **Wine also was a luxury:** McGovern, *Uncorking the Past,* 62–64.

p. 20   **A second jar analyzed:** Ibid., 74–75.

p. 20   **Further south, little evidence for viticulture:** Michal Dayagi-Mendels, *Drink and Be Merry: Wine and Beer in Ancient Times* (Jerusalem: Israel Museum, 1999), 16.

p. 20   **Mentions of wine in tablets:** S. F. Hallgarten, personal notes, 1962–77.

p. 21   **Free-standing vines:** William Younger, *Gods, Men and Wine* (London: Wine and Food Society, 1966), 61.

p. 21   **Drinking was a ritualized aspect:** Ibid., 58–60.

p. 21   **According to recent research:** Patrick E. McGovern, Armen Mirzoian, and Gretchen R. Hall, "Ancient Egyptian Herbal Wines," *Proceedings of the National Academy of Sciences of the United States of America* 106 (May 5, 2009): 7361–66.

p. 21   **Given recent linguistic findings:** José Vouillamoz, "Anatolia—Cradle of Wine?" presentation and slide 17 for: "Discover the Roots: Inaugural Wines of Turkey," Conference and Tasting, 2011, London.

p. 21   **Hittite royalty prized Anatolian wine:** Sedat Alp, *Grapes and Wine in Anatolia During the Hittite Period* (Ankara: Kavaklidere Cultural Publications, 2000), 68.

p. 22   **Cuneiform Hittite tablets:** A. Nedim Attila, *Western Anatolia Wine Culture* (Istanbul: Bilbi Matbaa Yayincilik, 2011), 14; Alp, *Grapes and Wine in Anatolia,* 69.

p. 23   **The historical evidence for wine:** Dayagi-Mendels, *Drink and Be Merry,* 15.

p. 24   **Haran also was not far:** Stephanie Dalley, *Mari and Karana: Two Old Babylonian Cities* (Piscataway, NJ: Gorgias Press, 2002), 26.

p. 24   **The archive contained letters:** Georges Dossin, "Benjamites dans les textes de Mari," *Melanges syriens offerts á M. Rene Dussaud* (Paris: Librairie Orientaliste Paul Geuthner, 1939), 986.

p. 25   **At the time Abraham settled:** H. Weiss et al., "The Genesis and Collapse of Third Millennium North Mesopotamian Civilization," *Science, New Series.* 261, no. 524 (August 20, 1993).

p. 26   **Some studies also conclude . . . The Nabateans:** A. S. Issar and H. J. Bruins, "Special Climatological Conditions in the Deserts of Sinai and the Negev During the Latest Pleistocene," *Paleaogeography, Palaeoclimatology, Palaeoecology* 43 (1983): 63–72. As cited in website www.mnemotrix.com/adasr/arch.html Archaeological Studies.

p. 26   **Just as the ancient prophets:** David Ben-Gurion, "Importance of the Negev" (in Hebrew), January 17, 1955, speech to Knesset, cited in Wikipedia.com biblio (see article on David Ben-Gurion).

p. 27   **Abraham acknowledges:** Hermann Gunkeland and Mark E. Biddle, eds. and trans., *Genesis* (Macon, GA: Mercer University Press, 1997), 203.

p. 27   **Abraham helped Melchizedek:** D. Steurnagel, *Die Einwanderung der israelitischen Stämme in Kanaan: historisch-kritische Untersuchungen* (Berlin: Schwetschke, 1901), 120.

p. 28   **Shalem is probably a wine god:** Eric Voegelin, *Israel and Revelation*, vol. 1 of *Order and History*, edited and introduced by Maurice P. Hogan (Columbia: University of Missouri Press, 2001), 325.

p. 29   **Thus the wine god Eshcol:** Morton Smith, "On the Wine God in Palestine (Gen 18, John 2, and Achilles Tatius)," in J. D. Shaye and E. J. Cohen, eds., *Studies in the Cult of Yahweh: Studies in Historical Method, Ancient Israel, Ancient Judaism* (Leiden, Netherlands: E. J. Brill, 1996), 1: 234–38.

p. 30   **In a ritual and prayer:** Billie Jean Collins, *A History of the Animal World in the Ancient Near East* (Leiden, Netherlands: E. J. Brill, 2001), 1:164. *Libate* means to pour wine as a sacrifice.

p. 30   **This method of preparing wine:** Homer, *The Iliad and the Odyssey*, trans. Samuel Butler (1897/1900; repr. Adelaide, Australia: University of Adelaide Ebook Library, 2007), *Iliad*, Book 11, generation.feedbooks.com/book/4959.pdf.

p. 30   **"A Second Soldier's Oath":** Text: CTH 427; KUB 43.38. Edition: Oettinger 1976: 52f., 58, 94.

p. 31   **In Genesis 27:25:** Walsh, *Fruit of the Vine*, 5.

p. 31   **The story says that in the land:** James Henry Breasted, *A History of Egypt from the Earliest Times to the Persian Conquest* (New York: Charles Scribner and Sons, 1906), 1:313.

p. 32   **Documents from Ugarit:** S. F. Hallgarten, personal notes, 1963–1977.

p. 33   **Elsewhere in the Levant:** Magen Broshi, "Wine in Ancient Palestine—Introductory Notes," *Israel Museum Journal* 3 (1984): 23.

p. 33   **Iron-rich terra rossa:** Walsh, *Fruit of the Vine*, 31.

p. 33   **"The idea of a two-handled pottery container":** Virginia R. Grace, *Amphoras and the Ancient Wine Trade* (Princeton, NJ: American School of Classical Studies at Athens, 1979), 8.

p. 33   **Aluntit was a mix:** Eva Davis, "The Importance of Wine in Talmudic and Biblical Times," talk at Talmud Shiur; NNLS Kol Hatazafon RH 1993, 31.

p. 34   **Wines from Petra, Tyre, Beirut:** Younger, *Gods, Men and Wine*, 75.

CHAPTER 3: JOSEPH AND THE CUPBEARER

p. 37   **Because the vine:** Peter Damian Akpunonu, "The Vine, Israel and the Church," in *Series: Studies in Biblical Literature*, vol. 51 (Peter Lang, 2003), 70.

p. 38   **When Joseph was in Egypt:** Michal Dayagi-Mendels, *Drink and Be Merry: Wine and Beer in Ancient Times* (Jerusalem: Israel Museum Press, 1999), 40; Magen Broshi, "Wine in Ancient Palestine—Introductory Notes," *Israel Museum Journal* 3 (1984): 23.

p. 38   **The baker most likely:** Delwin Samuel, "Beer Bread," in Donald B. Redford, ed., *The Oxford Encyclopedia of Ancient Egypt* (Oxford: Oxford University Press, 2001), 1:66; Zahi Hawass, *Mountains of the Pharoahs* (New York: Doubleday, 2006), 211.

p. 39   **Perhaps the cupbearer:** Dayagi-Mendels, *Drink and Be Merry*, 81.

p. 39   **As we know:** Patrick E. McGovern, *Ancient Wine: The Search for the Origins of Viniculture* (Princeton, NJ: Princeton University Press, 2003), 92–93.

p. 40   **The discovery:** On the molecular analysis of the clay in the amphoras, see McGovern, *Ancient Wine*, 101.

p. 42 **A fruitful bough:** Hermann Gunkeland and Mark E. Biddle, eds. and trans., *Genesis* (Macon, GA: Mercer University Press, 1997), 459.

p. 42 **The pharaohs used wine:** P. Dils, "Wine for Pouring and Purification in Ancient Egypt," in J. Quaegebeur, ed., *Ritual and Sacrifice in the Ancient Near East* (Leuven, Netherlands: Peeters, 1993), 107–23:111.

p. 42 **From an early time:** Jon D. Mikalson, *Ancient Greek Religion*, 1st ed. (Malden, MA: Wiley-Blackwell, 2005), 212; Herodotus, *The History of Herodotus, Book II*, trans. George Rawlinson, 144, available at http://classics.mit.edu/Herodotus/history.html.

p. 43 **The Temple of Amon-Re:** Margaret Marchiori-Bakos, "The Significance of Wine Drinking in Love and in Daily Life in Ancient Egypt," *Atti del VI Congresso Internazionale di Egittologia* 2 (1993): 320–21.

p. 43 **While Egyptian vineyards:** H. Kees, *Ancient Egypt* (London: Faber & Faber, 1961), 91; M. C. Poo, *Wine and Wine Offering in the Religion of Ancient Egypt* (London: Kegan Paul International, 1995).

p. 43 **Amenhotep III (1390–1352 BCE) had:** Charles Singer, E. J. Holmyard, and A. R. Hall, *A History of Technology* (Oxford: Oxford University Press, 1956), 1:283.

p. 43 **Erman suggests:** Adolf Erman, *Life in Ancient Egypt*, trans. H. M. Tirard (New York: Macmillan, 1894), 197.

p. 43 **Amphoras taken from Tutankhamun's tomb:** Maria Rosa Guasch Jané, *Wine in Ancient Egypt: A Cultural and Analytical Study* (Oxford: Archeopress, 2008), 59–60.

p. 43 **Tomb paintings depicted the lives:** Kees, *Ancient Egypt*, 82.

p. 43 **Poor Egyptian farmers:** John Baines, and Jaromir Malek, *Atlas of Ancient Egypt* (Oxford: Phaidon, 1984), 17.

p. 43 **The Chronicles of the voyages:** Asaph Goor, "Histoire de la vigne en Terre Sainte," *Bulletin de L'OIV* 378 (1962): 378; 344.

p. 44 **The wild grape:** McGovern, *Ancient Wine*, 85–89.

p. 44 **This new jar became common:** Dayagi-Mendels, *Drink and Be Merry*, 39.

p. 44 **Further evidence for the influence:** Patrick E. McGovern, *Uncorking the Past: The Quest for Wine, Beer, and Other Alcoholic Beverages* (Berkeley: University of California Press, 2009), 173–74.

p. 45 **As we noted earlier:** Guasch Jané, *Wine in Ancient Egypt*, 26.

p. 45 **Only a drawing of a grapevine:** P. Montet, *Every Day Life in Egypt in the Days of Ramesses the Great*, trans. A. R. Maxwell-Hyslop and M. S. Drowers (London: E. Arnold, 1958), 106–7.

p. 45 **Hieroglyphs even provide names:** McGovern, *Ancient Wine*, 87–88.

p. 45 **A fine example from Tutankhamun's tomb:** Guasch Jané, *Wine in Ancient Egypt*, 37.

p. 45 **An inspector:** L. H. Lesko, "Egyptian Wine Production During the New Kingdom," in Patrick McGovern, Stuart Fleming, and Solomon Katz, eds., *The Origins and Ancient History of Wine* (Amsterdam: Gordon and Breachm, 1995), 215–30.

p. 46 **A papyrus dating to the time:** Ibid., 230.

p. 47 **Red also is the color of the Nile:** Guash Jané, *Wine in Ancient Egypt*, 25.

p. 47 **Egyptians also made date wine:** Dayagi-Mendels, *Drink and Be Merry*, 36–37.

p. 47 **Paintings on walls:** Virginia R. Grace, *Amphoras and the Ancient Wine Trade* (Princeton, NJ: American School of Classical Studies at Athens, 1979), 7.

p. 47 **The Egyptians did not mix:** Lesko in McGovern, et al, *The Origins and Ancient History of Wine*, 225.

p. 47 **This statement is not conclusive:** Guasch Jané, *Wine in Ancient Egypt*, 55.

p. 47 **Athenaeus was describing a wine:** Ibid.

p. 48 **Papyrus scrolls:** Patrick E. McGovern et al., "Anticancer Activity of Botanical Compounds in Ancient Fermented Beverages (Review)," *International Journal of Oncology* 37 (2010): 5–14.

p. 48 **Sample residue:** McGovern, *Uncorking the Past*, 166.

p. 48 **He was the prototype of Asclepius:** George Sarton, *Ancient Science Through the Golden Age of Greece* (New York: Dover, 2011), 126.

p. 48 **One papyrus mentions:** Pieter Adriaan Aart Boeser, "Transkription und Übersetzung des Papyrus Insinger," *Internationales Archiv für Ethnographie* (Leiden, Netherlands: E. J. Brill, 1922).

p. 48   **To make a concoction to cure epilepsy:** McGovern, "Wine for Eternity," *Archaeology* 51, no. 4 (1998): 28-34.

p. 48   **The Egyptian treatment for asthma:** Dayagi-Mendels, *Drink and Be Merry,* 109.

p. 49   **Wine was also a social lubricator:** D. C. A. Hillman, *The Chemical Muse: Drug Use and the Roots of Western Civilization* (New York: Thomas Dunne Books, 2008), 210.

p. 49   **McGovern notes that:,** Patrick E. McGovern, M. Christofidou-Solomidou, W. Wang, F. Dukes, T. Davidson, and W. S. El-Deiry, "Anticancer Activity of Botanical Compounds in Ancient Fermented Beverages (Review)," *International Journal of Oncology* 37 (2010): 5–14.

p. 49   **The most interesting aspect:** Patrick E. McGovern, Armen Mirzoian, and Gretchen R. Hall, "Study: Herbs Added to 5,100-Year-Old Egyptian Wine," *Ancient Egyptian Herbal Wines, Proceedings of the National Academy of Sciences of the United States of America* (April 2009): 166.

p. 53   **The word *hemer*:** Jeffrey Tigay, *The JPS Torah Commentary: Deuteronomy* (Philadelphia: Jewish Publishing Society, 1996), 304.

CHAPTER 4: WINE UNDER SIEGE

p. 56   **Wine even served as a currency:** Thomas Pellechia, *Wine: The 8,000-Year-Old Story of the Wine Trade* (Philadelphia: Running Press, 2006), 66.

p. 56   **Wineries have been found:** David Schloen, "Recent Discoveries at Ashkelon," *Oriental Institute of the University of Chicago* 20 (1963): 113–39.

p. 56   **What the biblical writer is saying:** Carole R. Fontaine, *Traditional Sayings in the Old Testament* (Sheffield: UK: Almond Press, 1982), 76–86.

p. 57   **As in ancient Canaan:** William Younger, *Gods Men and Wine* (London: Wine and Food Society, 1966), 127.

p. 59   **The narrative does not reveal:** Carey Ellen Walsh, *The Fruit of the Vine: Viticulture in Ancient Israel,* Harvard Semitic Museum Publications (Winona Lake, IN: Eisenbrauns, 2000), 195–96.

p. 61   **Assyrian kings:** Tom Standage, *A History of the World in 6 Glasses* (New York: Walker, 2005), 49.

p. 61   **Wine provided currency:** Marvin Chaney, "Whose Sour Grapes? The Addresses of Isaiah 5:1–7 in the Light of Political Economy," in Ronald Simkins and Stephen L. Cook, eds., *Semeia 87, The Social World of the Hebrew Bible* (Atlanta: Society of Biblical Literature, 1999), 107.

p. 61   **As wine production increased:** Ibid., 106–211; Edward F. Campbell Jr., *Shechem II: Portrait of a Hill Country Vale: The Shechem Regional Survey* (Atlanta: Scholars Press, 1991), 109–112.

p. 62   **Ahab is rather polite:** Walsh, *Fruit of the Vine,* 78.

p. 62   **The words "May YHWH forbid":** Ibid., 71–78.

p. 65   **The so-called Isaiah apocalypse:** Randall Heskett, *Reading the Book of Isaiah: Destruction and Lament in the Holy Cities* (New York: Palgrave Macmillan, 2011), 49–63.

p. 66   **Trading slaves or selling children:** Elizabeth Fentress, "Slavers on Chariots," in A. Dowler and Elizabeth R. Galvin, eds., *Money, Trade and Trade-Routes in Pre-Islamic North Africa* (London: British Museum Press, 2011), 65.

p. 67   **Here the sowing of peace:** David L. Peterson, *Haggai and Zechariah 1–8: A Commentary* (Philadelphia: Westminster John Knox Press, 1984), 303–8.

p. 67   **For this reason:** Michal Dayagi-Mendels, *Drink and Be Merry: Wine and Beer in Ancient Times* (Jerusalem: Israel Museum Press, 1999).

p. 68   **His grandfather Nebuchadnezzar:** Marvin A. Powell, "Wine and the Vine in Ancient Mesopotamia: The Cuneiform Evidence," in Patrick McGovern, Stuart Fleming, and Solomon Katz, eds., *The Origins and Ancient History of Wine* (Amsterdam: Gordon and Breach, 1995), 102.

p. 68   **Other sources however, suggest:** Younger, *Gods Men and Wine,* 60.

pp. 68-69 **Yet a later remark:** Herodotus, *The Histories of Herodotus,* trans. G. C. Macaulay., n. p.: Halcyon Classics Series, n. d., e-book.

p. 69   **A tablet lists vineyards:** Younger, *Gods, Men and Wine,* 21; 31.

p. 69   **Still another entry:** Ibid., 61.

p. 69   **by the fourth century BCE:** Daniel Hillel, *The Natural History of the Bible* (New York: Columbia University Press, 2006), 125.

p. 70   **Paleoclimatologists also have noted:** www.israelweather.co.il/english; Catherine Kuzucuoğlu, "Climate and Environment in Times of Cultural Changes from the 4th to the 1st Millennium BC in the Near and Middle East," in *Scienze dell' Antichità: Storia Archeologia Antropologia 15* (2009), (Roma, Università degli Studi di Roma 'La Sapienza'; Edizioni Quasar di Severino Tognon srl 2010); 193–216.

p. 71   **The *marzēaḥ* represents:** John L. McLaughlin, *The Marzēaḥ in the Prophetic Literature: References and Allusions in Light of Extra-Biblical Evidence* (Leiden, Netherlands: E. J. Brill, 2001), 1.

p. 71   **It originated in Ugarit:** Patrick A. McGovern, Ancient *Wine: The Search for the Origins of Viniculture* (Princeton, NJ: Princeton University Press, 2003), 204.

p. 71   **The marzēaḥ festival:** Phillip J. King, "The Marzēaḥ Amos Denounces—Using Archaeology to Interpret a Biblical Text," *Biblical Archeology Review* 16, no. 4 (1988): 34–44; McLaughlin, *Marzēaḥ in the Prophetic Literature*, 110, 119.

p. 73   ***Shiraz* and hermitage:** Jancis Robinson, *Vines, Grapes and Wine* (London: Octopus, 1986), 90.

p. 73   **In 1999, however, DNA testing:** Carole Meredith, "Origins of Syrah," *Syrah Producers' Club* 19 (April 2004): 3–4.

p. 73   **Recent genetic studies reveal:** José F. Vouillamoz, et al., "Genetic Characterization and Relationships of Traditional Grape Cultivars from Transcaucasia and Anatolia," *Plant Genetic Resources* 4, no. 2 (2006): 144–58.

p. 73   **Ironically, today Iran deems:** Patrick E. McGovern, *Uncorking the Past: The Quest for Wine, Beer, and Other Alcoholic Beverages* (Berkeley: University of California Press, 2009), 62–64.

p. 74   **The Kaftari period cylinder seals:** Ibid., 112.

p. 74   **Persia produced its vintages:** Hugh Johnson, *Vintage: The Story of Wine* (New York: Simon & Schuster, 1989), 106.

p. 74   **Yet the residents of Susa:** Ibid., 111.

p. 74   **Then they reconsidered the matter:** Herodotus, *Histories of Herodotus*, 1:135.

p. 74   **It had the following effect:** Pliny the Elder, *Natural History* (Cambridge, MA: Loeb Classical Library, 2005), XXIII: 17.

p. 74   **We find ironic how little:** Johnson, *Vintage*, 101.

p. 74   **Some Persians:** Edward Hyams, *Dionysus: A Social History of the Wine Vine* (London: Sidgwick and Jackson, 1987), 211.

p. 75   **From eastern Turkey:** Xenophon, *Anabasis* (Barnes and Noble Edition, B&R Samidzdat Express, e-edition) 1.5, 2.3, 4.4.

p. 75   **The Persian wine world:** Homer, *The Odyssey*, 3:391, 10:234, our translation.

p. 75   **The Persians also would have:** Younger, *Gods, Men and Wine*, 146–47.

pp. 75-76 **The existence of rhytons:** P. Gignoux, "Matériaux pour une histoire de vin dans l'Iran ancien," in R. Gyselen and M. Szuppe, eds., *Matériaux pour l'histoire économique du monde iranien* (Paris: Association pour l'Avancement des Etudes Iraniennes, 1999), 39.

p. 76   **The oldest use:** Tom Stevenson, personal email communication with author, March 2, 2012.

CHAPTER 5: HOW THE WEST WAS WINED

p. 79   **By the early eighth century BCE:** Marvin Chaney, "Whose Sour Grapes? The Addresses of Isaiah 5:1–7 in the Light of Political Economy," in Ronald Simkins and Stephen L. Cook, eds., *Semeia 87, The Social World of the Hebrew Bible* (Atlanta: Society of Biblical Literature, 1999), 107; Michal Dayagi-Mendels, *Drink and Be Merry: Wine and Beer in Ancient Times* (Jerusalem: Israel Museum Press, 1999), 16.

p. 79   **A bath was about 36 liters:** cited in S. F. Hallgarten, personal notes 1963–1977; Henri Daniel-Rops, *Jésus en son temps* (Paris: A. Fayard, 1945), 192.

p. 80   **Wine residue from a jug:** Patrick A. McGovern, *Ancient Wine: The Search for the Origins of Viniculture* (Princeton, NJ: Princeton University Press, 2003), 235.